Praise for
EVERYTHING MATTERS, NOTHING MATTERS
and
GINA MAZZA HILLIER

"Prepare to be changed forever. *Everything Matters, Nothing Matters* will lead you to the place you desire, whether your goal is spiritual growth or just a life lived fully. Gina Mazza Hillier's beautiful book illuminates the road ahead in a fresh, inspired and joyful way."

—Nancy Mramor, PhD
author of the award winning book, *Spiritual Fitness*

"Reading *EM, NM* is like learning your creative-conscious path in one lesson. I was reminded of the profound simplicity of Ekhart Tolle and the heartfelt compassion of Wayne Dyer."

—Dr. Dan Wagner
**pharmacist/ethno-pharmacist, rainforest activist,
owner of Nutri-farmacy,
author, *Natural Medicine* Audio Series**

"Gina Mazza Hillier is *the* spiritual guide to watch your back."

—Tom Volkar
**life coach/business consultant
Founder of CoreU and *DelightfulWork.com***

"Gina Hillier's new book, *Everything Matters, Nothing Matters*, presents a wonderful opportunity to explore the world of intent, intuition, ceremony, karma, healing and harmony. The process, and the discussion it will inspire, is fascinating."
—**Lewis Mehl-Madrona, MD, PhD**
University of Saskatchewan College of Medicine;
author, *Narrative Medicine*

"*Everything Matters* is the Operating System on becoming fully alive and awake within the divine awareness of our human potential. Gina shows us how to recognize and trust our muse."
—**Steve Sciulli**
one-half of the ambient/global-dance musical duo
Life In Balance (Koch Records)

"Gina's energy is electrifying. She has inspired me to persevere on my own path of personal growth. Her writings will help you, the reader, reach higher, too."
—**Siri Heasley**
choreographer/dancer/singer/actor
founder, Siri's School of the Performing Arts

"*Everything Matters, Nothing Matters* provides us with a beautifully etched roadmap to the numinous. With honesty, wit, and compassionate insight, Gina Mazza Hillier offers practical techniques that we can use to our great benefit."
—**Ingrid Mundari**
Professor of English, University of Pittsburgh
kundalini yoga instructor

"Gina is one of the most authentic individuals I have ever met. I am so thrilled that she has written this book. It will help those of us on the path to crystalize the yearning within us and guide us in developing our own authenticity."

—Edy Hope
recipient of the President's Volunteer Service Award
by President Bush

"*Everything Matters, Nothing Matters* is for creative minds who want to be at peace with themselves and give higher meaning to their work and life."

—Sebastian Dominguez
Emmy Award-winning filmmaker/TV producer (PBS, NBC)

"This book is so valuable. It gives working women like me the tools to balance it all and find peace within myself—even when my baby dumps his porridge on the floor and my magazine editor is calling from London, asking me to fact check details."

—Debbi Gardiner McCullough
writer, editor

"The spiritual basics, fleshed out with the comedy-drama of Gina's own life. This book does what inspirational literature is supposed to do—inspire. A vibrant, breathing companion muse for anyone's journey."

—Sven Hosford
co-founder and publisher, Point of Light magazine

...and from the professional world of self-help and guidance, a letter to the author:

Dear Gina,

I just finished your wonderful book! I work with clients as a social worker in a practice integrating many of these concepts. You have created an inspirational book that supports and enhances spiritual exploration, growth and development.

One of the ways your writing stands out in the self-help field is your integration of earthy and spiritual perspectives—something that is too often portrayed as a false dichotomy. I know from my professional experience that in order for people to embrace and activate change, they have to feel it is both possible AND important. If it seems impossible or unimportant, then we'll just putter around keeping comfortably mediocre in our pursuits—because change seems too hard, we are too busy, or spiritual attainment falls too low on the hierarchy of our perceived daily life needs. However, to infuse our everyday actions and interactions with intention and purpose so that we consistently cultivate our personal growth, now that's living!

Your perspective on simple ways to implement everyday spiritual practices shows that change and growth are indeed possible and above all, important. I will certainly be recommending this exuberant, practical book to my clients.

Thank you for writing *Everything Matters, Nothing Matters*. It is a joy to read.

Warm regards,

Cinda Hocking, LMSW
Internal Energy Plus Consultant
www.cindahocking.blogspot.com

Everything

MATTERS

Nothing

MATTERS

Everything

MATTERS

Nothing

MATTERS

For Women Who Dare to Live with
Exquisite Calm, Euphoric Creativity & Divine Clarity

Gina Mazza Hillier

PITTSBURGH

Everything Matters, Nothing Matters
For Women Who Dare to Live with
Exquisite Calm, Euphoric Creativity & Divine Clarity

Copyright © 2008 by Gina Mazza Hillier

Grateful acknowledgment is given to Veritas Publishing,
www.veritaspub.com, for permission to quote from Dr. David R. Hawkins'
I: Reality and Subjectivity and Transcending the Levels of Consciousness.
Special gratitude to Dr. Hawkins for his kind approval of this
use of his words.

ISBN-13: 978-0-9767631-8-5

Library of Congress Control Number: 2007937948
CIP information available upon request

First Edition, 2008

St. Lynn's Press . POB 18680 . Pittsburgh, PA 15236
412.466.0790 . www.stlynnspress.com

Typesetting—Holly Wensel, Network Printing Services
Cover design—Nita Ybarra
Editor—Catherine Dees
©Author Photo—Becky Thurner

Printed in the United States of America
on recycled paper ♻

This title and all of St. Lynn's Press books may be purchased
for educational, business, or sales promotional use.
For information please write:
Special Markets Department, St. Lynn's Press, POB 18680,
Pittsburgh, PA 15236

10 9 8 7 6 5 4 3 2 1

To my three loves and my Beloved

IN MEMORY:

JOSEPH AUGUSTUS MAZZA

CONTENTS

I Have Learned So Much

I
Have
Learned
So much from God
That I can no longer
Call
Myself

A Christian, a Hindu, a Muslim,
A Buddhist, a Jew.

The Truth has shared so much of Itself
With me

That I can no longer call myself
A man, a woman, an angel,
Or even pure
Soul.

Love has
Befriended me so completely
It has turned to ash
And freed
Me

Of every concept and image
My mind has ever known.

—Hafiz, translated by Daniel Ladinsky,
The Gift: Poems by Hafiz the Great Sufi Master

INTRODUCTION

Something big is coming.
It's still secret, but arriving everywhere.

—Rumi

For many of us, heaven meets earth through creative inspiration. We may not all be working artists, yet each of us was born with a creative soul. Along the way, part of it may have become shrouded, squelched, devalued, injured or ignored altogether. Too often, we're forced to choose between our creative longings and everyday practicality. So we deny that part of ourselves, linger through our days obliquely, and wonder why we feel bitter. The current flows around us and we slowly drown in our own life.

How do we save our creative spirit? As a lifelong writer and student of consciousness, I have stumbled upon a workable, practical truth: real creative power is actualized from being clear, pure and wholly connected to Creation itself. When we embrace the sacred, we free our creative genius. Once free and open to the infinite, we can become as prolific as we choose to be—in our art, in our heart and in our daily life.

Because I'm a self-prescribed specimen on life's Petri dish, I sometimes want to be grabbed and shaken from my familiar, microscopic existence . . . levitated to a higher, fertile ground that contains the seeds of all my unrealized potential, awaiting germination. What takes me there again and again is faith

i

in the Unmanifest, the genesis of all that is. To be creative and conscious are synonymous in this way: both require that we acknowledge the presence of a transcendent energy that can take us to unimaginable places (yes, beyond the imagination). And yet, neither the spiritual nor the creative are known paths. Each must be sickled blade by blade through dedication and devotion.

Today's spiritual enthusiasts aren't necessarily seeking enlightenment or some fresh dose of woo-woo. We're more interested in being present now. We understand that a full-out integration of our physical and higher selves is simply part of our larger evolutionary process—the missing link between chaos and order. We appreciate that we can't "get there from here" by following a straight line towards some end point, because accessing our highest potential is an immeasurable, continual process, maybe even happening on multiple levels of reality at the same time. And when far-out things happen in our meditations and other daily practices (which they will), we immediately seek to make sense of their meaning and value. We do this to ultimately learn something new about ourselves, and reflect it back to the world through our chosen mode of creativity so that others, too, may learn about themselves.

First, let's define consciousness, the consciousness that is yours in this instant. In simplest terms, it's your state of awareness. No one has set the limits of your awareness; they are set by you alone—and the degree to which you are aware greatly determines your capacities within your human experience. Many of us come to certain moments in our lives when we realize that our self-imposed limits no longer serve us, that it's more appropriate to look beyond ourselves at a broader vision of reality. And when we have elevated our awareness to the highest degree, we reach a state that the ancient masters and modern-day mystics describe, where we can see through all conditions and circumstances, and the veil is completely removed between our mortal selves and Spirit.

* * *

While I may be accused by some of having a fantastic imagination—and, as a writer, I wouldn't necessarily take umbrage at this—I give you my best word that the stories on these pages are real. I am not so unlike you—a working-class American, married with children, focused daily on what needs to be done for my family. I was raised by hard-working, Italian-immigrant parents who passed down a rich ancestry of Catholic-based traditions and virtues of respect, humility and self-reliance. Parallel to this ordinary life, I nurtured within me a growing magnetic attraction to subjects related to metaphysics, parapsychology and human potential. From a young age, I had an impulse to ask epic questions: who am I? why am I? what am I here to do? As a journalist, I now write about consciousness studies, and after years of doing so have come to realize that the more we know, the more we don't know. "To live is so startling," Emily Dickinson wrote, "it leaves little time for anything else."

During my childhood years in the 70s, mainstream society hadn't yet embraced the exploration of realities beyond our five senses. The 80s eked its way through full-blown affluenza and by the arrival of the 90s, more of us seemed eager to abandon materialism for a simpler lifestyle. Around this time, I and many others had a (sixth?) sense that within a decade, the notion of higher consciousness would hit the mainstream and I wanted to be on the front lines, researching and hopefully reporting about it. So it happened. Just as I self-published a book on health intuition in 2000, topics related to integrative medicine (then a newly coined phrase), spiritual intelligence and the practical use of intuition were finally eliciting hoo-ha in conventional media outlets.

Meanwhile, the information I was reporting on began to seep into my own awareness, to the point that I started to experience the opening of my third eye, the entry gate of intuition, and it's been nothing but upward momentum ever since—a continual expansion of consciousness. I document my findings on these pages, an amalgam of what I've discovered to be the seven essential, overarching concepts to consider when we finally decide to take that leap of faith into the great unknown (and how the unknown can be extremely fruitful, creatively). It's a read that I wish I'd had when I set out, basically on my own, to blaze my personal trail towards finding meaningful answers to inquiries that haunted the recesses of my psyche—and that I knew had been waiting there for me all along.

This book is my offering to your own quest. It guides you through the seven incremental steps of Intention, Daily Practice, Paying Attention, Turning Within, Working with a Mentor, Witnessing—and finally, Integration. Integration is no small word, because in this context it means you will have succeeded in creating for yourself a gift beyond price:

**You will know who you are,
with the freedom to be it.**

**You will know what you want,
with the daring to go for it.**

*   *   *

So what exactly does "expansion of consciousness" mean, beyond sounding like so much physics department cocktail chatter? While these pages attempt to dissect the process, language seems inadequate to describe the concept of coming fully awake and aware. It must be experienced to be understood.

With this in mind, my intent is for this book to be a template upon which you may overlay your personal, subjective experiences. At best, you will find your own truth in these stories and take them as confirmation that, no, you're not crazy—unexplained phenomena happen every day, if we "stay tuned" and routinely "pause for station identification." In due course, the messages in these seven chapters will lead you to a creative encounter with your life's higher story. (To facilitate this, I've included action items at the end of the book, keyed to each chapter's themes. The Contemplations will serve to clear your creative channel; the Self-Creations will provide access to realms of higher creativity.)

I will do my best to articulate my own internal process of moving from what I call a sepia-tone version of life to a more vivid, multicolored, creative existence through the expansion of awareness. I will go deep, get quite intimate and may even surprise myself with what I choose to share—but I vow to reveal straight up as much as I can recollect because I believe that what's being communicated on these pages are matters of extreme relevance to each of us personally, as well as to the whole of humanity.

Our respective spiritual development goes through phases and everybody is in a different place along the road, so your experiences will be different from mine and anyone else's. Hopefully, we're at least on the same "interstate"—or cruising towards the same inner state. To guide your road trip, these chapters are about how awakening to both Creator and our own creative capacity helps us live more purposefully, and how expanding our intuitive and artistic abilities serves to ameliorate ALL of our life experiences—be it play, work, family, health, happiness, death, joy, sorrow, you name it. Being well connected to the Divine enriches every one of these things, and plenty more.

* * *

What is the meaning behind the book's title? As we ascend to higher levels of awareness, we reach a place where we realize that everything is for a purpose, that our time here is one of learning, and all situations that arise are specifically chosen by us for the purpose of mastery in some aspect of our humanity. While Everything Matters because everything is a perfect creation—every dewdrop, every triumph and tragedy, every emotion—it is equally so that Nothing Matters. Said another way, the more we're able to remove our ego/personality from situations, the clearer that perfection in everything becomes; we are, therefore, increasingly in a space of gratitude for whatever situations come our way. There really is no good or bad, right or wrong. Everything is a blessing. The beauty of this concept gives us a simple blueprint for how to approach each day: revere all life experiences and deny yourself nothing.

The Everything Matters, Nothing Matters life mantra relates directly to our innate link with the Divine, which is given voice through our intuition. As we take time to simply become aware of the characteristics and behaviors of people and things through our intuition, our higher self unfolds— much like the alchemical process that burns away the dross to reveal the gold beneath. What we are aiming to achieve with our own alchemical purification is not full enlightenment but a refined state of unconditional love, altruism, inner joy, creative abundance, and a sense of wisdom in our lives. Trust me, though, purification in itself is a life-changing, transformational process. By the time you've assimilated the seven concepts in this book, your life will not look, feel or be the same.

To help you on your way, I will speak candidly here about how my increasing awareness of other dimensions impacted my view—sometimes painfully so—of ordinary, 3-dimensional reality and my place in it. At times, spiritual development has sent me into the throes of an existential quandary. With vast internal shifts occurring inside me—everything from my personal identity to my fundamental understanding of what reality really is—questions about how to live my life have become, at times, simultaneously complex and peacefully simple. Add in the fact that others around me may not be privy to this internal process and you've got more quiet anxiety than a mother coming home from the hospital with her firstborn.

So far it's been an incredible journey, vertical in nature, tending towards transcendence. And how did I arrive at this point-of-know-return—by mistake? self-delusion? special privilege? No, no and no. I simply intended to get here. That's how I began. With inquisitiveness and a gut instinct that there was something larger TO life that was larger THAN life. These simple words from Spanish poet Antonio Machado express precisely what I felt:

Beyond living and dreaming
There is something more important:
Waking up.

I've worked and played at waking up. As a reward, greater mysteries have rained down on my life—this exquisite, sacred, euphoric, fierce, mysterious, crazy-juicy, treacherous, blessed, self-willed life. You, too, can savor the experience of awakening more fully into your own life. It's a matter of choice. So we begin at the beginning, with the first of the seven incremental steps: Intention.

one

INTENTION

Nothing is too wonderful to be true.

—CANDACE PERT, PhD, NEUROSCIENTIST

$\mathcal{F}$rom the outside, it appears to be an average day. It's 7 a.m. and my kids are off to school, my husband is on his way to the office, and multiple to-do lists are beckoning. My own commute is a dozen steps into my home office. But first, before the day's craziness begins, I settle into the meditation space in my living room. Nothing fancy about this space I've created for myself, nothing mysterious—just a comfy sofa where I'm surrounded by things that have special meaning for me. Behind me on the wall is a Roman stone sculpture of two horses at full gallop, suggesting power and grace. To the left of the sofa I've made an altar—mostly Catholic with an eclectic mix of relics, coins and talismans from India, Asia and Latin America. I light a candle on the coffee table before me, which burns next to a blessing bowl filled with gifts from nature: polished stones, sage and lavender from my garden, hawk and swan feathers, tree bark, sea shells, all resting on a bed of exotic-scented Jasmine loose tea. From the candle's flame, I light a stick of Satya Sai Baba Nag Champa and prop it on an incense

1

holder. Surrounded by hundreds of books and many framed pictures of family and friends around the room, I scooch back in my seat, contented, take a few deep breaths, and prepare for lift-off.

For the next 15 minutes or so, the ordinary and extraordinary intersect. From the inside, serenity and a sense of timelessness prevail. I open my mind and officially greet the day, expecting to be amazed and amused by how the splendorous intelligence of the universe will reveal itself to me in the coming 24 hours. Now, I ease into a state of heightened intuitive flow. In these moments, concepts like inadequacy, anxiety and struggle seem unfathomable; in their place rest compassion, acceptance, trust and a hint of invincibility. I let go of could-have-been's. I play with perhaps-ness. I toy with of-course-it-can's. I send love, love and more love to everyone and everything. All is peaceful on Planet Earth and in my heart.

One final prayer of gratitude (for life, for health, for all things) and I'm up from the sofa, eager to dive into the freshly born day. If there's writing to be done, I flip open my laptop, unabashedly commune with the muses-on-standby and allow their insights to fill my waiting being. As a creative person, it's a provocative place to be, a port of call like none other. I always cherish my arrival there. Regardless of the tasks ahead of me that day, my hours unfurl like a whimsical sonata, leaving in their wake a prism of superfluid ideas and inspiration.

Life can be like this, a gift re-presented each dawn with great flourish. It can be voluptuous, no matter what is occurring around us. Indeed, our moment-to-moment existence can be ecstasy, even when things happen that really suck big time. How is this possible? Because, truth be told, we don't just exist, we are *conscious beings*. As such, we are free to choose how to be: we can live, or . . . we can be Alive with a capital A.

* * *

"I write to learn what I know," Flannery O'Conner once said. As I connect to higher guidance and intentionally ask for today's insights, I reflect on the meaning of "knowing," an enormous word that has little to do with academics. (When the Oracle at Delphi said that Socrates was the wisest man in Greece, Socrates replied, "That can only mean that I know that I do not know.") Like a musician who masters scales and other melodic rules in order to break through them into virtuosity, I've come to understand that being well educated (formally or through books) is a firm foundation for sepia-tone living—while being able to crash through the known world into the "knowing" world of incisive clarity and unbounded creativity is where prismatic living really begins.

I cannot wait to share with you the sensations of living a lavishly creative, provocatively intuitive and ultra-conscious existence. I want this for you. It's too plush and lovely to conceal, too important to constrain. I wish for you to experience life (or at least moments, hours, or days of it) as the one big love rush that it is—in spite of what our outer circumstances might show.

WHAT IS INTENTION?

It all begins with intention. Intention is higher-consciousness thought. In other words, it's using the mind for a higher purpose—higher, meaning that you are not limiting yourself to certain outcomes or procedures. When you hold an intent, you call forth the actual consciousness (awareness) of the universe and therefore have at your disposal all the intelligence contained within it. Here is the difference between thought and intention: Thought is like tying up a care package with string and sending it for delivery to a specified address. Intention is more like being on the other end of a delivery, with or without knowing its sender or contents. An intention-based life is approached, always, with optimism that gifts are arriving all the time. As the recipient, we are only responsible for signing for the package, unraveling the string and accepting the gift. This realm of universal consciousness, where everything is a potential arriving gift, is where infinite creativity lives.

In order to access the extraordinary power of intent, it's important to realize that it operates in a limitless field of energy and cannot be contained within a narrow purpose. Paradoxical, I know, because you may think of setting an intention as focusing on a specific thing. This is where people become confused and misuse this concept—and say it doesn't work. Nonsense. Intent cannot NOT work; it's *that* energetically powerful. Yes, you have something in mind when you set an intention. Once done, however, this something is released like a vapor into the atmosphere and permeates the entire universal energy field. We're sending that package across the universe, quite intentionally, without a mailing label. Can you see what's happening when you do this? You're allowing all possibilities to occur and for that gift to be delivered where it best fits into the Creator's big passion play.

The initial step in fruitfully opening to higher consciousness is, quite simply, having the intention to do so. To be conscious means to live with intent and a desire to nurture a part of oneself that many people don't take time to do on a regular basis. It's so true, we can easily get caught up in the crush of daily living and allow ourselves to be overtaken by very human activities like paying bills, taking care of the house, feeding the kids, going to work—and generally keeping ourselves locked into a static routine that we eventually come to believe we can't break free from. The rewards are well worth whatever little time it takes to formulate an intent to become the best person you can be—physically, emotionally, spiritually and, yes, creatively.

Intention is Powered by Faith

Having an intention is empty unless it's accompanied by faith. In my humble experience, faith powers the entire process and, to be honest, these two things—intention and faith—are all that's really required to advance intuitively and artistically. Here's a guarantee: If you can find within yourself the capacity to retain faith and trust as daily mantras, you will progress at a rapid clip.

For most of us, faith is a winding road, not a rocket shot heavenward. I've had many moments when I've wondered, What is the difference between having faith and being naïve? Keeping the flame of faith burning can be extremely difficult, especially during trying times and "dark nights of the soul." And what happens when we follow our truest instincts and our dream *doesn't* come true? We will explore these and other questions of faith as we go along.

To begin on a dedicated spiritual path, no fundamental education or training is required. Commence with no care about your knowledge of the subject because what's necessary to know will be revealed to you as you go along. In fact, it's possible to bypass mental knowledge about intuition by simply engaging in the spiritual practices described in the next chapter. With deliberateness of purpose, you will come to discern that an intuitive lifestyle is one of daily discovery that becomes progressively self-revealing. In other words, you will naturally become "higher powered."

And yet, I understand so well that we often feel impelled to get our minds around matters of importance to us, to become mentally engaged. I've read my share of metaphysical books—at one point, averaging five per week (how did I ever find the time?). And I've dabbled in various workshops, conferences, discussion groups and such. This is all well and good. We are endowed by our Creator with incredible intel-lects, and we should use them to the fullest. What I'm sug-gesting is to not get caught up in a morass of data, or use the mind to the exclusion of your inner voice. It's more effective to have the mind balanced with the heart; in fact, I've found that *feeling* most often gets me to the truth of a matter faster than *thinking*. I've met individuals who are quite erudite in their intuitive search and have accumulated an impressive amount of book knowledge and education from a great variety of sources. Sometimes to my envy, these types have resources of time, money and influence to fly around the globe, attend every spiritual retreat, enroll in every course, and meet every mystic, philosopher, guru and shaman from India to the Ama-zon rainforest—but they still seem not to *get it*. They think that if they study long and hard enough, their desired goal will one day bonk them on the head (and maybe it will).

What they haven't yet assimilated, in my view, is the inner experience of the mind-knowledge that they've acquired. While astute in the head, they remain disconnected from the heart of it all. At this juncture, these "spiritual power shop-pers" would be best served by releasing their grasp on the tra-peze wire and free-falling into the experience. If not, the thing they've been diligently striving to achieve—mainly, getting to the miraculous by way of the mind—will eventually become an insidious obstruction to the entire process. At some point, the intellect must be transcended, and this cannot be done by the mind on its own behalf. (That would be like trying to cut your own hair without a mirror.) Only the heart, which contains something infinitely more powerful than the mind—love—can overcome long-held patterns, thoughts and beliefs. At some point, we must simply toss aside all the books, this one included, and just be. Surrender to the Divine without stipulations. Muster your courage and let go. God is the net that will catch you if and when you fall.

SURRENDER IS SINGULARLY IMPORTANT

To know higher consciousness is to know God. And to know God, devotion is sufficient. I'm not talking about selling all your worldly possessions and entering a seminary or monastery (unless that's your dharma). For all practical purposes of living within the world you've made for yourself, devotion in this context means to surrender to the idea that our spiritual development is based upon "allowing" and not "trying." A very powerful concept, indeed. This is a good place to start, with the idea that spiritual development is not something to be acquired, but surrendered to. In fact, the four most powerful words that we can speak are: **God's will be done.** That brief phrase explains the Everything Matters, Nothing Matters concept like nothing else can. With this simple intent, answers to any questions that plague you begin to reveal themselves without effort or worry.

Remember, the experience of the Divine is internal. When we take the phrase "let go and let God" and slice it thinner, what we really see is that God's will for us is our will for ourselves. In other words, consider that it isn't an external power that is causing anything to happen or interceding on your behalf. More accurately, the result of connecting to inner divinity and following this guidance shows up in your life as prayers answered, needs met, miracles abounding, abundance flowing. It's a fine distinction: God doesn't answer our prayers, God perpetually resides in our hearts and minds and we draw out God's will for us by being clear about who we are and what we want to bring into our lives.

Why do you exist? There is only one answer: to know you are God manifest in your unique time and place. You are the way God knows itself. You are the way God takes out the trash, walks the dog, cooks breakfast . . .
– *Rabbi Rami Shapiro,* The Hebrew Prophets: Selections Annotated and Explained

We let God know what our will is through our intentions. A few years ago, I was offered a writing assignment that seemingly (operative word) came out of the blue. When I checked in for internal guidance about whether I could handle the commitment of time and travel it would entail, I was cleverly given a common business term: ROI, or Return On Investment. (Clever, because the project being offered was co-authoring a book about a "transcendental organization"—an LA-based entrepreneurial venture that actively uses higher-consciousness business principles with much success.) Only, in this case, I was told that ROI stood for Return On Intent. Big difference! "This opportunity is the appearance of a gift that you've already asked for," I heard claircognizantly, and for emphasis, was told, "It is not a steak dinner or cable-knit sweater: you cannot send this one back!"

After reflecting on the project's potential, I realized that it fit all the requisites of a work situation that I had indeed wanted to draw towards myself. I marveled at how brilliantly the universe juxtaposed two things that I'm very interested in and put them together in the form of a writing project. It was definitely within my career track of writing about consciousness, but within a book category (business/entrepreneurship) that I hadn't considered on my own. I was intrigued to explore the integration of high-flying consciousness with grounded business practices.

Around that same time, I was grappling with changes going on within my own small "inspired event planning" company, an entrepreneurial venture that was consciously created within what I believed were attributes of this new business paradigm. In certain moments, I had actually thought, *This is nuts, I can't really run a business this way, how's this going to work?* So, writing about how this West Coast company prospered using futuristic business principles would be a brilliant means for me to discern how my own venture could thrive. The founder of this ahead-of-its-time organization is a spiritually intelligent, kind-hearted woman whom I had long admired; working with her would be an absolute joy, I just knew it. And so it was.

Point is, we can intend things and the universe gifts us with those intentions in forms that many times are so much more magnificent than we could have thought up on our own. The key is to surrender and realize that we are responsible for the intention and the effort, *but not the result.*

Spirituality and Religiosity
I have no desire to challenge the mystery and deep meaning of religion in its traditional forms. We have much to learn from ancient and modern theological teachings, and from the reverence and rituals that comprise the world's great religions. Religion and spirituality are not in conflict—this isn't so edgy a concept anymore. As you probably have already experienced, it's quite possible to embrace spiritual evolution and all it entails, and yet cleave to the essential teachings of one's known religion. When examined from the Everything Matters, Nothing Matters perspective, it's clear that we're all endorsing the same humanitarian concepts: love God, love your neighbor, love yourself. This is further buttressed by evidence that descriptions of ultimate reality by enlightened beings throughout history have been identical—

whether Jewish, Buddhist, Christian, Hindu or other.

The beauty of Catholicism passed down from my parents has given me a solid foundation for living in faith, and I was fortunate to be taught about Jesus Christ, Mary, Joseph, the Holy Spirit, archangels and saints, and many other facets of the Divine. I loved, and still do love, the formalities of entering a cathedral in all its glory, lighting candles, kneeling in front of the exquisitely marbled altar and staring at the sacristy where the holy hosts are kept, praying at the side altar to the Blessed Mother and leaving a sprig of lilacs at her feet, and of course reenacting Jesus' last supper on earth—transforming bread and wine into body and blood, the ultimate alchemy.

One thing I wasn't able to reconcile as a child with a catechism on my school desk was the teaching that we need an intermediary to connect us with our Creator, as well as to lay down adequate punishment in the form of penance when we allegedly do something to bring on His disfavor. I was taught to venerate Jesus, the son, but to me, God was always ultra-personal. I didn't want anything to intrude upon my intimate relationship with Him, and at times, the elaborate hierarchical framework through which I was learning about divinity (religion) seemed to do just that. It wasn't until my teenage years that I discovered that others took offense to this approach as well, and that while religion might be a safe harbor we seek, or even a watertight ship on life's tumultuous waters, this farther-reaching phenomenon called spirituality is actually the ocean that the vessel floats upon.

We are All Worthy to Receive God

In Catholic grade school, where conformity was encouraged over individual expression, I most assuredly would have been accused of blasphemy (or insanity) if I were to even casually mention that Mary Magdalene gives me personal messages, or

Archangel Gabriel whispers into my right ear. I know now that such connections are available to all of us—at least to those of us who believe, ask, and feel worthy to receive. As we say before Holy Communion: "Lord, I am not worthy to receive you but say the word and I shall be healed." The word has been given, people. You are worthy. You do not require God's forgiveness because He has never condemned you. Knowing this in your soul is a mature version of surrender—we are in gratitude for the fact that the Divine lives within us, and we are therefore tethered to it without exception.

Intuitive consciousness transcends religious dogma and, ultimately, usurps it because accessing our higher selves enables us to have a more focused connection and, therefore, more personal relationship with God. We don't stop worshipping our chosen form of a higher power, we simply transfer the onus for that adoration onto ourselves. It is up to us—not a priest, pastor or rabbi—to cherish our Creator. Said another way, religion is the intellect's way of grasping the Divine; spirituality is the soul's way, because no two people can experience God identically. For this reason, theology lacks the authenticity and authority of realized mystics, sages, avatars and ascended masters who have given us their accounts of transcendent knowing—based on absolute subjective experience.

Anyone who takes time to research the history of organized religion will eventually realize that it, too, is based on subjective experience—namely, that of enlightened beings such as Jesus, Buddha and Krishna, as well as their disciples. These individuals were inspired by a profound spiritual urge. (For example, Buddha sought to understand human suffering and brought forth a system for escaping it. Jesus focused on connecting ordinary consciousness and higher consciousness and achieved this through his death and resurrection.) To say that the subjective experience of Spirit is not real is to also challenge the very foundations of religion. God can be known, but not proven. What we're all going for is the *experience* of the Divine, and I'm suggesting that this isn't reserved for just a few enlightened beings, or even to the community of individuals who study about theological matters and become ordained. God is a personal revelation which extends far beyond ecclesiastical practices, even beyond the intellect, as Lao Tzu and so many others have said. I've also heard this: "Don't put your life in the ashram; put the ashram in your life." Excellent advice.

Driving in my car one day, I pondered how to approach these writings, and I got that their creation would be unlike any way I've written before. *Because it will be different, something new will come of it,* I heard. Was I basing the process of writing this book on projects that had come before it? Don't we all have a tendency to stick to the tried-and-true? In this case, I was being nudged to consider a new truth that I'd never tried. (For sure, the back story of how this manuscript fell together, found its way into the hands of such a caring publisher and became this book is a very good example of Intention bringing you what you need, even when you don't know exactly what that is. I invite you to read about it on the book's website: EverythingmattersNothingmatters.com.) This cosmic nudge made me think of the ultimate Creator, and how when He has appeared over the millennia in certain forms, people attribute to Him only that form. Then when he appears in a different way, no one believes it's God—as if God can take only a limited number of forms. "If you always imagine God in the same way," Carlos Valles is quoted in *This Our Exile* by James Martin, "no matter how true and beautiful it may be, you will not be able to receive the gift of the new ways he has ready for you." Clearly, living in faith requires a formlessness and a fearlessness. As soon as you ascribe to a certain outcome for something, you immediately limit yourself from potentially seeing anything else because it doesn't fit that mold. Perhaps this is the underlying cause of writer's block or an aspiring artist's belief that they only have one good song, novel or sculpture in them.

I'm still discovering how boundless creation can be, how many ways Spirit can reveal itself in our lives. How far I've come since those Catholic grade school days! I've had avatars, sages, Christ, the Blessed Mother, Isis, Ashtar (whom I affectionately call the ET Jesus, or cosmic Christ), and various saints and angels appear to me through my intuition—and I've discovered that each one is simply a reflection and aspect of the Divine. They all teach me about myself and how to best express my talents, which we all have. (We will talk about the purpose and usefulness of these various manifestations in later chapters.) There are countless ways to know God, and no one religion, spiritual school or source can claim that theirs is the only way. Every one of us has already been chosen by God—our acceptance of this truth, and our ultimate surrender to it, is up to us.

Invite the Inexplicable into Your Life

When we set an intention and have faith in the process of its fulfillment, miraculous things can happen. As a precursor, however, we must first invite the inexplicable into our lives through a suspension of disbelief that such things can indeed happen. Here's a random story to illustrate. My mom often gives me votive candles to place on my home altar. I generally light one on days when I'm working at home. I'm always super-careful to extinguish it and any other candles I might have burning when I leave the house. One morning shortly after my father fell ill, I lit a votive candle on the altar in my living room and asked for extra blessings for both my parents. Plans to work at home that day quickly changed with a phone call from my dad's caseworker. As I readied to leave the house, I blew out the candle, watched for a few seconds as the smoke spiraled up the side of the glass, then whisked myself out the door.

It turned into a stressful day of complex conversations with doctors and other caregivers, and numerous phone calls to long-term care facilities, during which I continued to ask for divine protection around my family. Arriving home that evening, I called my brothers and told them not to worry about Dad, as he was finally being moved to an assisted living home that could properly handle his illness. I hung up the phone and breathed a deep sigh that I'd been holding in all day. Subtly, I heard, "Go to the altar." So I did. To my surprise, that votive candle was burning brightly in the dimly lit living room.

I was accustomed to what one of those votives would look like after burning for approximately eight hours—there would be about two or three inches of liquid wax on the top. This candle looked like it had just been lit, with a pool of liquid so slight it barely reached the outer rim of the glass. In my opinion, there are two explanations for what happened: Either I didn't fully extinguish the candle that morning, or I was being given confirmation that my prayer to keep the light of hope burning on behalf of my parents was heard. The feeling that came upon me when I saw that beacon of light in the dark room, after being summoned to go to that room, is what made me lean towards the latter explanation.

INTENTION HAS HEALING PROPERTIES

In this 21st century, our inner skeptic is no longer at a loss for proof when it comes to claims of nonphysical manifestations of intention. Nowadays, there is plenty of evidence to support this as fact. For at least the past decade, modern science has been demonstrating in laboratory settings that intention and the use of intuition not only change the brain function and the body's physiology but are powerful and can heal. For now, I'll summarize a few recent studies (and you can ask any reliable search engine to provide many more).

The role of intent in healing is being studied, ah, intently these days. Marilyn Schlitz, PhD, senior scientist at California Pacific Medical Center and vice president for research and education at the Institute of Noetic Sciences (IONS), shared with me her broad definition of intentionality: "From a medical perspective, it is the projection of awareness, with purpose and efficacy, toward some object or outcome. Philosophically, it is consciousness *about* something or some content of consciousness such as belief, volition, expectation, attention, action, and even the unconscious." As for distance healing, she said, it simply involves holding a compassionate intention, such as a loving thought or saying a prayer, for another person at a distance. Changes are recorded by measures such as electrodermal (skin) activity, respiration, and heart rate. One IONS clinical study (under a National Institutes of Health grant) involved using intent as a therapeutic intervention to facilitate wound healing in mastectomy patients—with positive outcomes. Schlitz and her colleagues were encouraged by the findings of these and other studies. "What we found is that people with illnesses such as cancer, AIDS and heart disease are reacting, quite strongly actually, to positive intentional influences from [healer] targets. We're still in the early stages of this field, so I don't want to overstate our case," Schlitz cautioned. "What's important to note is that we feel confident enough [in evaluating our findings] to pursue this further. It challenges a lot of our assumptions."

In another IONS study, researchers Fred Sicher and the late Elisabeth Targ monitored distant healing intention to help late-stage AIDS patients. Distant treatment in this double-blind, controlled study was performed by healers throughout the United States, representing a variety of healing and spiritual traditions. The healers and subjects never met. Over the six-month study period—with both a control group and a distant healing group—the distant healing group experienced significantly fewer outpatient doctor visits, fewer hospitalizations, fewer new AIDS-defining illnesses, lower illness severity and improved mood, as compared to the control group. Clearly, the data support the possibility of a distant healing effect in AIDS and also warrant further research.

That is just one area where science is examining the nature of intention. Recently, it has begun probing the mysteries of consciousness as it affects the brain—specifically, investigating (and actually measuring) the dynamics of meditation. Not many years back, anyone submitting a funding proposal to investigate a subject as apparently woo woo as meditation, was on a futile mission. But thanks to people like Jack Kornfield, one of the early popularizers of meditation in the West (he holds a PhD in clinical psychology and trained as a Buddhist monk in Thailand, Burma and India) meditation has been brought out of the closet. My favorite among those pioneers is Jon Kabat-Zinn, who took mindfulness into the mainstream by developing a standardized teaching method of meditation. He is professor emeritus of the University of Massachusetts Memorial Medical Center and author of several practical books on mindfulness, including *Wherever You Go, There You Are*. And so we find ourselves, happily, in an era of serious exploration of how and why meditation works.

Neuroscientists today, and a very vocal population of scientist-meditators (such as Dr. James Austin, author of *Zen and the Brain: Toward an Understanding of Meditation and Consciousness*, who uses hard science to back up how meditation can "sculpt" the brain) have investigated meditation and mindfulness, which we will talk about in the next chapter. Scientists are taking advantage of new technologies to see exactly what goes on inside the brains of individuals who meditate regularly, and they are finding that it alters the way the brain is wired, leading to improved health and well being. One promising study that is underway at Oxford University's new Centre for Science of the Mind aims to shed light on the actual physiology of belief. The study, funded by the John Templeton Foundation, addresses the impact of faith on pain and suffering, hoping to answer the question: How do our spiritual and religious belief systems affect our state of consciousness? (Visit Oxcsom.ox.ac.uk to learn more.)

The Angst of Pain

We don't need elaborate double-blind protocols, random samplings and impressive research garb to experience the healing power of intent. I've heard it said that the body is the subconscious mind, or that the body and mind are one and the same. So any of us who have a body, ha, ha, can experience proof that intention works. Follow me through a personal tale of woe then whoa.

For several years, I had neck and shoulder pain and stiffness that went from mildly annoying to borderline debilitating. Early on, I consulted with my MD, whose solution was to write me two scripts—one for physical therapy and another for a horse dose of ibuprofen. The PT helped me to regain flexibility I'd lost from years of muscle tightness, but during the course of treatment I developed a lovely new pain that shot down my left arm and upper back. I ended the PT treatment feeling worse than when I started.

Out of desperation I contacted a colleague who happened to be a well-respected myofascial trigger point therapist who had trained under Dr. Jane Travell, President Kennedy's back doc. The TP work was excruciating, but after only one treatment, I would have a week or so reprieve from the pain. So, I'd venture to his office every couple of months and instruct him to "fix me good no matter how bad it hurts." During these years, I was raising my children and working full time. While I generally enjoy my life's freneticism, "stress" was a word mentioned too often in our household. My husband, children and I are high-energy individuals with diverse interests, so we have full plates almost every day. We're still high energy, but with an Everything Matters, Nothing Matters mindset I've learned to let most things roll off my back. But when I was a new bride and young mother, I was much more of a perfectionist in every area of my life—a fact that is central to my story here.

After a year or so of having infrequent TP appointments, the treatments lost their oomph. I wasn't experiencing pain relief and no one in his office could explain why I had this problem in the first place. They likened my symptoms to someone who'd been in a car accident or other jolting trauma, but I hadn't. I was doing everything they suggested: ensuring my computer work station was ergonomically sound, sliding a thin book under my left glutes to align my back; I had fun shopping for a fresh, firm bed pillow, and did gentle stretches to keep my scalene muscles loosened. In spite of these measures, the pain worsened. A constant, nagging ache prevented me from typing for any length of time. Most days, I couldn't sit, stand or lie down without a throbbing sensation in my left shoulder. Life goes on, and so did I, trying to keep up my normal pace even though my productivity had obviously fallen off—and I wished my left shoulder would have.

(I haven't yet mentioned that one of my greatest blessings is having a small collective of dear friends on the path—true soul connections. My daughter calls her best friends BGGs,

Best Friends Forever; I refer to my soul friendships as SFFs, Soul Friends Forever.)

One Saturday, I made plans with my SFF Jennifer to attend a health conference in our area to lend support to colleagues who were participating. Funny, because whatever healing happened that day took place during a conversation Jen and I had in my car. We parked and sat for a few minutes. I tried to make light of it but Jen knew I was suffering.

"Close your eyes," she instructed, "and let's figure this out."

Okay, eyes closed.

"Go into the pain. Ask when it started, the origin of the problem."

I immediately heard, "about 10 years ago." I tell Jen this.

"Good, what were you doing 10 years ago?"

"That's easy. Tomorrow is my son's birthday. He turns 10."

"Okay, how would you describe your life at that time?"

"I was very happy to have a healthy son and daughter. I loved that period of time when the children were babies! It was hectic though, too, because they're close in age." I knew Jen understood; she and her husband have three boys of their own.

Jen probed deeper. "Take yourself back to that time. Are you there?"

"Yes."

"What are you doing?"

"Hmm . . . I just flashed back to a day when something happened that was a little frightening for me as a new mom. Ha! I had forgotten about this incident! Gianne (my daughter) was about two and was becoming enamored with walking up steps. She was downstairs in the family room watching her favorite flick, Beauty and the Beast. I was upstairs in the kitchen with Carlin, then six months, in his walker. These steps connected the family room and kitchen, so I could hear Gianne from where I was standing at the sink, washing sippy cups and plastic plates.

"I heard her say 'Mama!' and by the time I rounded the corner she had teetered up four steps. She hadn't yet learned how to go down a staircase, only up, so I released the child gate at the top of the steps and scooted down to help her, afraid that she might lose her balance and take a hard tumble onto the floor below. Just then, I heard the ominous sound of that walker rolling across the kitchen floor. My daredevil son had managed to lap the L-shaped kitchen floor faster than Mario Andretti. I looked up and the front wheels of the walker were already hanging over the top step, with Carlin's feet a few inches from the edge. I bolted up the steps just as the walker started tumbling down and stopped it with my right hand. My heart was racing so fast!"

As I relayed this story to Jen, I got a mental image of myself stretched out on that flight of steps—one arm reaching up to stop Carlin from plummeting, the other extended downward to prevent Gianne from doing the same. "What a metaphor for my life at the time!" I blurted. "I was stretched thin—taking care of a baby and a toddler, working, helping to run my husband's business, renovating our house. I would say that's the period of time when something shifted in me. I went from successfully keeping all facets of my life in perfect order to realizing that something's got to give."

Jen asked, "So what happened to that area of your body in those moments?"

"Something snapped," I said, starting to get a clear intuitive image. "A piece of my energy broke off and is now aimlessly floating around in that region of my body."

"What does it look like?"

I was now "seeing" this area inside my body. "Hmm . . .

it's in the shape of a triangle, a pointy, rigid triangle that jabs me with its edges every time it moves!" I could clearly see this shape in my mind's eye, tumbling around the shoulder blade region.

"Does it have a name?" Jen deftly continued, letting her gut guide her and both of us knowing we were onto something meaningful.

"It DOES have a name," I said, surprised that a word came to me so quickly. "Its name is Angst, as in 'angular,' as in 'anxiety'."

One final directive from Jen: "Ask Angst what you need to do to release this rambling piece of energy."

I asked. "It's telling me that it's not a matter of releasing it from my body but reintegrating it back into that area." I was left to ponder how in God's name I'd be able to take this triangle image, this Angst piece of me, and make it "fit."

If anything, the immediate result of that intuitive dialogue with my source of pain was learning that this condition had gradually manifested over a much longer time period than I believed, which made me take it more seriously. There I was, trying to solve a 10-year-old, chronic problem by occasionally going for a treatment. Most patients at the center were coming in at least two or three times each week for several weeks or longer.

So I ramped up my schedule to once a week and switched to a younger, more aggressive therapist. After the first week, I noticed a slight improvement and was anxious to see how I felt after the second treatment. I walked in, hopeful, and the second round, though excruciating, went well. I left with the therapist's assurance that I was on the right track, yet my intuition was pushing me to solve the re-integration mystery.

I did nothing to heed this inner-voice advice, and that week I relapsed into severe pain. I couldn't help feeling disappointment; I was now getting more frequent treatments but wasn't improving. What was next for me to do? Physical therapy hadn't helped. My doctor wanted me to consult with an orthopedic specialist, but I knew the problem was muscular in nature. Acupuncture might work, I was told, but none of the health professionals around me seemed to know how to solve the problem because there wasn't a logical explanation for why it was "there." "It's probably something you'll have to deal with the rest of your life," the TP therapist told me, wanting to be realistic. "You may have to manage it by babying those muscles and getting more treatments whenever you have flare-ups."

Not what I wanted to hear. I was young and couldn't accept that I'd have to cope with this forever. Finally, I was ready to follow the internal calling to chat with Angst for answers.

"I don't want to talk today," I told my therapist at our third session. "I just want to lie still and meditate." No problem, she said. As she pressed deeply into hot spots along my scapular muscles, I tried to relax and tune in. What came to me were specific instructions on measures to take, like applying arnica gel, using heat, etc.—as well as the need to adjust my attitude towards this pain—and how to thank it for alerting me to bad habits in my life. I was also told to bless the pain and send it away because I had learned the necessary lesson and was working to rectify these unhealthy patterns. In other words, I was told to have faith that I would be healed of this affliction. I left for a planned beach vacation the next day and held the intent to be fully healed by the time of my return. Of course, I met the universe halfway by slathering on arnica gel, lying with a heating pad every evening and being consistent with stretching exercises. Further, with the sun rising over the ocean each dawn, I did a meditation in which I reaffirmed that I was healing, and I envisioned this triangle of broken-off energy reintegrating into my shoulder area. Every day, the pain lessened. By the flight home, I was 98 percent back to normal. This was five years ago. The pain has not returned since.

Since then, I've successfully self-healed other minor conditions through intuition and focused intent. Always, the ailment has a metaphysical reason for being and serves as a clarion call to some greater self-actualization. For instance, when dealing with recurring urinary tract infections (around the same time that I was working with root chakra / kundalini energy—no coincidence), I wanted to rid myself of them without the constant use of antibiotics. One week, after a round of Macrobid, I was feeling no better. So I took it to God. I simply asked, "Why do I have this problem now and what can I do about it?" What came through surprised me because it related to something that was to occur in my near future, something for which I was "being prepared."

First, I was told that the pain in my urine was to make me ultra-aware of what I was ingesting. In retrospect, I realized it was happening in response to an intention I had recently set: I had asked to be taken to the next threshold of my spiritual development—whatever that might be and in whatever form it would occur. I intuited that in order to elevate my energy vibration and heighten my connection to the Source, a process of purification would be required. I clearly followed the specific dietary instructions that were intuitively given to me; as a result, I was cured of these recurring infections without the further use of antibiotics—and haven't had one since. For anyone who suffers from UTIs, you know how huge a feat this is!

Quite naturally, I've seen intention heal others. Sometimes I assist in the process—rather, I hold the intent for higher energy to assist—and other times I share with others that the potential for self-healing exists. With such food for thought, many individuals figure out for themselves how to self-heal. You can, too. Even my son (who was 12 years old at the time), after experiencing (through my guidance) the overnight disappearance of a painful bruise on his knee from a hockey game, opened his mind to the possibility that he can play a role in his own healing.

I mention all of this here because in fulfilling our creative potential it sure helps to feel good physically and be balanced emotionally. In fact, I don't subscribe to the stereotype of the tormented artist who needs addictions to plunge into the depths of his imagination. Real creative power and genius is fully actualized from being clear, pure and whole.

EVERYDAY INTENTIONS:
THE TAMING POWER OF THE SMALL

In the Tao Oracle cards, beautifully written and illustrated by Ma Deva Padma, she talks about the "taming power of the small," or "learning to appreciate and work with times of having little influence" due to circumstances beyond our control. There are times when all our attempts seem to fail, she says, leaving us frustrated and feeling powerless. "This is a precious time for . . . making repairs in preparation for greater possibilities of influence that will arise later on." Padma advises us to work quietly behind the scenes with passive alertness. She offers the metaphor of a spider who works tirelessly to prepare her web. While many times her work may become damaged, she tends to the repairs without postponement, all the while blending into her surroundings. Once her web is made, she is utterly still, alert and waits in trust that some tasty opportunities will come her way.

I love this analogy in relation to both intention setting and the creative process. While I encourage grandiose imaginings that enable us all to live large, there is beauty in the small. In my experience, the universe most readily provides the things that we ask for with humility and self-restraint, things that we have carefully prepared for in some way. Case in point: Early on in my editing practice, I set the intention to manifest "one steady client who pays me handsomely to do a small amount of easy work each month"—easy, meaning work that wouldn't tax my creative faculties to the point where it detracted from other, more precious writing projects that required full immersion with the muses. I wasn't asking for fame, glory and great fortune, just a little extra reliable cash flow that would allow me to feel justified in spending time on my own writing endeavors.

I spun the groundwork by marketing my services to a variety of outlets—wire services, PR firms and such. Nothing seemed to stick but I continued to "repair the web" every time I reached a dead end. Then one day, a woman in my writers group informed me that she'd given my name to a magazine publisher in my area that I'd never thought to approach. "Their managing editor is leaving and they're looking for a replacement ASAP," she said. At first, it didn't dawn on me that this could be the answer to my intent. It didn't take long to figure out that it was the tasty opportunity I'd been waiting for once the publisher explained the position to me—practically a carbon copy of my intention. Our personalities clicked right away and my name hit the masthead the following month. The assignment is a breeze and I continue to very much enjoy working with this publisher, whose mission provides a tremendous service to their targeted readership.

I've found that divine manifestations of our intentions have a certain hallmark: Most often, they arrive effortlessly, out of the blue, with a touch of humor, and—like both this story and the ROI project mentioned earlier—in a way that we cannot imagine for ourselves.

LOGIC-DEFYING INTENTIONS:
THE LIMITLESS POWER OF THE GREAT

The Gnostic Gospel of Thomas preserves the words of Jesus, telling us: "If you do not bring forth the genius within you, it will destroy you. If you do bring forth the genius within you, it will free you." My corollary to this is that there is magic in remaining open to the largesse of the universe and danger in always sweating the small stuff and playing life safe. We all need regular doses of vastness in our lives; one of my favorite lines of modern day poetry by David Whyte says it well: "Anything that does not bring you alive is too small for you." Existing with higher consciousness and creative abandon allows us to discover new parts of ourselves and more fully explore our own magnificence. With choices based on integrity, we can manifest anything we can imagine. ANYTHING.

I'm willing to be dazzled, to cast aside the weight of so-called facts and float above "reality" for a while. In fact, I've been having fun recently with setting intentions for things that don't seem humanly possible. It came to me one day, for instance, that one talent I wish I had is a good singing voice. I grew up around a mom, two brothers, uncles and cousins who all have gorgeous voices—raw, inborn talent. My children are also blessed with natural singing voices and perform in their school's chorus ensemble, talent shows, summer rock bands and such. My singing voice, however, leaves much to be desired.

A *Course in Miracles* says, "There is no order of difficulty in miracles. One is not harder or bigger than another. . . . Miracles arise from a miraculous state of mind, or a state of miracle-readiness." Bearing that in mind, yes, I could take vocal lessons to improve my skill but that's not what I'm going for. I'm holding out for an utter metamorphosis of my singing ability (notice the "meta" part of that word). One day, I intend to open my mouth and the voice I always wished I had will pour out in all its magnificence. My inner voice will truly find a new level of external expression on that day. Think I'm nuts? The mind cannot conceive of that which is beyond the mind. This is clearly beyond-the-mind stuff, so don't ponder it too long. Try it on for size. It requires that suspension of disbelief. If we THINK, even subconsciously, that something is impossible, it will most likely never happen. On the other hand (we've touched on this already, yet it bears repeating), anything is possible with God.

Intentions Can Manifest Outside of Time and Space

Living in the realm of infinite possibility means that we're not limited to laws of physics and science. On a handful of occasions, for example, I've had time-warping incidents that remain unfathomable to me from a left-brain-only perspective. The first occurred when I was hopelessly (apparently not!) late for an airplane flight to Manhattan for an important meeting. I left my house less than an hour before the flight was scheduled to depart. Ordinarily, it's a good 45-minute drive to the airport and at least another 15 minutes to park and go through security (this was pre-9/11). As I walked through the airport to the gate, prepared to beg for a seat on the next departing flight to LaGuardia, I looked at my watch and realized that only 20 minutes had passed since I pulled out of my driveway. Sure enough, passengers were still boarding the plane. I couldn't make sense of this and, subconsciously, wanted verification of what had happened. Was it real?

I was given a "second chance to believe" the following evening while having a drink with a colleague in the hotel lounge.

"It's 9:30—let's make it a quick one because we both need to get a decent night's sleep," I said to her.

This former coworker was a very spiritually aligned person, and I enjoyed being in her company, conversing about all things metaphysical. Despite our agreement to turn in early, we quickly became engrossed in conversation and after what seemed like an intense, lengthy discussion about the direction and purpose of our respective lives, I glanced at my watch, expecting to see 11:30 or 12. It was 9:30. Something whirled inside my head (I physically felt this sensation) and I KNEW this was confirmation that time bending is possible. Of course, my immediate reaction was to think that the battery in my watch had gone kaput.

"What time do you have?" I asked folks at a neighboring table.

"Nine-thirty," they replied.

The two of us pondered this in silence—me transfixed, and my spiritually knowledgeable coworker amused.

"Oh, where has the time gone?!" we jested. When I shared with her my experience at the airport the day before, she encouraged me to simply accept the possibility of timelessness—and agelessness, for that matter.

I glanced again at my watch. 9:32. Battery okay.

In both cases, my underlying intention was clear. That meeting was the culmination of years of hard work and there's no way I was going to miss it, despite being unavoidably delayed that morning. The universe offered a supporting role by manipulating time and, in my disbelief, further demonstrated that such a phenomenon is possible.

Since then, I've learned to acknowledge when similar things happen and give thanks for the fact that time (and space) are more malleable and unfixed than we believe them to be. Master illusionist Christopher Howell says, "Magic is the pure belief that anything is possible. The answer is right in front of everybody's eyes. The possibility is always there, we just don't see it. Now you don't see it, now you do." This is similar to how I would describe the unseen power of universal intelligence—it's there all along; we just don't realize it . . . until we do.

*   *   *

And so, intention, when combined with attention, not only accelerates the development of consciousness, it enables us to become wildly generative receptacles through which creative inspiration flows. In the next two chapters, we will look at what happens when intention and attention are combined with regular dedication—taking some action in everyday life to open to a direct experience with Spirit. "Authentic spirituality does involve practice," says Ken Wilber, one of the most influential American philosophers of our time. "This is not to deny that for many people beliefs are important, faith is important, religious mythology is important. It is simply to add that, as the testimony of the world's great yogis, saints and sages has made quite clear, authentic spirituality can also involve direct experience of a living Reality, disclosed immediately and intimately in the heart and consciousness of individuals, and fostered by diligent, sincere, prolonged spiritual practice."

Having said that, remember: Intention should be effortless, a no-brainer. There is no struggle, no-thing to gain. Intention is about being in play with the free fall, and ravishing the results, no matter what. Ritual around intention-setting helps to solidify its meaning and level of importance in your life—that is not to say you need to DO anything. For now, simply intend to let the ideas in this chapter settle into your consciousness, into your heart, into your cells . . . and let's see what happens.

NOTE: At the end of the book, you will find Contemplations and Self-Creation exercises relating to each chapter. I welcome you to join me there at any time.

two

DAILY PRACTICE

Once you taste of the Divine, you become an addict for life.
Nothing else will ever satisfy your hunger in the same way.

—JOHN O'DONOHUE, POET AND AUTHOR

*T*he opening of one's consciousness is not unlike the unfolding of a flower into full splendor: it happens slowly, over time, when conditions are fertile and we give nourishment to the process. The art of awakening is like any other art; the only way to master it is through practice.

We all have a star seed, a magnificent cosmic gift, contained within our DNA. When conditions are right—when we have our first aha! moment and realize there's so much more we can become—that seed sparks forth and starts the growth process that is its birthright. What causes us to bloom into the ripeness and rightness of our personal selves is a daily practice of introspection and contemplation on the inner workings of the ego-self and soul-self, so as to understand not only who we are, but *why* we are. This takes dedication and devotion.

So, the second step in the process is to allow time to be still, meditate or have a daily practice where you're nurturing that part of yourself and bringing it to the forefront.

Most of us would agree that anything worthwhile takes work. When we take time for daily practice, we're essentially saying to God, "I want the essence of Creation to sing itself into me." This alone brings great rewards. When you're able to move through your days in a sort of contemplation—meaning, you are paying attention to the big picture and not the minutia—your intentions become more powerful.

The practices that I've used and recommend are practical, classic techniques that have stood the test of time. They've all been written about before—in fact, they've entered the mainstream vernacular to the point that they risk being watered down. What I want to emphasize is that these spiritual practices, though simple, are powerful and should be approached with respect. The more you work with them the more you hold them in reverence, because you come to fully comprehend just how potent they are. In fact, looking back upon the start of my spiritual life, I see how naïve I was to the realization of their power. If you yearn to connect with Creation and stay connected, these techniques will go a long way in helping you.

Opening to higher consciousness and creative flow requires leaving behind the mind for moments at a time or longer. Meditation is the means for successfully tipping you, at will, into a state of no-mind. As you adopt the Everything Matters, Nothing Matters life mantra, you will begin to experience every moment as a meditation. Gradually, your life turns into a prayer during which you are in constant communication with the Divine, ever confident that what you need to understand at that time will be revealed to you in the proper degree. It becomes a lifestyle, a way of being in the world. What I'm referring to specifically is mindfulness and the ability to "witness" your own existence. This occurs further along in the process of expanding one's consciousness (we will explore Witnessing in Chapter 6).

The first step for those just starting out is to commit to giving yourself quiet time to meditate/pray, spend time in nature, walk quietly through a museum or just be still. This will help clear the mind and, in return, allow the universe to fill you. Once you get out of the mind and into the universal consciousness, this is when miracles begin to occur.

MEDITATION: SILENCE BECOMES YOU

I've always savored that glorious space between wakefulness and sleep. It's always held intrigue for me—drifting off from a busy day, finally able to drop into the intoxicatingly pure silence between thoughts as they empty from my consciousness. In the evanescent seconds before sleep, there's nowhere to go, nothing to do except embrace pure rest. As a child, I remember lying in bed, listening to the rhythm of my breath as my lungs voluntarily welcomed and released it, until overtaken by slumber. Unwittingly, I was in training for what was to become a meditation practice many years later. Whether dozing during a catnap or floating along the slipstream of meditation, we are brought to stillness by the breath.

> **Silence is the root of everything. If you spiral into its void a hundred voices will thunder messages you long to hear.**
> **– Rumi**

Times change, the world spins on, souls come and go, but the experience of silence remains the same—one of the few true constants in this human existence. It blows my mind to think that the silence I hear when nodding off to dreamland every night or sitting in daily meditation is the same silence that Buddha experienced, the same silence that urges blades of grass to grow, the same silence that fell seconds before Jesus died on the Cross, the same silence before a star is born in outer space, the same silence that swept the streets of Auschwitz after the Germans were driven out, the same silence that existed before the universe was created. It contains everything.

Silence can be at once provocative and disorienting. No wonder it makes some people uncomfortable, accustomed as we are to the accelerating din and activity levels of our modern culture. We fill every minute of our time with actions that lead to some semblance of gratification or accomplishment. "I don't have time to meditate," I hear people say. (Of course you do!) "I'm not doing anything when I'm meditating," some insist, as if doing nothing is a plague to be avoided at all costs. "It's a waste of time." I assure you, clearing the decks and cleansing the mind isn't a waste of time.

During my early 30s, I'd heard about the benefits of meditation and decided to give it a formal go. I wanted to know what all the fuss was about, why disciples would sit on teensy zafu-cushions in ashrams, or monks in Himalayan caves, for days, weeks, years. It hinted of escapism, something done to avoid reality and certainly not an activity that hard-working, carpooling, home-owning, politically correct people engage in. I knew that The Beatles and 60s beatniks had been into it, and I rationalized that any voodoo resulting in the *The White Album* and Kerouac's bohemian *On The Road* odyssey must have *some* perverse, poetic value.

At that stage in my life—with two babies in tow, a marketing career, marriage and a home to tend—being still in body or mind for more than five minutes was a foreign concept. Time to "do nothing" seemed to never arrive on its own. I had to create it. Once I finally did honor my commitment to carve out slices of solitude, though, I had a tough time winding down my mind. So much chatter! I found myself filling this initial meditation time with mental to-do lists that seemed to go on forever. But as I began to meditate on a regular basis, I was gradually able to put the eraser to the big chalkboard in my head, although it still took a minimum of 30 minutes to wipe away the mental clutter. Admittedly, meditation seemed boring at first. I wondered why I wasn't feeling transported, why a Roman candle wasn't igniting underneath my cushion and shooting me to the stars. (I've since learned to always respect the way a meditation comes to me, without expectation.)

You Will Only Know Meditation by Doing It

I turned to books in order to unlock the deeper mysteries of meditation. Would I go that route again? No. Why not? Because the only way to know meditation is to do it, just do it (and then keep doing it). There have been hundreds of books written and audiotapes produced about meditation, when really all it comes down to is this: breathing.

Want to learn how to meditate? Here's everything you need to know in a single strand of declarative statements: sit straight, close your eyes, follow your breath, allow thoughts to come as they may, release them one by one, continue to follow your breath and say bye-bye to thoughts until there are no thoughts and your mind is a clean slate. Do this . . . well, until you can do it. (It might take an hour each time for several months or longer; it might take a minute each time later on.) The mind is meant to be your servant, not your master. You are in control of it and can train it to do what you want.

You Can't Do It Wrong

Nothing can "go wrong" when you meditate. You cannot do it wrong. If you fall asleep, enjoy the rest—you need it. If you cannot clear your mind of thoughts, stop telling yourself you can't and return to the breath. In, out. In, out. In, out. You can do it. There are no other requirements. Everything else is ritual designed to get you to the gap: lighting a candle, listening to shakuhatchi flute music, chanting a mantra, visualizing a mandala, repeating an affirmation, clutching prayer beads, placing your hands in a mudra position. All these things are ultimately unnecessary, but engage in them if you are inclined, as sacred ritual is important in its own right. If you stick with meditating long enough, you'll be able to do it standing on your head, up a tree, in a crowded airplane or on your bed with the children screaming in the next room.

If you're new to this, don't expect anything to "happen" when you meditate. In fact, having an expectation is similar to holding a thought—and you already know that what we're going for here is only going to be discernable "between" thoughts. Most of the benefits from meditation—clarity of mind, acute awareness, pure knowledge, perfect balance, infinite peacefulness, increased vitality, the ability to simply *be* (pretty groovy stuff)—happen primarily when you're NOT sitting in a lotus position. Yes, you awaken from each meditation more alive than when you entered it. Over time, you begin to feel better and look better. You discover that flirting with silence becomes you—a sort of spiritual facelift with no risk of side effects. So, enter your still point with as little attachment to the outcome as possible, and realize that most benefits will be recognized over time in the higher quality of your daily life.

The Depth Eventually Deepens
Not to say that things *can't* occur when you meditate. If you're practicing regularly, I promise you a day will invariably come when something WILL unfurl when you are in meditation—a scent, a sound, a vision, a voice, a taste, a touch, a color, a wisp of insight—and, best of all, flashes of creative brilliance.

In short, your perception of what you think is possible will be instantaneously expanded. There you'll be, merrily going along, meditating in your usual manner, spiraling away any thought remnants that bubble up, just grateful for 15 minutes of relaxation in your day, then . . . bam! The silence widens and the expanse in your head becomes borderless. You're still in your room, sitting cross-legged in the chair, but your consciousness has just rappelled into a deeper depth with an incomprehensible vastness. Peripherally, you're able to hear the dog bark in the back yard or the cell phone thrum on the hallway table, but you're light years away, cordlessly bungee jumping off an ethereal cliff toward a distant netherworld of beckoning possibility. The atmosphere into which you've leapt consists only of the absence of everything; exhilarated, you allow yourself to be swallowed up in a safety net of absolute trust.

As a reward for such trust, anything can arise, including that Roman candle thing. Eureka can strike. Travel on the space-time continuum can take place (current passport not required and no schlepping through customs upon reentry). Insights can plummet forward, showing you the way where there once was none. From the stillness, a tremendous pulsating force can arise, taking any number of splendorous forms. Here's one: the sublime essence of purest love can shimmer up and permeate every cell in your body, reducing you to rapturous tears. Or, you can reach that exotic place where you're entirely out of your head, just observant and amused, as if your life belongs to someone else.

A Queen Emerges

When I first started a meditation practice many years ago, I would only see colors—vivid purple, green and blue. Then one morning, about six months into my regular practice, an unmistakable image flashed through the nothingness. The vision was a stone statue of an Egyptian queen, adorned with an ornate headdress, and it rotated 360 degrees in my mind's eye, enabling me to get a full glimpse of her profile. I was sufficiently freaked out by this uninvited simulacrum, and its appearance shocked me out of my relaxed state. I sat up straight, eyes like salad plates, and pondered what it meant.

Gradually, I connected enough mental dots to draw a loose conclusion about why THIS image, why NOW. Around that time, I'd made the monumental decision to transition from toiling in advertising and corporate marketing to work that focused solely on journalism and narrative writing. It was a bold declaration (to myself) that I wished to follow my true vocation as a nonfiction writer—not just penning ad copy, company newsletters, media releases and such, but really being a writer in *every* sense of the word. You know, scribbling on tablets into the wee of the night like Virginia Woolf in *The Hours*, extrapolating the soul, losing myself between lines of Kafka and Nabokov. This decision brought me miles closer to who I really was (and had always been—for goodness sakes, my favorite childhood book was the *Merriam-Webster Dictionary!*). This is how I wanted to live, with creativity at the fore.

As I've intuitively discovered over the years, it also was a return to who I once was in other lifetimes. (I've experienced conscious memories of having lived in ancient Egypt as a scribe to the queen. I will speak more about this later.) This meditation talisman of an Egyptian queen—Nefertiti, I believe—was a simple confirmation that my choice to go forward with righting full time was the write one (two words purposely transposed to see if you're awake), as it's something that's been an important part of me for a long, long, long time.

Now, far from being boring (because all sorts of crazy, cool stuff has transpired since my visit with the queen), meditation is something I crave. The feeling it imparts is addictive in a healthy way. I know that it's possible to do nothing yet still feel powerful and exquisitely peaceful. And after a dozen or so years of practicing, it takes only minutes, even seconds, to tune into my center of stillness. Meditation is not a waste of time any more than sleep is; conversely, it makes every moment count and its resulting clarity makes you more efficient in daily life.

Meditation is the most effective way to expand your consciousness because it creates a direct, unbridled link to your higher self and the creative intelligence of the universe. Like intuition, meditation is innate; your body already knows how to shift into a state of profound rest. You do this every night. Yet meditation differs from sleep in one distinct way: you are resting more deeply than you do when you sleep; and paradoxically, you are consciously awake. Instead of falling asleep, you fall awake.

All you type-As out there, trust me on this. If I can master the concept of mingling with silence, so can you. Create time in your life to give it a try, and just begin, bearing in mind the words of Zen philosopher Dogen: "When you walk in the mist, you get wet." In other words, by simply engaging in the practice of meditation, you will inevitably absorb the great teachings that exist in the sound of silence, and you'll agree that there's no place like OM.

CONTEMPLATION: LIFE AS A WHISPERED PRAYER

If meditation serves to crack open the cosmic door, then the art of contemplation—in which every moment is a whispered meditation—is the door swung wide open. Being able to live in perpetual contemplation (I imagine, as I'm still getting there) would lead us to the peak human experience of living with unconditional love—which is the hinges of the door being blown off. After this stage, we don't need a door, we have transcended.

I use the word "imagine" because my desire several years ago had been to successfully jump the chasm from occasional higher and blissful states to a leveling off in which I can realize those higher states all the time. In 2004, I had the pleasure of interviewing teacher, scientist and modern day mystic David Hawkins, MD, PhD, a prolific author and authority on the nature of consciousness. I was really curious about this level-ing-off effect at the time, so I queried him. "Can we stay in this heightened state or is it more likely that we experience brief periods of it then return to our *normal* state?"

"It ebbs and flows," he responded. "It's not linear. It's more like the stock market—up and down, up and down."

I'd had peak experiences leading up to that time and since then have discovered that as our spiritual practice becomes dedicated and long term, our connection to higher conscious-ness evolves from simply being a passing phase into a perma-nent characteristic—something that, if done enough, becomes part of who we are. I've found this to be a self-perpetuating phenomenon: as we begin to experience the oneness of the universe very profoundly through repeated practices and train-ing that reinforce those peak states, the more effortlessly and naturally the heightened and integrated state of contempla-tion occurs. I would describe this "oneness of the universe" as feeling totally connected with the one centrifugal energy that flows through all of creation with no sense of separateness. Everything Matters! With contemplation, the focused aware-ness that we realize through meditation becomes much more than (and everything *other* than) simply sitting in silence in a room with candles and incense. Our everyday activity becomes infused with it—whether we're folding laundry, mowing the lawn or walking the dog—and it brings us more fully alive.

I'm now in my car on the way to a meeting in Ohio. It's a crisp, blue-sky autumn day. The sun is glistening through colorful foliage. Shadows of already barren trees reflect off the road. Yellow school buses blend with the bright yellow leaves. As I drive along, my car whips the leaves aside and creates a path, literally and figuratively. What a perfect time to keep the radio OFF and tune in (no singing today!). So often we fill our time with noise. Road trips are a great chance to get into a contemplative state. Of course, I'm paying attention to my driving because as we know about meditation, it's about heightened awareness, not a sleep state. Focusing on driving becomes like chanting a mantra, which allows my mind to clear itself of everything else that I might be thinking and float into contemplation. I've found this to be an effective means for being creatively productive. In fact, this book project began with notes that I tape recorded while driving north by north-east. I outlined the entire manuscript by keeping the radio off, entering a contemplative state and allowing the information to pour through my voice into the tape recorder.

A Simple Daily Routine

I'm not advocating something rare or exotic. To date, at least 1,600 scientific studies have established the benefits of having a spiritual practice. The form that your practice takes should be whatever has the most meaning for you.

Here is my own typical daily routine: I do a morning meditation when time permits. I call in the energy of God, Christ, Divine Mother, the Holy Spirit and any other energies from Divine beings, mother earth, nature, heaven or the cosmos that seem "appropriate" that day or that I sense are present and willing to work with me. I ask for only the highest and purest energies to come through. I give thanks for life, health, family and friends, and the infinite forms of abundance bestowed upon me—from the ability to have a clear mind to the cup of coffee I savor upon waking each morning (and the fact that my husband lovingly takes care of brewing the coffee). I silently announce my intentions for the day and send prayers to those who've either requested that I do so, or who I feel may need a healing boost.

Then I settle into the silence and see what shows up. Oftentimes, insights for the day will bubble forth. On days when life is frenetic, all I can manage is a brain dump; keeping a notepad nearby allows me to write down things that I need to remember. (Be mindful of these subconscious thoughts, as they are oftentimes emergent intentions—whether we intend them consciously or not.) Sometimes, a message will download for me or someone else—which I usually type right into my laptop. Other days, I simply relish the nothingness because I realize it's probably going to be the calmest, quietest piece of my day. I close the meditation by once again expressing gratitude for life. When I don't have time for an a.m. meditation, I can at least take a moment in the shower, or even upon waking, to ask for the highest and best outcome for the day ahead. I ask the universe to amaze and amuse me with its wisdom and whimsy. If I desire guidance on a particular issue for the day, I will either ask Spirit to be with me when confronting that situation or will simply say "show me the truth of what I need to know about this circumstance now." Then, I go on with my day, moving more into contemplation. At random times throughout the day, I stop, connect and observe whatever comes through my consciousness. This generally doesn't take any longer than a few seconds. Stop, connect, observe. This keeps my day on its truest course.

With enough practice of living in contemplation, there is no seam between formal tuning in and all other everyday pursuits. Intentions can go from being specific statements made at the dawning of a new day or during a special moonlit ritual, to ongoing, evolving, moment-to-moment contemplations that bend and sway like reeds on a breeze. I check my "voice messages" in this contemplative manner with no interruption of the tasks I'm doing—whether it's preparing dinner for my family or producing a public event for hundreds of people.

CHAKRA BREATHING: FACILITATING THE CONNECTION

Breathing is not only necessary to being alive (and an important part of meditation), it's also one of the simplest, best things you can do to facilitate the expansion of your consciousness and creative faculties. Since ancient times, various breathwork techniques have been practiced to promote physical, mental and spiritual health—pranayama, ujai breath and chanting, to name a few—but one basic yet effective technique that has brought me worlds closer to feeling consciousness in the physical body is chakra breathing. By meditating on the chakras, the key energy centers, significant breakthroughs in self-understanding, personal healing and artistic inspiration are possible. (To utilize this breathing exercise, it's necessary to have a basic understanding of the etheric body and the chakra energy system. One of the best modern day resources on this topic is the work of former NASA research scientist and healer Barbara Ann Brennan; read *Hands of Light* and *Light Emerging*.)

Chakra breathing is a blessed event, not unlike taking communion at church or lying supine in the Redwood Forest to fathom the enormity of those Grandmother Spirits. It is holy because it forms a direct link between your energetic body and the Creator. In this practice, you are breathing life force energy, or chi, up the spinal channel—from your root chakra at the base of the spine, up through the solar plexus and heart, to the crown chakra at the top of the head, and beyond to the universe. As you inhale and visualize each of these seven energy centers coming alive and pulsating, your energy shifts—sometimes subtly, other times, markedly—to a quicker, higher level. I also envision the additional chakras that extend above the crown as a column of light reaching up to heaven. It's a beautiful way to rejuvenate your energy field and prepare to receive creative downloads. If chakra breathing is done consistently enough, a moment will come when there is no physical separation between your energetic field and everything else that extends beyond it.

Chakras as Gateways to Your Life Story

When you begin to experiment with the chakra system (and your personal energy field in general), what awaits is a world of rich symbology, meaning and great learning about the self. These energy vortices not only represent our mental, emotional and etheric aspects (root: material; sacral: sexual; solar plexus: power center/ego; heart: love and community; throat: verbal/ rational mind; third eye: psychic-mind; and crown: light and transcendence), they also correlate to our human lifeline. And so we have root: birth; sacral: adolescence and puberty; solar plexus, coming-of-age years; heart: young adulthood; throat: finding our voice and place in the world; third eye: opening to spiritual vision and maturity; and crown: death. As such, each chakra retains the experiences of the life development stage it represents—including any traumas or unresolved dynamics. I believe that each of us has all ages and stages contained within us, even those we have yet to experience. As creative beings, our essential work is to reveal these layers. When we tune into the energetic biography of our lives, we remember circumstances in which we lost or found ourselves. Through our chosen art or craft, we're given opportunities to reshape these experiences, using wisdom, maturity, forgiveness and deeper self-awareness as our (re)construction materials.

I came into this realization about the chakras and their equivalence to the human timeline during a weekend retreat in which 25 of us from all walks of life and geographic locations experienced intensive energy work interspersed with chakra meditations. In sharing a few of my experiences from that weekend, I hope to illustrate more fully for you the value of this type of internal work.

As we honed in on the second chakra (creativity/sensuality, ages 6 to 12) during a guided meditation, I revisited an incident in my early childhood that helped me understand and reaffirm the importance of one of my core values as an adult. In my inner sight, I was transported back to a neighborhood tree house at the edge of my childhood friend Sally's backyard. Sally and another childhood friend, Ann, were there, along with two girls I didn't know very well. We were, for whatever reason, playing dentist. I wanted nothing more than to fit in and was devastated when Sally (one of my best friends, I thought) began to make fun of me in front of the other girls. I was forced into the "patient's chair" and the bed sheet we'd tacked along the tree for privacy was whipped away. Sally stuck her fingers in my mouth and began counting.

"Yuck, she has 50 teeth!" Sally exaggerated. It was her attempt to embarrass me in front of Ann, hopefully replacing me as Ann's best friend. (Wow, girls can be catty!)

"She's a freak! Get her out of my office!" Ann chimed in, willing to play along.

I ran home crying, and believing that I had a mouthful of big choppers. As I reconnected with this humiliating moment in my young life (which I hadn't even remembered until that day), I pondered why I felt it so necessary to fit in. My mind zoomed forward to my grade school years. I was often taunted about my curly hair and olive-toned skin, but by the time I reached seventh grade I started to not care about being like everyone else. In high school, I actually *wanted* to be different. Now in my life, I appreciate the beauty of being unique, knowing we are all aspects of God. Reflecting on that day at the tree house as a little girl led me to clearly identify with one of my most precious core values, which is to innovate, be original . . . and be different! I'm not always going to fit in (by someone else's standards) and that's okay, even preferable. Now, I'm just happy to be me.

I'd like to spend just another minute on the second (sacral) chakra, as it is the emotional center of the body that energizes both our biological creativity (reproduction and procreation) and our psychological-emotional-spiritual expression of creativity. "Since our culture is challenged around supporting children's emotional and creative expression," suggests Susan J. Wright in *The Chakras in Shamanic Practice*, "from a shamanic perspective there is much to be healed in this chakra." I agree that we've all taken some shrapnel in this area—a hit here or shot there from someone telling us we cannot or should not express ourselves or be who we are, even forbidding us to do so. Do you have a story to tell about how you were suppressed or shunned in this way, particularly during the ages of 6 to 12? I sure do. (For a contemplation exercise on this subject, please see p. 239.)

During the next day of that retreat, we connected with the third eye (intuition/spirituality) and crown (mastery/unconditional love/freedom/miracles) chakras. Both meditations brought forth beautiful experiences. The third-eye meditation took me out into a blue-lit cosmos, where I saw a multitude of complex layers of live matter; each had its own paper thin pattern, and they overlaid each other. Their patterns were light, almost transparent, and I could see the blue of the universe through them. All of these layers and patterns were extraordinarily alive, aware and breathing with life force energy. They all eloquently came together to form a superconsciousness that I can only describe as Oneness. I stared in awe at this inner vision for what seemed like hours until a vortex opened in the middle of it. I thought I might be taken to another place in the cosmos; instead, I was drawn down to our beloved planet and shown depictions of earthly scenes: a 1950s kitchen, an open window, a murder site, a field of poppies, a cemetery headstone, a Vegas casino, a dilapidated village with sick, starving children sitting along a wall. I knew this all represented the human experience. This vision left me with two unforgettable impressions: 1) From the grandest perspective of the cosmos, it is evident that we are but a speck of "living matter." From this mega-view, truly, Nothing Matters because all is exactly as it should be. The things we fret about—even death—are insignificant. And 2) Truly, Everything Matters because all details of our human experience—including every living being and thing (even inanimate objects are alive)—deserve respect, compassion and reverence for the miracles they are. Both impressions, taken together, illustrated to me the value of integrating our human and spiritual natures.

At the crown chakra, I received a powerful message of guidance. As I saw myself walking into an intense ball of divine light, my logical left brain bumped into the moment and I thought, *Oh, a ball of light, how trite.* So I cleared my mind and asked for another symbol. As I waited, waited, waited, I began to notice a feeling of bliss in my physical body, a sublime energy pulsating up and down my spinal column. Then the message came: "Don't look for external symbols of I AM, as I AM inside of you." When we came out of that meditation,

I was so completely tapped up with pure light that I could literally feel it beaming out of me—very cool, indeed. From that day forward, I have never forgotten that the ultimate confirmation of the existence of the Divine is always internal.

* * *

Consistent practice of meditation, contemplation and chakra breathing will undoubtedly facilitate higher states of consciousness. As you raise your vibration through these practices, you will begin to discover frontiers beyond the thought process, a sacred new land in which awareness rises directly from your intuition. Your dedication to Daily Practice will be rewarded tenfold with spontaneous realizations—about people, things and situations—that arrive in a form of knowingness or creative sparks. This direct knowing, which originates from the third eye and connects us to higher realms, is typically referred to as claircognizance.

INTUITION EXPANDING INTO CLAIRCOGNIZANCE

As a child, I dreamed of traveling to distant lands and seeing for myself all the things that I read about in books. I'd scour whatever texts I could find and study everything from ancient civilizations to modern pop culture. But that's all it was: passive learning. I yearned for the day when I could experience for myself the mysteries of this oblate sphere we call Earth. And so, in the past 20 years, I've had the good fortune of traveling to the ancient ruins in Rome, Stonehenge and other stone circles in England, the mystical Aran Islands off the coast of Ireland, the historic forts and lush rainforest of Puerto Rico, the mountain ranges and volcanos in the South American Andes and the Hawaiian Islands. I will never tire of crossing time zones.

Now, as a student of intuition, I realize that I don't need to hop a plane to get to my destination. I've come full circle— back in that chair like when I was a kid with a book in my lap. Expanding my consciousness has brought me to a point where I'm now able to do what I once thought unimaginable: travel to, and actually *experience*, distant worlds without leaving my living room. I never thought it was possible to sit in one place and go so far away.

Intuitive travel isn't limited by geography. I call it Inter-galactic Geographic, because of its ability to travel outside of time and space as we know it. Back to the future, forward to the past, inside the body, into another's mind. In this book I will be your travel writer, describing to you the places I've been, reporting on what I've seen, and (I hope) making sense of the reasons behind it all. And you won't have to take my word for it because you'll know that you can do it yourself.

We all exist in a larger, invisible dynamic of which our physical reality is a part. As our intuition matures, we learn to perceive, appreciate and act in accordance with this larger perspective. Eventually, we will begin to notice that our real-ity has become reoriented to include a greater reality beyond the physical plane. I'm far from being the only person who can access this greater reality. In fact, during the past five years in particular, I've noticed that more and more individuals are experiencing an opening of their intuitive faculties or obvious expansion of their attitudes. It's all part of our natural societal progression as we move through the current planetary intuitive evolution.

An intelligent intellect becomes aware of its limitations and thus seeks answers outside itself.
– David R. Hawkins

Yes, spiritual study utilizes the intellect. Eventually, as Dr. Hawkins tells us, we understand that the mind has its own inherent limitations and must be transcended. Little by little, we become comfortable with being outside of the mind and into the true essence of things. Once we're able to shift from reliance on being in the mind to not, this leaves space for our spiritual and creative vision to emerge. It seems to me that one of the fundamentally dynamic characteristics of using intuition is that it challenges us to either accept or reject that there are dimensions of ourselves that may not have previously been included in our self-concept, and that life is much deeper, broader and more heightened than we perceive it to be. It makes us undeniably aware that we are living yet an inkling of what we really are. But, we can exist in that deeper, broader dimension all the time, if we choose.

The Value of Voyages to Other Realms

Like travel on the earth plane, voyages to unseen worlds are most beneficial if we learn something from them. All of this spiritual aspiration and practice does have a great purpose, I've found, and tremendous healing ability. At first, I didn't understand this, until I met an energy healer from Brazil who would become my spiritual mentor—Edemir Rossi.

As I began to work alongside him in his client energy healing sessions (which I did for first-hand experience, not to someday become a licensed practitioner), a lot of information would start funneling through my consciousness; yet I couldn't correlate exactly how what was coming through me was relevant to helping the person on the healing table. I began to realize that the clients aren't always able to work on a subconscious level for themselves to heal certain issues. In many cases, a person may not even be aware that he has a subconscious issue that needs to be resolved or healed in some way.

With practice, I've found that I'm able to access these deeper levels and effect positive change in some way that is unique to each individual. When I'm working in tandem with other healers, we are simultaneously directing energy to all levels of the client's energy field—whether conscious, subconscious, etheric, auric, mental or emotional. No wonder people leave their sessions feeling rejuvenated from the inside out!

In Chapter 5, we will revisit some of my travel destinations in more detail, including some of the very first healing sessions that I participated in. During those early months, I was fascinated and intensely gratified to receive third-eye visions that seemed so complete, as if I were passively watching a TV movie or feature film in a theater. As a writer, I was riveted by these living mysteries. This was spiritual storytelling in its truest, most authentic form. The client's subconscious would speak to me with such clarity and vibrancy that I felt awed and humbled by the opportunity to connect with each person on such an intimate level. What came up for the person wasn't always pleasant—sometimes what I tuned into was heart-wrenching or gruesome—but it always had great purpose. Something, or some aspect of that person, was crying out to be healed.

In the beginning, this kind of visceral storytelling usually happened in the presence of my mentor, Edemir (we will discuss why this is so in Chapter 5, as well). As my vibration heightened over time, I found that my mind's eye was always open, and information would come unbidden at any time. A quick example: About five years ago, I started what I call a monthly Intuitive Dialogue group. My intent was to invite others in the community to experiment with refining our intuition and share our experiences based on this. When I met Marilyn (a woman in our group) for the first time, I saw Our Lady of Guadalupe on her right side and a Native elder on her left. Not knowing Marilyn, I hesitated to say what I saw. Then she told me that she'd just returned from a trip to Mexico with her church group. So I spoke up. Marilyn's face brightened when she explained that she had felt an affinity towards Our Lady of Guadalupe on her trip, and had brought home a statue of her for inspiration. She went on to discuss her long-term interest in Native American medicine and spirituality. Through hundreds of little incidents like this, I've learned to trust the information that comes from Spirit. It's become a vital part of my daily spiritual practice.

DREAMS: INTUITION WITH THE LIGHTS OUT

I peered out the picture window at Mom's house, watching fish and insects rain down on the concrete driveway. They poured onto the ground as if buckets were being tipped here and there, contents splattering to the pavement with sharp, slapping sounds. Fish flopped and insects scurried about. I wasn't unnerved, only observant. Just then, I became aware that the necklace I was wearing felt very front-heavy. It was a porcelain egg on a string, the kind that opens in the middle with a little golden latch. The egg was so heavy it strained my neck. Afraid the string would snap, I gently cupped the egg in my hands and opened it. Inside, fish and insects floated in water. As I dumped them out onto a clean, white surface, I thought, *Gee, I'm going to have to empty this every so often so the string doesn't break.*

If I told you that I'd just witnessed a deluge of fish and insects from the sky, you'd call me certifiable. Truth is, I *did* experience it, only on a subconscious level. Does this make it any less real? Does the fact that this scene unfolded while I was asleep disallow its power to help me understand the part of my life that transpires while I'm not asleep? Besides, who among us is completely awake? Some of us are more catatonic than others, but none of us is fully enlightened. We spend, on average, one-third of our lives in a subconscious state. We're asleep yet we're still alive, therefore our dreams are lived experiences. Why not learn what this level of existence has to teach us.

Dreams Show Us that the Subconscious is Real

Dreams awaken our intuition. Not everyone gives credence to the little voice inside, but everyone involuntarily dreams. If you're honoring your internal voice and want greater clarification on any matter of significance large or small, your dreams will lovingly blow you a message on your matter of inquiry. If you discount your sixth sense, believe me, your dreams will eventually scream at you like the fool you are for not listening to it.

My fish-and-insect dream came at a time when I'd acknowledged my desire to bring forth my own inner stories. I'd begun writing a series of essays that were autobiographical in nature—an emotionally charged activity, since I'd chosen to excavate an unpleasant time in my younger life. Water represents emotion (so elemental in my dream life, because I'm an emotion-based person and a water sign, Scorpio). Fish swim in water and are symbolic of reaching into one's own depths, penetrating the subconscious in search of personal truth. Insects are often busy, determined and active, so dreaming of them at that time was a testament to my own hard work and professional goals. Necklaces generally suggest wish-fulfillment, and it was definitely an urgent wish of mine to plumb my emotional depths and transform these emotions into written content. It's true, I was determined and active in this pursuit, busy like a bee. And yes, at times, the emotional weight of it all seemed too much to bear. The responsibility of following through on my desire (or worry of not being able to do so) weighed heavily on me, like a noose around my neck.

That egg—the shape of conception, genesis, fertility— held the potential for what would ultimately hatch into little scoops of stories. If properly fertilized with the creative force and incubated, an egg germinates new life (in my case, a new project). It was my imperative to empty the egg every so often onto the page—to get at the truth of a situation or emotion. The egg's white color lends it the association of perfection. I sought perfection for this project because it would serve as a standard bearer of my work. Mom's house indicates my child-hood home, my younger years, going back to retrieve memories. Every element in the dream meant something and contributed to the whole, like pieces in an ethereal jigsaw puzzle.

By respecting what my dream wanted to tell me, I clearly understood that I didn't have to get drenched in a torrent of unsettling emotions about the past, and I didn't need to feel overwhelmed about the enormity of the project. Rather, my task was to "open up and empty out" vignettes of my life story, bit by bit. In other words, no need to feel stressed or urgent about the work, just look upon it lovingly and be willing to unzip my soul onto the page.

Swiss psychiatrist Carl Jung was the first to suggest that there is such a thing as the "collective unconscious"—a por-tion of the mind that warehouses information common to all humans. This was his rationale for the fact that an African aborigine who speaks only Swahili and a coal miner from the backwoods of West Virginia could have dreams with specific symbols that have the same apparent meaning. Jung identified our waking selves, with our ego-based posturing and regalia, as the persona. Because we humans are nauseatingly con-cerned with outward appearances and what others think of us, the mind gifts us with dream characters that represent our hidden selves.

Austrian psychiatrist Sigmund Freud was one of my heroes

up through my sophomore year of studying psychology in college. As a young woman in the throes of ravenous coming-of-age hormonal fluctuations, I tended to agree with Freud's assessment that we're all repressed, neurotic and oversexed, and our dreams are symptomatic of this unfortunate nature. Now that I know more, I believe that it was Freud who was repressed, neurotic and oversexed. Another of my early heroes, Plato, had his own thoughts about what waits for us in sleep: "In all of us, even in good men," he wrote, "there is a lawless wild beast nature which peers out in sleep."

I have no wish to take on Plato, Aristotle, Jung, Freud and other good people who've philosophized over the millennia about the meaning and metaphor of dreams. Let's keep all their research (including that of Hippocrates, the founder of modern medicine and a believer that dreams are a reflection of the bodily state and therefore can be used as a diagnostic apparatus); and let's add to it the possibility that our egoless sleep state allows us to gain entry into other higher states of consciousness and creativity—states that we normally deny ourselves access to because of our limited thinking. No jacket required in dreams. A backstage pass with your name always awaits.

To Pee or Not to Pee

Your intuition naturally expands during dream state. In fact, it is the closest that many of us come to experiencing union with our psychic selves. All dreams have meaning, but they're not all equally important. In many instances, dreams are your mind's clearinghouse for insignificant thoughts, events, beliefs or fears in waking life, and can be easily dismissed. Others are so striking that they remain in your memory for years, even a lifetime. These dreams generally have intuitive overtones and are likely to have greater consequence. They are your inner voice speaking to you, and are worthy of reflection.

When I'm preparing to write a lengthy project that I have to immerse myself in, I typically dream of urination or defecation (sorry to be gross!). I've had many variations on this pee-theme over the years. In 1996, while working on my first book, I'd dream of doing my duty in public restrooms, a sure sign that I was concerned about what the public's reaction to my ideas was going to be. Usually, during the weeks when I was diligently drafting the manuscript, I'd dream that I was letting out such copious amounts that the flow resembled a faucet being turned on, directly onto the floor, swooshing down a drain in the floor. Just when I'd made a sloppy mess, a stranger would walk in and shoot me a nasty look, naturally.

Months later, when I was approaching literary agents for representation, my dreams on this topic altered in tone and content. In one, for example, I'm in a college class (denotes learning) and I can't find a bathroom before the lecture begins. I leave the lecture hall and enter a huge, formal office. A woman appears and scolds me for entering the headmaster's house. I plead to use her bathroom, and she reluctantly allows me to because the headmaster isn't home. I try to not make my usual mess and thank her for allowing me access. Clearly, this dream connotes my desire to unleash my "creative juices" in the office of an authority figure—at that time, a literary agent.

In 2001, I began another writing project that required emotional submersion. So now what happens? A few weeks into the process, I dream that I'm at college (still learning) and pleased to be there. It's the beginning of the school year. I'm shown, of course, the *bathroom*, since that's where my creative output will occur. I'm happy and surprised to see that it looks more like an executive washroom than a dank, dark, smelly place. I was especially taken with the commode, which had ornate brass handles, a mahogany seat, and was pristine and private (not like before, where I had to go in the middle of an open room). I say to myself, "Now here's a toilet I can get comfortable sitting on!" Problem solved; anxiety gone. The following week, I plunge into outlining the project and have great fun doing it.

Within a month, I'd refined the concept, drafted chapter outlines and felt good about what I'd produced thus far. Right on cue, a dream arrives in the night. I'm at a friend's house, someone who, in real life, is supportive of my work. I show her a wooden toy, a block of wood with a face on it, like a Tinker Toy or Lego head. I hold it lovingly in the palm of my hand and say, "Meet my baby!" I mention something about being afraid to leave the head too long without the body, that it might die. I'd birthed the head—the rational, vital part (concept, structure)—but must now give birth to the "body" of the manuscript. I'm afraid that if I don't do that soon, my enthusiasm for the project will die. The toy clearly meant that I was much more playful with the process of writing this project compared to the previous one.

"Guided" Dreams

My mom has said to me on several occasions, "I have three mothers: the Blessed Mother, my birth mother, and my sister Rose." (Aunt Rose had died of cancer when I was a girl.)

It is possible to call on higher guidance and connect with loved ones in your dreams. One night, after I went to bed asking to be shown my intuitive guide at that time, I dreamt that I was walking towards my house with Mom and her older sister, my Aunt Rose. I walked into the kitchen and was overwhelmed to see it filled with hundreds of flowering plants in clay pots. My aunt told me that she had picked them up for me. As I walked closer to observe them, I realized they were miniature red roses. Before this dream, I half-expected to be shown an angel or Native guide. Upon awakening that morning, I knew my guide was my Aunt Rose.

This was further confirmed a short while later when I had to go to a business event that I was anxious about attending. Someone would be there whose difficult and unpredictable behavior made me dread the occasion. I wanted to just quietly go about doing my job and not allow this person to pull me into his drama, as I'd seen him do with others in the past. I asked in my journal, "How should I be at this event?" My aunt came through clearly on the page: ". . . be as soft and gentle as a rose on the vine. Observe and give of yourself, as a rose gives its scent to the air. Those who get drift of it will be touched by it in a beautiful way. Those who sense it but don't acknowledge it will still realize it's there. This is your goal, to be still and yet very present, as a rose." My aunt was a soft-hearted, gentle soul, unpretentious and always ready to help others. Her essence filled me that day with calmness and a light heart in the midst of a potentially explosive situation. I knew that I didn't have to prove myself, or even speak, in order to be present and noticed.

(An aside: once a spirit being has made a connection, I've discovered that it becomes easier to reestablish the link at any time. While at my mom's house recently, she said, "We're using Rose's wine glasses today," and explained that her sister had gifted her with the crystal goblets on her wedding day. Immediately, I felt Rose's presence and the importance of that date for her—but I didn't know why. So, I asked Mom, "What is today? Is it Aunt Rose's birthday?" "No," she confirmed, "today is the anniversary of her death." A small wave of sorrow passed through us as we took a moment of silence to remember this great lady, then raised those glasses for a toast in her honor.)

Pay attention when others dream of you, as well. I've found that confirmation for what I'm doing in my life can come through some else's mind. An example: around the time I began freelance writing almost exclusively about integrative medicine and consciousness studies, I received an email from a woman I see only a few times a year. "What are you up to?" she asked in greeting. "I dreamt about you last night. You were lying in a very large, purple bathtub."

"Well, I'm not at a honeymoon resort!" I responded in jest, and explained that I was immersing myself (huge tub) in research about topics related to intuition and spirituality (purple).

Dreams can foretell the future, explain the past and pro-vide an inlet through which other realms can enter your con-sciousness (yes, I've been "visited"). We can even create and control our dreams. We won't get into the definitions and inter-pretive process here—there are many excellent guidebooks on the subject. I simply want to suggest that no matter how bizarre, shocking or insignificant your dreams may seem, don't dismiss them. "The voice of the unconscious so easily goes unheard," Carl Jung noted. Take time to figure out what your dreams are showing you, and I promise it will lead you many steps closer to self-knowledge and more refined states of awareness.

CREATIVITY AND CONSCIOUSNESS: WIDENING THE PVC PIPE

I have always thought of creativity as a connection to a higher source, a muse, an energy of pure potentiality that enables us to gather inspiration from the universal mind. As human artists, our task is to assign form to these inspirations—whether it's words on a page, choreography set to music, tulips arranged in a perennial bed, a dessert recipe, the architecture and engineer-ing of a building. We become divine when we create, because we are, in essence, replicating the act of our Creator. The more intuitively connected we are, the greater access we have to material that can be used to invent or produce something. This process, by its very nature, makes us more creative—or, more accurately, draws out the inherent creative force that is always inside us. We begin to live more often in the space of pure potential. Is it any wonder I admire the haunting imagery of the poet Rilke: "In one creative thought a thousand forgotten nights of love revive." Eventually, our entire life becomes our own creation. At that point, we are aligned with and living in the essence of God.

"Books don't happen in my mind, they happen somewhere in my belly," says acclaimed novelist Isabel Allende. In *Writers Dreaming*, she shares how a book grows inside her, slowly revealing itself. She gives total credence to her intuition: "It is as if I have this terrible confidence that something that is beyond myself knows why I'm writing this book. And what the end of the book will be. And how the book will develop. But if you ask me what the book is about or where I am going I can't tell you. I can't even tell myself . . . I trust that there are voices outside myself that talk through me. So the voices know. And sooner or later I will listen to the whole message."

Consciously or subconsciously, we all crave the peace of mind that creative acts can bring to our lives. We capture glimpses of soul-level peace when knitting by the fire, sketching a still life, playing the piano, photographing wildlife or writing haiku. When fully engrossed in an activity that you love, your mind becomes silent and you happily lose yourself. Your creative PVC pipeline is most clear and pure in these pleasurable moments. When you become practiced at a certain activity, you can consciously take your awareness into this heightened intuitive state almost at will. It's a matter of training your mind to trust your gut, and remaining in that open space for increasingly longer periods of time.

INTUITIVE WRITING: SOUL PAGES

This process can happen through any form of creativity. For me, I naturally turned to writing when I wanted to strengthen my intuitive link—and vice versa. And writing (at least in the form of journaling) is something we can all do. So I'd like to focus on this now.

"Art is not about thinking something up," says Julia Cameron in *The Artist's Way.* "It is about the opposite—getting something down. The directions are important here. If we are trying to think something up, we are straining to reach for something that's just beyond our grasp. When we get something down, there is no strain. We're not doing; we're getting. Someone or something else is doing the doing . . . We are more the conduit than the creator of what we express."

In my life and especially in the years since I've said yes to Spirit, journaling has often served as my own brand of what I call "rule-lined psychoanalysis." And while writing is an emotional and intellectual pursuit, I view it foremost as a spiritual act. Creative inspiration and divination funnel through the same channel. If this were a TV station, it would be Channel One; if it were a satellite, the docking station would be situated somewhere far beyond our known cosmos. Its transmission is that incalculable.

Writing comes naturally to me, but this is not to say that my earliest attempts at intuitive journaling were fluid and revolutionary. I would like to recount how this process unfolded for me; maybe it will help you make clearer sense of yours. Typical of most people, I would journal more when things weren't going so well in my life. On stacks of yellow legal pads that I've accumulated from as far back as my teen years, I can see that I was speaking to myself, mind-dumping the myriad thoughts that seemed to constantly swirl around my noggin. In one sense, this was a rudimentary form of meditation—a simple attempt to sit quietly, clear my head and drop-kick whatever minutia was bothering me on any given day. Revisiting my early journals is good for comic relief—so much time spent circling around issues that I now get immediate insights on!

A subtle shift in tone started to occur in these journals around the time I began reading voraciously on the subject of metaphysics: I seemed to stop asking myself questions and began stating them to the universe. A minor chord of desperation bleeds through the text every so often: "I don't know how to proceed with my dilemma . . . answers, please!" Or, "No synchronicities have occurred this week, I must be clogged . . . HELP!"

In the early 90s, I was introduced to a woman who gave angel readings. I now think it's preposterous to ask someone to connect to my angels when I can do this anytime I desire. But she gave me a valuable tool at the time. She had me sit across the table from her with a sheet of white paper and a pen, and write, on the spot, what my guardian angel was telling me. As thoughts came into my head, I'd scribble them down and show her. She'd confirm when I was correct in interpreting what she said my angel was saying. It seemed contrived and I walked out of there highly doubtful that anything meaningful had occurred, yet jazzed about the idea of talking directly to a "source" in my writings. So much of discovering our spiritual nature is about self-reliance. Seeing is NOT believing, *feeling* is believing. I wasn't going to take as my truth what someone else was saying my alleged angel was saying to me, especially if I felt underwhelmed by it all.

Intuitive Writing Takes Practice

So, I committed to the process on my own. I started with a meditation in which I asked for only the highest and purest energies, those closest to God, to assist in the writing, and that I be protected from any unwelcome influences that might try to interfere. (This is really important because, as I'll address later on, when we open to higher consciousness we open to everything.) My first attempts came in fits and starts, with passages scribbled or X-ed out. These early messages instructed me to ease up and let it rip: "To heed our advice, start by having no motive;" "Do not judge the message as we say it to you;" "Relax and listen to how my voice sounds in your mind."

Other passages were stunted and inchoate, as if I'd grasped the ethereal brass ring for a moment but my grip loosened before I could finish a sentence. I remember awaiting each word like a Labrador for a retrieval command; I'd quickly jot down the message before I forgot it or judged it with my rational mind. It was a feat for me to bypass thinking long enough to allow snippets of information to reach the page unscathed. It felt like a mechanical switching back and forth between sound mind and no-mind. I was scolded about this in one writing: "Do not think about the words as they put themselves on the page! How do you expect the knowledge to come through if you think about what's coming? Be calm and don't have a conditioned response. Open your heart and expect miracles. See how easy?" The writing went on to instruct me to "look upon all messages as though you're tuning a radio into a frequency; the closer the waves, the finer the focus."

It did get easier. I'd return to the journal when the spirit moved me and eventually the information began to click into place. I'd pose questions and get answers—first, about myself, then about others. The writings would tell me how others felt about situations and struggles in their lives—personal information that I wouldn't have known otherwise. The insights were small yet profound. To a dear friend who was grappling with making major life changes, I wrote: "She will achieve unimaginable things once she has the courage and will to leave behind the notion that she has to be safe and sure at all times. Strength comes from knowing you are unsure, but safe anyway." Sharing the journal entry with her touched a deep chord within her and opened a dialogue between us that ultimately led her to leave an unfulfilling career and find a job in a field that she loves. To another dear friend who had been diagnosed with clinical depression: "His healing will begin with the realization that the self is unique and able to create its own identity, in spite of experiences that sway us to believe that we are parts of other people and their behaviors. Your friend struggles because he holds onto the idea that he is controlled by past events. Therapy showed him this. Now he must release old ideas and begin his life anew in the knowledge that we are what we intend ourselves to be, and no one can decide for us what our intentions should be. He will grow to believe that he can become the man he knows in his heart he can be, regard-less of what exterior influences may have or will tell him." When my friend read this, he was stunned. "It captures the theme of what I've been dealing with in my life," he said. It seemed to summarize that he was on the right track with how to purge the demons that were destroying his life at that time.

When others caught wind that I was journaling in this manner, they'd ask me do writings for them on matters of importance to them. I did a handful then stopped, because I preferred to tell them how they could do it themselves. Shortly thereafter, I started offering workshops on intuitive journal-ing, and the number of people who turned out showed me that others wanted to learn this for themselves. Meanwhile, I refined my own process: ask a question, await inspiration. It became a breeze to clear my head long enough to be free on the keyboard (I had since switched to journaling directly onto my PC), allowing my fingers to flow and form whatever words appeared in my consciousness. The less I cared about what came through, the more I produced.

At first, I didn't think to ask details about the source of the information, something I now know to always do. Back then, I just thought of it as a dialogue with my higher self and the collective unconsciousness—an intuitive dialogue. Either way, the content of the answers helped me. I would call forth the creative muses and get insights. One example:

"It matters not how you begin this dialogue, so long as you continue with the passionate nature that brings you here to write. These are trying times, not from external suffering, necessarily, but from lack of spiritual meaning. People are not particular about how the message gets through to them—however, they are in need of the message and searching for it at every turn, consciously or not. Continue with your writings and never doubt that a greater context is shaping your thought process. See the world, really see it, be in it, and recollect what you see and feel on the page. You will be amazed at what comes forth if you fully trust this. And your worries about what to write will dissolve in a mist of your own accomplishment. What you most deeply desire is to be pure in thought and for that purity to be an expression of beauty in written form. We know this! You have to believe that it's obtainable. Just begin and be in your glory."

When I needed to laugh and lighten up the most, the passages came through with humor. (The more we open to higher consciousness, the lighter we become, able to look at all things with playfulness and Lila.) Here's an excerpt from a day when I was attempting to put a time constraint on my burgeoning creative process:

"What's with the artificial deadline, Gigi? Why not a lifeline? We're giving you one right now. This is a period of reflection, transition, clearing, renewal, gentle shifting. Ha, you want a 17-second building implosion but you just ordered the dynamite last week. Give it time to be delivered, set up the groundwork, get in your safe place, put on your hard hat and then get the heck out of the way because we're going to blow your panty hose off. We can't help but chuckle up here that you're trying to rock the building without waiting for us. Silly girl! Haven't learned that patience thing yet? Don't make us back-order the dynamite!"

By the end of that summer, I was slowly building a freelance writing and editing practice yet was still in an unknown place about what my next major work assignment would be. Fretting about this was causing me to lose perspective on the good things happening in my life. Then 9/11 happened and, like everyone else, I stopped in my tracks and reevaluated portions of my life. My "guides" (I didn't know what else to call them then) gave their two-cents worth:

"The tragedies of this historic week will serve to show many things to many people for the collective betterment, though it's hard to imagine this now. For you personally, doesn't it put into perspective what you are attempting to do in your own life? You have a beautiful existence just as it is, and all of this striving [with your work] is icing on the cake, not the cake itself. We're not belittling your endeavors, just wanting to show you that it needs to be kept in its proper place, not overblown such that it affects areas of your life in which you've achieved contentment and fulfillment. You have a sweet tooth, we know, and you crave the cake, the icing and ice cream on the side. But tell me what happens physically when you eat too much chocolate. You get a headache, right? Same as what happens when you are consumed by your aspirations. There's really no need to be hyperglycemic over this.

"Go on with your writing, because you see in it a kernel of hope and healing. There are many ways that people get through tragedies in their lives and in many instances it takes writers to help others make sense of it all. You are already immersed in writing about the human condition—it's your highest area of interest—and suffering is part of it, right? It's okay to write about the suffering. Stop and recollect times when you've felt devastated or overcome with grief, sorrow, rage, even hate. Feel these feelings again, as you write. This is where compassion lives, this is how you get to it. But don't give up your vision of writing from the perspective of beauty. In good times and bad, people want to hold to images (visual or written) of hope, happiness and goodness. Those who've lost loved ones will, in the long run, remember and cherish most the beauty of their lost relationships, more bittersweet than bitter."

After a while of journaling in this manner, it truly became an intuitive dialogue, with both parties (me and a higher source) quipping back and forth. One passage:

"My dear, you've gone through many layers of emotion over the past month about the specific path you must take to fulfill your life purpose. We are proud of how you have allowed yourself to open doors that you've kept shut for so long, and to meander down pathways that may be off the beaten track that you've so stridently set for yourself—but nonetheless lead to the fulfillment you most desire.

Which is what? I write. *Remind me what I want.*

"You want to be heard. You have something meaningful to say."

Who will listen?

"You will be surprised. We mean that literally. You will find outlets for your authentic voice in the most unconventional places. Keep going, love. You are continuing to mature into yourself and we know that you can feel this optimism growing inside you, even if others say that the fruits of your daily labor are not yet obvious."

I'm more confident in my abilities but that doesn't seem to pay off in today's world. It's discouraging.

"Would you have it any other way? Would you rather lead a lackluster existence where you had no impetus for striving in the passionate manner that you're known for? Don't you see that the fulfillment of all your grandest desires would bring with it a contentment that would lead to apathy?"

No, I don't see that. I could use a little contentment—okay, as I write this, I know I already have contentment. Let me rephrase . . . I could do away with the struggle to be handsomely rewarded for my work.

"Then do away with it."

Okay, I need to rephrase again. I have, in great part, done away with it. I choose over and over again, day after day, to continue with the work I'm doing, because I see great potential in it—even if others don't . . . yet.

"And so the struggle has been mitigated . . . and so the lack of contentment has left you . . . and so what is left for you to fume about?"

Lots of things that I can think of or nothing at all . . . and I get to choose which one, right?

"Indeed. Tell me, what do you want more than anything?"

It's not a material thing, it's that rapturous place that I sometimes go to where I feel completely nourished and shamelessly able to allow multitudinous sensations to pass through my body and soul—there isn't a word that encapsulates it other than passion, the feeling that overtakes me.

And so the dialogue went. When I look back on these early intuitive writings, I can clearly sense that I was connecting with the angelic realm, a loving maternal essence that was the appropriate energy to be guiding me at that time. As the last few lines indicate, I was beginning to play with the Everything Matters, Nothing Matters concept. In the last paragraph, I am referring to the creative writing process, but nowadays, I can evoke that same feeling in my daily life any time I tune in and strengthen my connection to the Divine.

* * *

All of us who work at expanding our consciousness go through various stages, ranging from doubt and despair to delight and even ecstasy. At times, nothing seems to happen and we feel as if we aren't getting anywhere. These periods of stagnation and frustration are normal. This is where Daily Practice comes in. Dedication and perseverance carry us through to greater and greater insights. The way is easier if we connect with a group of like-minded individuals, and even more so if an authentic mentor is available (which we will talk about later on).

When we combine Intention upon a foundation of surrender, then build upon that base with a solid daily practice, we undoubtedly see results. Subtle shifts will occur and, suddenly, you will find yourself at a level of awareness that is a notch above where you'd been previously. You will discover your own truths about the existence of higher realms and will have experiences that are separate and distinct from what you may have heard, read or felt about the subject. As an outcome of your daily practice, you will become acutely aware of the relevance of being present and appreciating that Everything Matters.

Now let's talk now about what unfolds when you do just this.

three

PAYING ATTENTION

Everything in the world is full of signs. All events are coordinated.
All things depend on each other. Everything breathes together.

—PLOTINUS, GREEK PHILOSOPHER

*O*nce you open to the intelligence of the universe, you cannot help but notice that it echoes back. We are all having
conversations with the Creator every moment of every day.
After all, Everything Matters. Nothing goes unnoticed from
above. This doesn't mean that God is a voyeur watching our
every move; rather, our choices are the construction materials
that we use to assemble our days and nights—we are the archi-
tects of our own lives. When we consistently tune in during
our daily practice and pay attention during our waking hours,
we are given the necessary blueprints to proceed with building
our personal "high rise."

"We each have our own pyramid," my intuitive mentor,
Edemir, once told me. "There is no need to strive to get to
the top of anyone else's pyramid. Each of us is unique, and our
life's work is not to compete with others, but to know our own
upward path."

In other words, we should aspire to our own spire.

The universe goes to great lengths, with impressive grandeur, to help us do just that. When you pay attention, miracles begin to show themselves. The universal intelligence threads together information, knowledge and material occurrences to magnify our intentions and manifest results from them. This is where the Everything Matters, Nothing Matters viewpoint really comes into play, and I do mean play. You will start to notice as your consciousness expands that everything does have a meaning—numbers, signs, colors, words—and most often, the way these meanings appear can be quite humorous. What makes this subject so mind-boggling is that these seemingly disparate events involve the free will of every living being on the planet. Everything is interconnected, and whether or not we see the connections, all outcomes are based on this reality.

A small example that comes to mind: my family and I were running odious errands one Sunday afternoon and decided to make it more enjoyable by stopping for lunch. My daughter wanted to go to a Chick-Fil-A, which was a bit of a drive from where we were shopping. I returned some merchandise to Target then waited for my husband and kids to pick me up for lunch. As I waited inside the front doors contemplating restaurants that were closer by, a husband and wife walked in. Just as he opened the door, he said to his wife loud and clear: "You know, honey, Chick-Fil-A is closed on Sundays." Something so simple—yet serendipities like this keep us in flow and add grace and levity to our ordinary lives.

When I sat down to write on this topic, I was overwhelmed with where to begin, because once you focus on synchronistic events in your life, you realize that *everything* is synchronistic. For me, the stories are too many to count: I reluctantly move to a different city and within a week meet the love of my life. I sit by my living room picture window, asking for a sign about the rightness of a recent decision, and

suddenly hundreds of grackles flock to my front yard, transforming it into a sea of iridescent blue. Nine months pregnant
and stranded on the interstate with my infant daughter during
an unexpected blizzard, I fling open my car door to see the
only moving car in sight coming towards me—a yellow taxi
with good tire chains.

I used to view fluky events as awesome and unusual coincidences that only happen when the Big Cheese really wants
to get our attention. Now, they are more often and more
immediate—practically continuous! By putting our focus on
the present moment and observing what occurs, we get a clue
that every moment contains an infinite splay of potentialities
that basket-weave together to form yet another infinite array of
outcomes. In other words, anything can happen, at any time,
in any way, any shape, any form. We can carefully plan our
lives to the point of hyperbole, but underlying it all is a greater
force at work (and play). It's quite amusing to flow along with
it and appreciate it as our daily dose of the miraculous.

Angels Can Help with (Cash) Flow

At some point along the way, I stopped waiting for synchronicities to occur and started using my awareness of universal
mind to create them. It's a matter of being perceptive, listening and—perhaps most important of all—following through
on whatever insights present themselves. The following story
illustrates this point.

I love to grocery shop at Whole Foods Market whenever
I can. It's located on the east side of the city, about 45 minutes away in a part of town that I don't go to very often. One
day while shopping there, I made a stop in the restroom. As I
came out, I noticed a large community bulletin board and felt
impelled to post my business cards on it. For the past several
years I thankfully hadn't had a need to market myself, since

I seem to attract a steady stream of work. Yet I heard very clearly, "Someone in this part of town needs you." (For whatever reason, the message felt like it came from the angelic realm.) So I tacked a handful of cards on the board.

A week later, I got an email from a woman named Dana inquiring about my services. "I've been a repressed writer for 15 years," she later explained. "My degree is in English and my lifelong desire is to write. I've taken a backwards path." She worked as a family therapist but wasn't feeling fulfilled. As Dana described it, "Writing was screaming out to me." However, being years removed from this type of work, she didn't know where to begin.

"I had just about reached the end of my rope one day with my therapy work. In fact, I was having lunch with a friend at Whole Foods and was expressing my frustration with my career. I was fidgety and wanted to get going but she asked me to wait for her while she was in the ladies' room. As I stood outside the door, I was literally thinking *Gosh darn it, I want to pursue writing. The time is now. How in the world can I find a local writing coach, someone who's right for me?* Just then, I looked up at the bulletin board and saw Gina's card. The words 'writing coach' jumped out at me and a chill ran down my spine."

"How many cards did you tack on that board?" Dana later asked me. Four or five, I recalled. "Well, I got the last one!"

So Dana and I began working together. Within a few months, she had sold her first piece to our daily city newspaper; I screamed an emphatic "YES!" when I flipped the page and saw her byline. Not only did her writing continue to develop but her physical and emotional health improved considerably as a result of embracing her true calling. Another synchronicity: Dana was most interested in topics related to alternative medicine—particularly homeopathy. What are the odds that she'd find someone who not only understands this subject matter but can guide her down the right avenues for publishing this category of writing? When angels are involved, the odds are pretty good.

Fourteen Gifts

I've had numerous experiences just like that one, in which I marvel at the confluence of serendipitous events, small (or big) miracles, and humble pleasures that come as a result of simply listening to higher guidance.

Another example: To this day, I continue to host the monthly Intuitive Dialogue group that I mentioned previously—which is now co-facilitated by one of my dearest SFFs, Nancy. Because our collective goal is to fine-tune and utilize our intuition, we typically don't pre-plan what we do each month. Sure, we pull together an agenda but we remain open to whatever is meant to unfold at these meetings, and no one objects if we veer off course. Many times over, we've discovered that, in the cocoon of the safe, intimate environment we create for ourselves, everything happens with good reason and Everything Matters.

A few years ago, we assembled for a final June meeting before our summer break. In my meditation that morning, I was given instruction to walk around my home and gather items with special significance, to be gifted to the group members that evening. My immediate reaction was, *Gosh, I don't have time for this*, but I took 30 minutes and followed through. It was an interesting exercise for me. As I scanned the contents of each room in my house, I was drawn to certain things: a pillow with gold fringe, a purple butterfly brooch, a pocket-size Webster's dictionary, a gold money clip in the shape of an angel.

As these items "chose themselves," I placed each one on the chess table in my living room. While most of them weren't valuable in terms of dollar amount, some were quite sentimental—such as a collection of bird feathers in a delicate sweetgrass basket I'd bought in a marketplace in Chile, South America. Nonetheless, I was encouraged by my guidance to "release attachment to earthly possessions" and pass them on to others. A few minutes into this process, I began to receive insights about the significance of each item. The pillow represented the need for rest, relaxation and self-care. An assortment of lollipops and hard-tack candy symbolized the desire for more sweetness in one's life. A hand-crafted, wooden kazoo meant to lighten up, have fun, blow off some steam and dance to one's own tune. And so on.

When I sensed that this task was complete, I dug up some tissue paper and ribbon, and asked my daughter—who would attend the meeting with me that evening—to wrap each item the same way so none of them appeared more important than the others. Later in the day, I got word from Nancy that we may have a larger-than-usual turnout. *Hmm, I wonder if I have enough items.* I certainly didn't want anyone to feel left out. I quickly rustled up a handful of additional things, wrapped them and put everything into a large bag.

Towards the end of our meeting, Nancy led us through a beautiful guided meditation in which she asked us to hold in our minds a special intention, goal or wish for the coming summer months. Afterwards, as we settled back into our bodies and opened our eyes, I passed the bag to my left and asked that each person choose one gift. No one knew I planned to do this, not even Nancy, and everybody seemed happily surprised. I delightedly watched each person's expression as they unwrapped their gifts—seeing smiles, tears and even calm looks of knowing.

We went around the room and shared our thoughts. Marilyn revealed that her intention was to take a beach vacation for the first time in decades. She giggled upon opening her package; it contained a conch seashell and mermaid's purse from the Atlantic Ocean. Kathy was contemplating a career change and whether to pursue a long-held dream, to purchase a tract of commercial real estate and open a first-of-its-kind holistic center. The gift she selected, a silver-plated acorn, was a small yet profound confirmation that planting a seed can lead to the emergence of something as strong and enduring as a mighty oak. "How perfect and inspiring," she said.

Jack was also incubating a new business venture. Appropriate, then, that he chose a hand-painted box containing a tiny bird's nest with a cracked-open eggshell. Susan picked a toy model of a yellow Volkswagen Beetle. Her face lit up as she explained that not only was this the first-ever car she'd owned as a teenager, but that she and her new husband had decided to take a "major road trip"—to relocate in North Carolina. That car epitomized the rightness of what was transpiring in her life: movement, freedom, a return to youthful folly, a future filled with sunshine (the color yellow) and reinvigorated self-esteem (yellow also represents the solar plexus chakra, the center of self-worth and personal power).

Judy chose the brooch, the butterfly signifying her recent transformation as a result of leaving an abusive marriage, and its purple color representing a rediscovery of her spiritual self—something she'd been stifling for many years. Dan received the angel money clip, an encouraging sign that his intention to trust in financial abundance from Spirit had been heard. "Money has usually taught me my hardest lessons," Dan confessed. "My intention was that money can also represent some loving lessons, as well. I will carry this angel with me until further notice—from her."

The pocket dictionary ended up with an aspiring writer in our group. The pillow? It landed in the lap of Pat, the very person who puts everyone's needs before her own to the peril of her health. "I get it loud and clear," Pat sighed. "I need to take time for myself."

And on it went, around the room—everything (miraculously?) finding its intended new home. Oh, and the feather collection? It went to the exact right person too: Annie, whose goal was to heal through her brother's suicide and release her need to cling to him on the spiritual realm. She shared this with us: "For months now, my deceased brother has been leaving bird feathers in obvious places in order to make my family members aware of his presence. Now, it's time for us to let him fly away and move on."

But it was Edy's explanation of her items that really got me. She received four antique coins: a Kennedy quarter and three foreign coins from Canada, Brazil and Fiji—and a card that read "A thing is only impossible until it's not."

"I asked in the meditation about a recent job offer my husband had received and whether he should take it," she explained, adding that the significance of each coin was not lost on her. "The Kennedy coin represents me because I'm American and my son was born in 1965, the same year that quarter was minted. The Canadian coin is my husband—he's Canadian. The company that is offering him this position is Brazilian, an indication that joining this firm is a good move for him. And the coin from Fiji, well, my husband has been saying for as long as I've known him that he wants to retire in Fiji!"

Edy further noted that this new high-powered position came with a generous compensation package that would enable them to indeed retire on a tropical island, something that had been just a dream months earlier. A thing is only impossible until it's not!

As I listened in awe to everyone describe in rich detail

the personal meaning of their gifts, it all seemed divinely precise. Remember my momentary panic at not having enough gifts? We had 14 people at the meeting—exactly the amount of items that my daughter and I wrapped that afternoon.

The next day, Dan, who participates in a Joseph Campbell-inspired group called The Hero's Journey, emailed this to me: "We do a gift-giving ceremony at my workshop where you bring a gift you thought you would never ever give away. It's similar to last night and quite special. The thought is, by giving something precious away you take one step towards the gods and they in turn will take 10 steps towards you. Hmm . . . 14 gifts times 10 = 140. Hold onto your seat, sister, you've just dropped a bunch of quarters in the ride of Spirit!"

It's true. The following week, I met a shaman from Australia and was gifted with an impressive and rare Night Whitehawk feather—a more than ample replacement for Annie's feather collection. "It's meant to assist individuals who work in other realms," he informed me. I couldn't wait to discover how the feather from this magnificent animal totem would work its magic! This shaman's simple gesture was one of many ways in which the universe continued to re-gift me with whimsical iterations of the precious items I passed on to others that evening.

PAY ATTENTION TO OTHER PEOPLE

People are involved in God's plot to guide us towards what's best for us, as the following story illustrates. My children were babies when we bought a new home. Shortly after moving in, my husband decided to build them a play cottage in the back yard. An acquaintance had offered to give us roofing materials that were left over from a construction job; the only stipulation was that we pick them up at his property about 20 miles north. As I mentioned earlier, it was a stressful year—in addition to having two children in 18 months, working, and setting up a new residence, I'd taken it upon my already weary self to impersonate Martha Stewart, wanting everything to be perfect in our new home. One Friday afternoon, I picked the children up from day care and set off to squeeze in errands before dinnertime, including a drive north to pick up those roofing shingles.

Soon, my one-year-old was fidgeting in his car seat and I became anxious to get to our destination. Halfway there, an unmarked police car appeared out of nowhere and flagged me over. Now both children are full-out crying—my son because he wants out of that seat, and my daughter because she's old enough to understand that Mommy did a no-no. I'm upset too, knowing that my husband is not going to be happy that those shingles are now costing him $190, the result of going 60 in a 45. The pressure of that year seemed to culminate in those few moments. As I fought back tears, the officer handed me the ticket, looked intently at me with radiant blue eyes, and said in the most sincere, compassionate (almost pleading) way, "Please, please SLOW DOWN."

I was momentarily transfixed. The crying in the backseat faded into the background and I sat very still for a moment, contemplating how his words were a signpost for my life at that time. Later, I arrived home to find a package propped against my front door, a surprise gift from my dearest SFF Lee Ann with a note attached, "For some reason, I saw this and thought of you, love you!" I unwrapped the brown packaging to reveal a hand-painted plaque that read (drum roll, please): *Never drive faster than your angels can fly.*

Tribute to Philomena

My bond with my paternal grandmother Philomena has grown

increasingly stronger over the years. She was instrumental in helping me find the love of my life. Grandma is often here to softly offer maternal advice and encourage me with my work. Oftentimes, she beams with pride about the way I've grown as a woman, and her unwavering love makes me feel like I can take on the world. How comforting it's been to have her in my life. In many ways, ours is a typical grandmother/granddaughter relationship, with one possible exception: Philomena died when I was 10 years old. It's been my experience that loved ones and others who support us don't have to be in a physical body.

I didn't have the opportunity to know her very well when she was on earth because I didn't get to see her that often. In the window of my mind, I remember Philomena as mostly a silent presence, yet in spite of her reserved nature, I sensed an implicit, fearsome strength about her. She'd sit in a rigid metal chair beside her living room corner altar and call me to her. I'd perch on her generous lap and, feeling shy that this woman I barely knew could love me so completely, I'd gaze beyond her at the blood-red votive candle flickering in the corner and fixate on the picture of a honey-brown-haired Jesus, left hand pointing at his exposed sacred heart. Grandma's death was the first such experience in my young life, which probably explains why I'm left with a vivid impression of her burial.

That February day was brisk but sunny. We processed to the cemetery in silence and exited our Cadillacs and Buicks. Our shoe heels clipped against the unforgiving concrete pad leading up to the wall of vaults, one of which was open, waiting to receive Grandma. Although I grew up across the street from a Jewish cemetery with traditional graves and headstones, I'd never seen above-ground interment. Her casket stretched out before us, perpendicular to the wall. All the while, I stared at the row of red votive candles along the wall of vaults, imagining Grandma's casket trapped forever in its steely vortex.

Many years later, in my mid-20s, I'd created an adequate life for myself. I'd graduated from Florida State University and had a great job in DC. Still, I felt unsettled. Several disappointments had rocked my world during those years, leaving me emotionally vulnerable and unsure of my proper place in the world. One weekend, I drove up to Pittsburgh to visit my parents, and my car practically steered itself to Grandma's final resting site. I hadn't been to that cemetery since I was a child but had no problem finding my way to the gates and down the narrow, circular road leading to the vaults. Feeling fragile and hypersensitive to everything around me, I was overtaken with a sensation of coming home to someone who'd been awaiting my arrival for many moons—so much so that I began to quiver inside. I shuffled up to the towering vaults and pressed my hand against the marker that bore Philomena's name. At my feet was a green vase of wilted roses. To the right of the vaults, hundreds of red votives glowed a soft hush of remembrance.

I sat on a concrete bench nearby, arms around my knees, and began to talk aloud. "Hear me, Grandma. Help me know who I am," I said, and the tears came fast. "I want more, if that's okay. I'm getting by, but is this all there is? My destiny, what is it? Where is it? How long to it?" I buried my head in my knees and wept, feeling puny and isolated in the expansiveness of the cemetery grounds. Finally settling long enough to be silent, I heard Philomena's voice: "Go home."

I sat perfectly still, immediately knowing that she meant "move back to Pittsburgh."

"Go home. It will all work out." I resisted the message but couldn't deny that I felt cleansed and set free. There was a whisper of a promise that I'd find absolute contentment if I allowed myself to give it a go. Ultimately, I took Philomena's advice, and she was right, of course. Within a month of the move, I landed a good job, met the man who is now my husband of nearly 20 years, and found a sense of peace about my future. Every so often over the years, especially when my children were little, I got a sense that Grandma was there soothing my baby to sleep on a tough night, or helping me find it within myself to be a good wife and mother. Over the years, Philomena has lovingly connected with me and has even told me things I never knew about my ancestors, which my mom later confirmed. While Mom is, and always will be, my best friend and greatest example of pure maternal love, I'm further blessed to have Philomena in the ethers as a continual source of grandmotherly support and protection.

PAY ATTENTION TO NATURE AND THE ANIMAL WORLD

The natural world is an expression of Creation, so being in nature brings us close to that higher connection. This is why walks in the woods, in the mountains or along a beach are so cleansing—and why even finding a special seashell, rock, seed pod or snakeskin can be powerful. One day, while weeding my flowerbeds, surrounded by a purple-orange fusion of irises, Oriental poppies and bachelor buttons, the flowers spoke to me. In their silence, they told me:

> *True beauty is quietly present, not anxious or ostentatious; be still, and shine in subtle eloquence.*
>
> *True creativity is patient, happening in its own time. If we allow necessary elements to come together when conditions are right, the fullest possible bloom presents itself.*
>
> *Open to the sun, turn toward its light, bask in the glory of being.*

Remain open, even if rain or darkness falls.
There is a dying, so necessary for continued
rebirth. It's the cycle of all things creative.

These profoundly simple insights about creative expression helped me through a period during which I was dying from old patterns, being stripped bare of that which had served me in my previous flowering. I was feeling sad, and the wisdom of the flowers seemed to give me permission to allow the sadness to fill me. I had the distinct impression of not just seeing the flowers and apprehending their innate wisdom as it applied to my human life, but also *knowing* them in their flowering-ness completely.

Animals and other living beings are also harbingers of synchronistic messages. I've had numerous encounters with animal totems over the years—demonstrating to me how pets, wildlife and other creatures intervene on our behalf and teach us about ourselves and our place in the natural world. I could fill a book just with stories of the great wisdom that plants, animals, insects, bird, trees, lightning, sunsets and many other aspects of nature have imparted to me—blue jays screeching at me to speak my truth, crickets on my walk when I'm taking great leaps forward, swan energy around during a year when I was penning poetry and writing about ballet. Horses, panthers, butterflies, bats, dragonflies, skunks, turtles, even gazelles and buffalo have taught me great lessons. For the purpose of this chapter, I will delight in telling just a few of my experiences.

Around the time of my daughter's 13th birthday, I had a brief, amazing encounter with a particularly rare insect that I've been fascinated with since the first time I saw one as a child. It happened this way. Our birthday gift to our daughter that year was to redecorate her bedroom to more accurately reflect her becoming a young lady. She chose a beautiful (and mature!) color scheme—magenta, olive green and pebble stone, with splashes of lime green—and we painted away after tearing down the former pastel pink ballerina wallpaper in her room. Her choice of vibrant colors was, I think, symbolic of her emergence as a teenager and the expressive young woman she was becoming. (By age 14, she was already a prolific songwriter.)

Even though that month was a busy time for all of us, I was determined to have that room finished and decorated before her birthday, as she had planned a sleepover party with a few friends. I was putting unnecessary pressure on myself—after all, Nothing Matters—and the natural world was about to remind me of this. Days before the party, I ran into a home store to purchase new bed linens and throw pillows for her bed. I felt almost "led" to the magenta sheets that I'd been looking for in other stores, then straight towards a pile of fuzzy, lime-green pillows. As I reached for the pillows, I was startled to see a praying mantis, of all things, mysteriously perched on one of them. *What the—?* Hauntingly motionless, it spoke to me without words: "Stop with the odious errands, go home, be still." After depositing the praying mantis on a tree outside, I did just that: went home, lit a fire in the fireplace, and enjoyed a glass of wine and leisurely conversation with my husband. By the time of my daughter's party most of the room was pulled together, and what wasn't . . . well, it didn't matter. And everyone had a good time.

Have you ever had a surprise insect or animal experience such as this? An inexplicable dog bond? Repeated day sightings of an owl? Dolphin fascination? "Everyone has an animal tale to tell," Ted Andrews told me over the phone during an interview. Ted is a world-known animal educator and author of the bestselling classic *Animal Speak*, in which he encourages us to spread our wings and recognize what animal encounters mean when we have them—in waking hours or dreams. Ted's writings aren't about deciphering the meaning of Rover's yip. "It's not about animal communication," he explained, "it's about the natural world's inherent symbology and how understanding it can work to our advantage." Hawks caution us to see the big picture. Squirrels teach us preparedness. Ants are masters of order and discipline. Hummingbirds mean happiness. And the ass encourages, well, humility. When these creatures show up in our lives, we need more of what they have. "Anytime I'm confused about anything," Ted shared with me, "I take a walk in the woods and see what animal stands out. This always helps resolve my situation." What if you lose your way during contemplation? I asked him, and he replied, "Ravens have shown me the right direction out of the woods."

My Blue Sentinel

We're fortunate to have a lovely, natural-spring pond on our property, visible from the kitchen window. I've lived in this home for 13 years and for about a year was blessed to have a blue heron visit that pond on a regular basis. It was a year in which circumstances forced me to rely primarily on myself.

In the glow of predawn, this great blue sentinel would glide in on wings that spanned six feet, right when I was feeling "blue" and questioning the course of my life. It would stand still for long periods of time in the pond's center, allowing me ample time to study it. All angles and curves, herons have a body language without peer. Their collapsible, extensible frames can shift from shrunken to regal in a trice. They write their own ancient language, posing with a gangly delicacy.

I saw in this bird, with its sinuous neck and unblinking eyes, a primordial creature that had survived millions of years of evolution. And I came to intuit that it was giving me courage to be a survivor, as well. Its long, thin legs confirmed that I didn't need massive pillars to remain stable, but that I must be able to stand on my own. This feeling was validated when I flipped open *Animal Speak*. Blue herons "stand out in their uniqueness," the book explained. The heron "reflects a need for those with this totem to follow their own innate wisdom and path of self-determination. You know what is best for you and should follow it, rather than the promptings of others."

After a while, I learned to call forth this beautiful bird and it would return, right on cue, to my little pond. I would absorb its wisdom for a matter of minutes, and then it would flap off, breaking the stillness, and fly to its tangled, stick-built nest that crowned the uppermost branches of a nearby tree. For years following this series of visitations, I didn't see a blue heron on my pond; maybe I had no more need to. I had moved through that period of standing on my own two feet and into a phase of outward collaboration with others, both personally and professionally.

PAY ATTENTION TO
(ALLEGEDLY) INANIMATE OBJECTS

Inanimate objects can participate in the symphony of synchronicity, as well. A few years ago, I was deciding whether to buy a new car. My vehicle at the time was 15 years old but still in good shape, a fine specimen of German engineering. My husband prodded me to trade it in, but doing so involved test driving different makes and models. I had no idea what type of car I wanted to buy even if I wanted one. My dad had just taken ill and I was devoting any spare time to helping my mom deal with an onslaught of medical, legal and other personal matters. Don lovingly went online to research different models and even stopped after work to test drive a few of them on my behalf. I still didn't heed his advice to upgrade to a newer vehicle. Finally one morning, things literally came to blows.

"We're going to look at cars this weekend, like it or not!" Don announced.

"I don't have time to talk about this right now," I responded. "Gianne can't carry her science project on the bus so I'm driving her to school." And that, for the moment, was that. After pulling away from the school grounds I finally had a chance to collect my thoughts about the car situation. "Okay, God," I said under my breath while I waited for a red light, "I don't have time to debate this, so give it to me straight. Should I spend the money on a new car or keep this one? Is it still safe to drive? Or should I make time to shop for a new one? Tell me what to do, and make it pretty obvious because you know how dense I can be."

Just then, the light turned green, I pressed the accelerator, the car over-revved, drifted into the intersection and died. I had just created a traffic jam during morning rush hour—cars coming at the intersection in four directions—but all I could do at first was sit in the middle of that mess and laugh out loud. Needless to say, I'd made my decision to get rid of the car even before word came back later that day that the transmission was shot. I was grateful this hadn't happened days earlier when I was driving Mom through a busy, unfamiliar part of the city, and her in the front seat, white-knuckling the dashboard. There was also a deeper, more emotional reason why that car had to be out of my life. In my stubbornness about letting it go, the universe presented me with what I affectionately call a "cosmic duh!"

PAY ATTENTION TO YOUR OWN CHOICES

Lastly, pay attention to how your intentions, small to great, manifest. It can be insignificant things like driving along a crowded urban street and nabbing a parking spot directly in front of your destination (parking karma!), or having the intention to quickly find the perfect greeting card for a loved one and it's the first card you happen to pick out (Hallmark karma!). It can be groups you're led to join, books you're impelled to read, quirky things that happen—they all have a meaning because Everything Matters.

One April, while doing a round of intensive spiritual work, I was being nudged to live outside of time, for lack of a better way to explain it. I was receiving cosmic instruction on how "we humans" constrain ourselves with this notion of time, instead of living in the eternal now. As fate would have it, that week (pre-Blackberry) I lost the leather-bound calendar that contained all my appointments, meetings and other daily details. I couldn't imagine where it might be, as the only two places I had carried it were my office and my car. Nonetheless, it disappeared. I immediately got the cosmic joke and trusted that anything of true importance would be retained in my memory. As any multi-tasking, working parent knows, this is quite a leap of faith.

I knew that I was supposed to experiment with living in a happy-go-lucky fashion through the upcoming summer months. As my schedule-less days went on, I felt increasingly liberated from my former time-constrictedness. It's true, any meetings and other commitments of absolute necessity were either retrieved from my memory or I conveniently received a reminder email or phone call. Granted, it was easier to play with this concept when the children were on school vacation.

Sometime that June, I was in an office supply store and happened to stroll by a big display of date books. It was too convenient to pick one up and buy it. I tuned in and got this impression: *well, go ahead and buy one if you must—it's not going to make a difference.* So I did. Only after I arrived home did

I realize that the gods had won again—the months on the calendar started with September!

As we begin to live with greater awareness, details become ultra-meaningful—said again, Everything Matters. (Indeed, God is in the details.) Early on, as I slowly ramped up my regular practice of meditation and intuitive writing, they seemed at times to converge. Every word, every metaphor, every symbol took on significance. As my connection became sharper, insights poured into these writings that helped me make sense of my life purpose.

Scribe Advice

I shared with you in Chapter 2 my first ever third-eye vision. Now, I glean knowledge through my intuition on an almost continuous basis. Then, it was a revelation. I couldn't foresee the depth and breadth of wisdom this initial foray into expanded consciousness would ultimately afford me. At the time, I was probably thinking, okay, so I saw the profile of an Egyptian queen in a meditation. What does that have to do with real life? Bills need to be paid, the kids have to be raised, the house still should be renovated, and so on. This is what's real, not some obscure, drop-in vision of a long-dead female aristocrat. Of what relevance is it to HERE and NOW? In time, I got my answer.

The years rolled forward and my predilection towards discerning and fulfilling my dharma grew stronger. I began writing for my life—literally. As I matured through my 30s, the urge to express sentiment through the written word steadily brought me more fully alive. I knew in my bones that my personal imperative was to refine my writing voice, then work hard to help it find its place in the world. My babies were growing strong and well, and while my priority was to be the best mother I could be, I also inherently understood that part of responsible parenting was showing them, through example, that personal growth and the nourishment of one's abilities is a lifelong pursuit—not something that ends after formal schooling. I couldn't teach them to lunge towards life with gusto if I wasn't doing this myself.

So I pressed on and pursued the writing of my first book, which explores (as you might have guessed) the use of intuition as a tool for healing and human evolution. The drafting of that manuscript involved a lot of tuning-in, and along the way I stumbled across inklings about my own personal history, including past lives. (Note: my belief in the possibility of reincarnation isn't tied to any particular religious conviction or any evidence presented to me by others; it stems purely from an empirical knowing that arose within me as a result of allowing myself to be open to all possibilities regarding the meaning of life, death, rebirth, re-death, and everything in between and beyond.) This past life information came in snatches over the course of several years, and is still evolving.

Briefly: My human existence commenced in Egypt, actually, before that; I came to Egypt by way of the star system Sirius—I am, ahem, serious about this—although I wasn't "human" yet. (This was confirmed for me many years later by Edemir. I didn't know him that well at the time and, being from Brazil, his English back then wasn't fluent. We were sitting in a courtyard with some friends when I felt him staring at me. I looked at him and he said, "What star are you from?" I wasn't sure he meant to say "star" but I discerned that he was asking where I was from before this lifetime. So I said, "Egypt." And he corrected me: "Egypt by way of Sirius. You're from Sirius." No more conversation needed to be had. I was stunned into silence that he confirmed what I'd felt about myself . . . anyway, I digress.)

Here's what I've intuited about my Egyptian connection: I once worked as a scribe in service to the queen and high priests of that day. I was male, dark, sharp minded, small boned. I excelled at my occupation and was respected for my skills, especially since most people of that era could neither read nor write. I could do both. My ability with language put me on par with aristocracy. I was content, well taken care of and had everything I needed—physically, intellectually, spiritually. I may have lived several lifetimes in this manner, I'm not sure, but one thing of which I AM certain: in the recesses of my vascular walls, strains of Egyptian blood still course through me. The majesty of the pharaohs continues to reign in me. (And as you'll read later, Isis and I are tight.) Memories of the skill I once mastered still reside in my psyche. I came to this present life encapsulated in a womb that contained, among other vital building blocks, remembered proficiencies from past lives. (It happens; how else could Mozart write symphonies at age five?)

These intimations about my former life simmered to the surface during the research and drafting of that first manuscript, and I put them to good use. How? I used to believe that writing a book is a cliff's-edge leap that can either result in flying without aid of hallucinogens or winding up splat on life's pavement like so many chewing tobacco stains. I was of the mindset that many modern-day scribes scribble in isolation for long periods of time, not knowing whether the fruits of their labor will ever see the light of day. As I strapped on that same yoke of wanna-be authordom, there were many days of doubt and despair—especially since I had forsaken a hard-won marketing consulting practice to devote full time to finishing the manuscript. There were moments when I couldn't fathom how I'd find my way out of the paper-pile morass, how in God's name, or the devil's, this research would ever pull together in logical fashion. Up to that point, the lengthiest piece of writing I'd published was a newspaper series (on the proliferation of a new category of books called "inspirational literature" such as *The Celestine Prophecy* and *Embraced by the Light*, an assignment that portended my writing future). No one—not my husband, dear mother, my SFFs, not even my Siamese cat, Geisha (and she was extremely empathetic)—appeared to understand what I was going through. For all they knew (with the possible exception of Geisha), the act of book writing was transforming me into a whiny, psychopathic basket case with dubious potential for spinning my threads of mania into monetary gold.

In those moments of desperation, I did the only thing I knew how to do: go within. And who was there to greet me? Scribe. In those years, he didn't speak with words, but his assured presence kept me on course, and reminded me of why I had chosen to enter the competitive bastion of book publishing. *I am what I am: a writer, just accept it . . .* and then, in the process of finalizing the manuscript and book proposal, the internal voice shifted to his:

> "Don't stop, no turning back, keep your eyes peeled, your mind unfettered. I'm here, so just ask. To ask is human, to receive is divine—you're poised for divinity."
>
> *Okay, lay it on me, Scribe. Why did I want to write this book again?*
>
> "We are humans, evolving," he told me. "People want to know this. You can tell them, because you have IT, a way with words. You know you do, so no fear, okay? No more away with words. You are here for this, believe me when I tell you. But you know you are, so I'm redundant."

"A way with words" . . . instead of . . . "away with words." What a difference a single character space can make. Scribe helped me to see my writer-consciousness at this level of detail.

Still, I so badly lacked confidence in my ability that I rebuffed this powerful message, thinking it was just me telling myself something I wanted or needed to hear. But I continued to write anyway. And write and write and write and rewrite and rewrite and rewrite and chop this and add that and fret here and worry there and Scribe would say:

> "Keep going, you're on a roll, can't stop now even though you want to but this isn't complete even though your patience wore out last year but, you see, those lessons aren't learned yet because you're resisting, because you're too 'human' and not enough 'being,' so scratch and claw if you must but you MUST get this, it's why you're here."

He would send thoughts to me in this calm, resolute manner. Though resistant, I did listen. His essence became steadily stronger. By the time I was pushing through final chapter rewrites, I could feel him infusing me with sustained energy. During the final stretch, I wrote for three days with virtually no sleep—hadn't done that since university finals week.

Many times since then, whenever I'd sit down to write something important but was too intimidated to begin (as Stephen King says, "The scariest moment is always just before you start"), I'd call in Scribe and honor him for helping me with the creative process. In March 2004, he fused into me through my third eye and I realized that I was Scribe, Scribe was me. What he told me that day began to mitigate my doubts about earning a living through writing:

> "As a scribe, I was on call with the queen and therefore had to always stay in the flow of what was happening. I became adept at being in the moment because my job was to record events—documenting knowledge, rituals,

speeches, history. It was easy for me to not get caught up in the what-ifs that sometimes seem to stymie you.

"One way in which you and I differ: you write to influence people's lives through your words. You write for others and want to be read by them. During my time on earth, my writings didn't help the masses, and I didn't long for them to. Most of society was illiterate and for this reason, I knew that my work would never be read by most people. I was there to serve the queen and the hierarchy. What kept me so engaged in my life's work was status, clout, being on that inner circle of society. It afforded me many privileges. But even beyond that, I had a knowing that future generations would benefit from it; I was reporting on present 'history' so that others, in the future, could know what my civilization was all about. In this sense, I was writing Future History. I was writing it in the now for the queen and her hierarchy, but 'later' for others.

"This is one way in which we're similar: I had a sense of the future, and so do you. What you're doing is the same as what I did, with a different twist: you are writing in the now for others to get a glimpse of their own future. So, you must work with a sense of the future."

Around the same time I "combined" with Scribe, I read Natalie Goldberg's *Long Quiet Highway*, in which she recounts what her spiritual teacher Suzuki Roshi once said about questioning one's life purpose: "It's like putting a horse on top of a horse and then climbing on and trying to ride. Riding a horse by itself is hard enough. Why add another horse? Then it's impossible." By reminding me of who I really am in *this* life, Scribe gave me the spunk and daring to at least get on the darn horse and grab the reins.

*   *   *

As we ascend in consciousness, we begin to make choices based on this heightened state of awareness. We're able to more readily make sense of the intimate connection among all things, and are drawn to specific people, circumstances and experiences for very specific reasons. You'll know why things happen and even be able to foresee outcomes. You'll realize that no event—good or bad—is wasted, because every one of them is manna for our creative soul and part of a finely choreographed universal dance of energy. Small occurrences that once seemed like mere coincidences will hold more meaning. In fact, you will recognize most events as synchronistic, each playing a part in the greater pattern of your life. You will see that each experience serves to ameliorate the next experience, and your life continually spirals to even higher levels of awareness.

"Think how it is to have a conversation with an embryo," wrote the poet Rumi (as translated by Coleman Barks). "You might say, 'The world outside is vast and intricate. There are wheat fields and mountain passes and orchards in bloom. At night there are millions of galaxies, and in sunlight the beauty of friends dancing at a wedding.' You ask the embryo why he or she stays cooped up in the dark with eyes closed. Listen to the answer. 'There is no other world. I only know what I've experienced. You must be hallucinating'."

Paying attention requires us to imagine that we are the embryo that Rumi is addressing. It lures us from the safety of our amniotic sac into a greater consciousness. It grants us courage to come out and take a look around. It urges us to feel more, think less, bring forth all that we have inside us, and birth ourselves, naked, to the vast and intricate truth. The rewards are immeasurable—I promise.

four

TURNING WITHIN

The time will come
When, with elation,
You will greet yourself arriving
At your own door, your own mirror,
And each will smile at the other's welcome.

--DEREK WALCOTT, FROM THE POEM, "LOVE AFTER LOVE"

I marvel each autumn as the hills around my home come alive with breathtaking foliage. How can anyone observe nature and not believe in a supreme Creator? Here in the Northeast, the leaves crescendo with colorful splendor about the first week of October, in all their ephemeral vividness. Then, shorter days and a cool snap in the air signal the denouement of another season of our lives and, perhaps, the prospect of barren months ahead—even a death, of sorts.

What intrigues me most about the leaves' perennial transformation is this: the true (and often wild) color of each leaf is contained underneath the green chlorophyll all along; in fact, the cold is what causes a leaf to reveal its natural color. What a great analogy for those of us who commit to a spiritual expedition and announce our intentions to run towards this great adventure called life. To fully become what we're meant to be

all along requires encountering harsh conditions and imperil-
ing ourselves along the way. In the grips of life situations that
chill us to the marrow, we recognize—at first with fright, and
then with great peace—that we have only ourselves to count
on. We come into this life, and leave it, alone. Which is why
the next imperative step in our conscious evolution is Turning
Within.

As we embark on this next step and raise our energetic
vibration, we begin to encounter intense challenges—a sure
sign that we're kissing the lip of the next level of our awakening. Because spiritual development can bring on strife, soul
friendships with others of like mind are paramount. The hidden
gift—and paradox—of this step is that as we face these inner
challenges, we are alone but we are not alone. With cherished
SFFs, we can share our scariest parts and heal through them
without fear of being judged or ridiculed. No matter how nihil-
istic you become, how blissed-up or bottomed-out you might
feel during the stages of opening to higher consciousness, a
true SFF is someone who will lovingly hold the "child" of you
in her heart when you go off on some dark rant or wail with
deep sorrow. SFFs know that spiritual commitment can sometimes feel like throwing fuel on the same fire that's consuming
us, only to offer the salvation of rising like a phoenix from
its ashes. Please bear in mind that those who haven't (yet)
been ouch-ed by this psychic burn don't understand what this
process looks like, and aren't quite sure how to respond to it.
(Even my husband, Don, who always does his best to support
me in whatever I choose to endeavor, has been admittedly
perplexed at times, attempting to understand my growth process. God bless him—he certainly couldn't have foreseen when
he said "I do" that, years later, his bride would be taking a
cosmic magic carpet ride.) As we will discuss in this and the
next chapter, it helps tremendously to be fully seen in all your

emerging complexity by safe people. If not for this, I believe, many spiritual aspirants would probably feel so isolated, bewildered and damaged that they'd choose to step off the path entirely.

Poet, philosopher and scholar John O'Donohue speaks beautifully about this level of friendship as it's understood in the Celtic tradition. In old Gaelic, the term for "soul friend" is *anam cara*. In the Celtic church, this originally referred to a spiritual teacher to whom you confessed the hidden intimacies of your life. "This friendship was an act of recognition and belonging," he says. "When you had an *anam cara*, your friendship cut across all convention, morality, and category. You were joined in an ancient and eternal way." With *anam cara*, you are "understood as you are without mask or pretension. The superficial and functional lies and half-truths of social acquaintance fall away, you can be as you really are. Love allows understanding to dawn, and understanding is precious. Where you are understood, you are home [and] you feel free to release yourself into the trust and shelter of the other person's soul."

Even so, we eventually reach a point where no one can really help us, not even *anam cara*. We have to help ourselves. We have to stop calling counselors, psychics, psychotherapists, MDs and others (even friends) who are on the periphery of what's really at the center of ourselves, and find the capacity to turn within. I'm not suggesting that you stop consulting with people. In fact, as we bravely traverse a geography of hot, shifting sands that can sear our confidence, it's helpful to take the guiding hand of someone who has already survived the desert (we will soon be speaking about mentors). What I'm referring to here is the mistaken belief that you can find truth outside yourself. It's just not possible. We all have to find our own truth, and the only way to do so is by connecting with our inner divinity and ultimately finding our own best answers. Zen wisdom says: "Think of all the great words and great teachings as your deadly enemy. Avoid them, because you have to find your own source."

Let's talk about what happens when we're given situations that profoundly challenge us. It WILL happen because embracing higher consciousness does not mean that things magically become better, stress-free and more pleasurable, or that there are no conflicts or pain in our lives. It's not all love and light—more accurately, it is the light, the dark and the shadow (more to come regarding the shadow). As Ram Dass has said, "The shadow is the greatest teacher for how to come to the light."

Why does embracing a fully conscious life have to be tumultuous, you might ask? As we fall into the well of our own heart and face the eyes of "ghosts both intimate and unidentifiable," as T. S. Eliot wrote, we unleash all the suppressed situations and accompanying emotions that we've been ignoring or denying. Hawkins advises us to intend love and joy but know that that intention triggers the surfacing of all that obstructs it and prevents its appearance. In *I: Reality and Subjectivity*, he writes: "Those who dedicate themselves to peace and love automatically pull up from the unconscious all that is cruel, unloving and hateful to be healed . . . This process of spirituality, in which one works through the obstacles, may seem painful at times but is only transitional."

I have mentioned David Hawkins already on these pages. In my studies and in my work as a journalist, I read, meet and have the great pleasure of interviewing modern day mystics and New Thought leaders and reporting on their work. Each one has had a positive impact on me, yet the teachings of several particular individuals have influenced me profoundly. Dr. Hawkins is one such person. A bestselling author of many books on higher consciousness, including the seminal *Power vs. Force* and my personal favorite, *Transcending the Levels of Consciousness*, his main premise is that truth is subjective, and directly related to one's level of consciousness. In his far-reaching, multi-disciplinary research he has developed a groundbreaking protocol to map consciousness in a way that can actually calibrate the whole of the human condition—the emotional and spiritual development of individuals, communities and cultures. He has documented his uniquely insightful work not only in his acclaimed books but in numerous scientific papers.

Hawkins' own journey of personal transformation is astonishing. He left a successful psychiatric practice in New York City at age 38 after contracting a seemingly terminal illness. "If there is a God, I ask him to help me now," he prayed. He fell unconscious; when he awoke, "the person I had been no longer existed. There was no personal self or ego left—just an Infinite Presence of such unlimited power that it was all that was." Longer and longer periods of bliss precluded him from continuing his practice. He sequestered himself in a cabin near Sedona and spent seven years as a recluse, meditating and studying. Finally, he reintegrated into society and began teaching others about transcendent levels of consciousness. I met him in Sedona in 2005. As he walked into the room, he had such an aura of a high priest / prophet that it rendered me temporarily speechless. He is a slight (almost frail), unassuming man, with a magnanimous light around him. Reading his explanations of the process of spiritual ascension has been, for me, like coming home. A crucial part of my own process of turning within has been the comfort I find in reading what others have encountered in their spiritual progression.

What I've observed (and experienced) is that our lessons become increasingly personal, intimate and often more difficult. You've heard the saying, "God never gives us more than we can handle." It appears to be true: as we ascend, our courage amplifies and we can handle more. Courage is not the absence of fear but our fortitude in breaking through it. Hindu mystic Osho once said, "It's the greatest adventure in life to go through a breakdown consciously and it is the greatest risk because there is no guarantee that the breakdown will become a breakthrough." I'm telling you now, there are no guarantees—which is precisely why faith must power the process. As the following story demonstrates, breakdowns can lead to breakthroughs of awareness, and life is never the same afterwards.

ZEUS' TEMPLE:
REFLECTIONS OF ANCIENT EGYPT

Before I get into this story, a little background information: In 2003, SFF Jennifer introduced me to an energy healer from southern Brazil, Edemir Rossi. He is but one of many natural intuitives and trained healers on the planet whose life's work is to touch higher realms and connect with Divine energy in order to facilitate profound, positive shifts in clients who ask for guidance in doing just this. (These shifts can occur on any or all levels of our being: physical, mental, emotional, psychic and spiritual.) In the next chapter, I will describe my one-on-one work with Edemir, as well as my impromptu apprenticeship in healing sessions with his clients in DC—his home while in the States—and, later on, in Pittsburgh where Jennifer and I have assisted him in establishing a client base. What I'm about to tell occurred within a year of my meeting Edemir; it illustrates that sometimes "the most beautiful things are those that madness prompts," to quote André Gide.

Immediately leading up to this experience, Jennifer and I had spent a week working alongside Edemir in Pittsburgh—an almost indescribable series of client healing sessions, where I witnessed how each person—either consciously or unconsciously—would bring deep, unspoken questions to the healing table, to be uncovered and elucidated. I had been privileged to have my own sessions with Edemir and was in a generally positive state of mind (I thought) as Jen and I packed up for the drive south to return Edemir to DC.

The story: We all arrive at our dear friend Kathy Pasley's home in Georgetown (she handles public information and outreach for Edemir in the U.S., and is his host when he works in DC). She greets us with open arms, the scent of French perfume, and 40s band music flowing from her living room. I love all the accoutrements at Pasley's place (everyone calls her Pasley), and being there once again feels like home. Later that evening, we linger over Turkish food in her garden courtyard. Candles dangle from the trees, softly spotlighting red and pink impatiens around our dining tableau. The patch of sky overhead is clear; moonlight reflects off the richly colored Tuscan plates that fill up as we pass around one entrée after another. I'm ensconced in a warm cocoon of friendship, fine wine, exotic food and meaningful conversation, and life couldn't be any sweeter.

But, wait . . . something is happening here. Emotions begin to bubble up from a deep place inside me. I start to feel strange, overly self-conscious. As our dinner conversation continues, I feel myself slowly becoming consumed with dark feelings of unworthiness. I can't stop them and I don't know quite what's happening to me.

In so many words, Edemir had cautioned me earlier in the week that this kind of thing might occur. In my personal healing sessions with him, I had encountered long-term, hidden thought patterns that were potentially blocking me from moving forward with a very personal writing project that I was incubating at the time. Up until then, I had only published work (news articles, magazine features, etc.) about other people—never myself. Even my first book was about someone else. Through a series of meditations, I'd concluded that at my energetic core, I was holding onto feelings of unworthiness brought on by circumstances in my childhood. If I hoped to bring my writing life to its fullest flowering, I'd have to crash my way through a small yet insidious inner attachment to the self-defeating notion that I'll never be good enough to achieve my own dreams. ER's energy work that week had helped extract these entrenched psychological and cellular memories from their hiding place, and he admonished me to be aware of a possible short period of unsettledness on the horizon. Even with warning, I couldn't have fathomed what was about to unfold in the next 24 hours.

By the time the dishes are cleared and dessert is served, Pasley's elegant courtyard soiree has segued into one of those ghastly dreams where everyone has clothes on except for me. I stop contributing to the conversation entirely, because whatever leaves my lips seems sophomoric and trivial. I feel stupid, ugly and worthless. The chaos swirling madly inside me isn't perceptible to anyone except Edemir, who occasionally slides me a sideways glance, a knowing glint in his eye—or maybe I imaged that, too; perhaps, in my neurosis, I needed a rope to stop short of slipping into a crevice of despair, so I conveniently deluded myself that someone understood I was two steps from plummeting. Finally, I push away from the table, walk into another room, wrap myself in a down-filled comforter, and go to sleep with my day clothes still on, hating myself.

I awake six hours later in the same pathetic state, only now my self-loathing is overlaid with a generalized antipathy. Last night, I cared what the others thought of me; this morning, I don't give a damn, which freaks me out even more. After breakfast, all of us, including Edemir, sit around the living room drawing rune cards. Everyone pulls illustrious runes that speak of abundance, healing and joy. My runes suck (word reflective of the mood I was in). Two are inverse and hint at sadness, rebellion, and more emotional theatrics to come. *Don't make me read these cards aloud.* Thank God I didn't have to. Everyone readies to head out for the day, no one asking what my runes foretold.

We pile into Jen's SUV and make our way to Zeus' Temple—Edemir's name for the Lincoln Memorial. "We must go there today," he insists (and with ER, Everything Matters so we agree to take that temple walk). I plod along with the rest, really wanting to be left alone. I sense an emotional avalanche coming on like nothing I've ever experienced, and I don't want to smother anyone when the torrent inside decides to rush forth. We stand at the foot of the Lincoln Memorial, gazing beyond the reflecting pool to the Washington Monument. Jen, Pasley and Edemir are engrossed in reading the intricacies of the aura around the gleaming obelisk, commenting on its color, shape, meaning. I'm the lame duck, standing to the left, only vaguely seeing the monument's energy field, if at all. *Of course, I'm too dumb to see such things, too unevolved, so incompetent.*

I don't know what's flowing through Jennifer at this time but I can see from her face that she's in a zone—a state of grace? Edemir stands nearby, paying silent respects to Zeus, Lincoln...whoever. Pasley is already inside the monument and I'm left standing with Jen and ER, who are both clearly having a moment. And then there's me. Without a word, I walk away and slowly start up the steps. *What's wrong with me? Why am I so bitter?* On one level, I'm observing myself being this way; on the physical level, emotions are moving through my body at mach speed, searching for an exit point. Tears build behind my eyes but I refuse to cry because then I would have to explain why I'm crying and I have no logical explanation.

As I ascend the white marble steps, I try to convince myself that this isn't really happening. *Stop being so emotional,* I reprimand myself. *Straighten up and get your shit together right now.* I should have known that no amount of mental exertion would stave off the inevitable. The locked-in energy that ER helped me release that week was leaving on its own recognizance and I was powerless to stop it.

By the time I reach the top flight of steps leading to the Great Emancipator, my reality shifts from being at a DC monument to ascending an ancient Egyptian temple. I take in the architectural beauty of this presidential memorial as I have many times before (I used to live near DC), yet I'm aware of being inside a sacred pyramid-shaped structure, my body clothed in a loose-fitting beige tunic and sandals. I'm so transfixed by this alternative reality that when I spot Pasley, I purposely walk past her, pretending to look at the murals on the north and south walls of the monument. I can't talk. I don't even want to look at anyone. People mill around, but I'm not with them. I'm worlds away.

As I place my eyes on the murals, I can't believe what I see. Before me, a scene from ancient Egypt begins to reveal itself, and I see a community that feels like a distant home. I can almost walk into it, it's that real. I stare at every familiar detail, knowing full well that the *actual* image on the wall (which depicts the Angel of Truth giving freedom and liberty to the slaves, and represents immortality, among other things) is not really what I'm seeing in this moment. I blink my eyes repeatedly in an attempt to reshuffle my brain. I force myself to look away. I stand, bewildered, for a long moment before the statue of Lincoln as he gazes out towards the U.S. Capitol, feeling small in his 19-foot-tall shadow.

Just then, a resounding voice hits my inner ear. It's

Scribe, the guide that had been with me since I made the decision several years prior to quit working in advertising and go full-time writer. He reminds me that this is my destiny, and I'm worthy of it. "It all began with this," he says, referring to ancient Egypt.

The tears won't hold back any longer. They stream down my face so copiously that my hands become soaked from swiping my palms against my cheeks. I walk in front of Abe and pay my respects, then turn to stare at the famous landscape stretching before me on the National Mall. I had returned to the here-and-now, and my friends had found me. By now, it's obvious to them that I'm processing something major. Jen offers a compassionate hug, which makes me weep harder. ER is steady as always, and I know that he knows why this is happening.

We all descend the steps of the monument and Edemir lags behind to walk with me. Pity, sorrow and anger have found their exit points and are slowly seeping out, but I'm still speechless. We walk in silence for what seems like an eternity (in this case, eternity equals one city block), then E speaks.

"My dearest Gina, you have a bright future and much to look forward to."

I think, *yeah right.*

"You will write many books and they will be successful, if that's what you choose to do."

"But who would CARE?" I shoot back, the only time I expressed anger towards my teacher. "I could write a hundred books but if no one cares, what's the use? It's a waste of my time, a waste of my life."

ER doesn't disagree, he simply and calmly says, "Yes, yes." I realize in retrospect that he was holding a space for me to feel what I was feeling. He knew this had to occur.

At our car Jen and I hug goodbye to Pasley and Edemir,

who are going to walk the short distance back to Pasley's house. ER very deliberately wishes me "good luck." We set off for the ride home to Pittsburgh, with me still shaken and crying uncontrollably. So what happened next? Jen, my much-needed SFF, was there to help me make sense of it all. I came to see that that week of healing through the unworthiness had come full circle. Now it was up to me to take this breakthrough and utilize it in a purposeful, pragmatic way in my life—no one could do it for me. That walk up Zeus' temple, the emotional breakdown, my connection to the Egyptian energy—it was all a crucial piece of myself echoing back at me that my ability to articulate truths (particularly in written form) to others is part of my karmic legacy from the past and is my birthright in this lifetime. The lesson has been extremely powerful and practical for me; it's given me confidence to move forward in my life and in my work. I don't mean to sound grandiose, as if I think my writings are particularly important to humanity. What I do want to say is that, yes, every one of us has a brilliant legacy, a rich karmic past and the birthright to make an important contribution to the world—that's why we're here!

The Shift Begins (and Has Already Happened)

Mine is but one story. People everywhere are turning within and having incredible experiences of personal transformation. Each story is remarkable in its own way. What weaves them into a beautiful tapestry of oneness is that they all speak to an experience of turning towards not only the Divine but one's own divine self. How we open to ultimate awareness happens to us in countless ways. As the Buddha said, there are (at least) 84,000 doors to enlightenment.

If you doubt that this shift is happening, just observe your own personal growth and how you've matured spiritually in the past 10 or 20 years. How have your views of the world, your relationships—yourself—changed in that time? Do you think differently? Have you had a "change of heart?" Are you now doing work that is for the greater good in some way, or do you yearn to? How many "awake" people do you know now compared to back then? Do you feel an urge to align more closely with other conscious individuals? Perhaps you've already accumulated an earthly soul group that shares a life purpose/reason for being that is similar to yours.

This turn of the spiritual tide became evident to me in a big way when I worked at the 11th annual Institute of Noetic Sciences (IONS) international conference in 2005 called "Consciousness and Healing: The Shift Begins," which was held—not coincidentally—in Crystal City, Virginia. The cast of characters I met that week all had personal epiphanies to share and I listened to each with rapt attention. Steve, an actor who was jokingly "only wearing black until he found a darker color," was unapologetically living from the seat of his Harley, traveling from city to city, staying in one place only long enough to complete whatever acting gigs he got. He'd finally broken free of his fear of losing his many acquired possessions—in fact, had sold some of them to buy his motorcycle. He was light, liberated and so living in the moment. Then there was Miles, a gentle soul who started a business importing eco-friendly clothing products from Latin America. In his former career incarnation, he was a party planner for Paramount Pictures. Then 9/11 hit, big budgets fell out and Miles got real with himself. "Looking back, producing huge galas for Hollywood moguls all seems so superficial and insignificant. Now, at least, I'm doing my small part to better the world."

Even before the conference began, I met two amazing women—one from Ecuador and another from the eastern shore. Talk about instant connection! We three met for lunch and were blown away by the synchronicities that led us each to that moment in time. The feeling was "we've known each other forever, and today we happen to meet in bodily form." With the incredible lightness of being in each other's company, we shared the genesis points of our spiritual awakenings. For Patricia, it was the breakdown of her marriage (while carrying twins) and how she lived with her estranged husband for two years after their separation. "In those two years, I was transformed from the inside out," she said with conviction. "My lesson to learn was this: no man will ever dominate me. I didn't run from this situation, I stayed with him and we healed through it together. In the end, I was whole and with this confidence, I chose to leave the marriage for good. Now, my ex and I have a solid friendship. The next man I love will be my equal partner."

Marisol's awakening centered around a male relationship, as well. "When I met Dean, I had a life-altering experience of euphoria that sent me reeling," she confided. "As the bliss between us continued, I started to think I was invincible. Ego took over. I went from feeling on top of the world to crashing so low that I lost myself." (In fact, around that time, Marisol was in a severe car accident that partly shattered her face.) "I mistakenly thought that Dean was giving me that sensation of bliss." In the months of recuperation from the accident, during which time Dean broke off their relationship, Marisol turned inward, determined to find that same feeling from within—which she did.

What strikes me about the transformation stories that people share with me in my journalism work is their individuality, and the fact that opening to our greatest potential is always, ultimately, an inside job, even if externally precipitated. Each person's tale involves some moment of trauma or questioning that leads them into a "shattering of the self"—which is what happens when "we don't know who we are," according to

Deepak Chopra, who spoke at this conference. "It's not know-ing who we are that causes suffering," he articulated. "The two most important questions in life are: Who am I? and What do I want? They sound simple yet they're complex and sometimes take a lifetime to answer. That is the mystery and meaning of life, to find out who we are and what we want."

While most of us can reflect back on our lives and point to certain thresholds that we've crossed within the dwelling of our spiritual awakening, the shift is, for others of us, sub-tler and longer term. Perhaps this is why the mid-life crisis is a prevalent social phenomenon—a red flag thrown up by our subconscious that we've finally reached a breaking point at which we HAVE to discover who we are, we simply can't fake it any more. We can no longer support the illusion, so we deconstruct ourselves and start anew. Wake-up calls like this occur more often than we might think. Hopefully, we're not letting them go to voice mail, because there are few things more powerful than breaking free of your own preconceptions of how life should be.

ON A PRECIPICE: LEAPING WITHIN

Whether long term or in an instant, when we reach that preci-pice, no one can really help us. We must find strength within. These are the places where we grow the most and, when we're on the verge of an epiphany of sorts, the times when we feel like our foundation is being rocked. As we advance, adversity begins to be viewed from a higher perspective, as well—an Everything Matters, Nothing Matters vantage point. We bring our expanding creative awareness with us, as well. "All suffer-ing [becomes] bearable if it is seen as part of a story," as writer Isak Dinesen believed.

When so-called misfortune strikes, we begin to understand

the nuanced distinction between a reactionary "Why did this happen to ME?" and an introspective "Why DID this happen to me?" Even if the "thing" that is happening is happening to someone else, on some level it's there to show us some aspect of ourselves. By turning within, we discover that the source of the challenging situation we're facing can be more easily and adequately addressed and corrected. Hawkins would say that our beliefs, and not external causes, determine what we experience. What we perceive as lacking in our lives is turned around and projected onto others. In other words, a comment such as "I don't feel loved" stems from not loving others or yourself; or, "people disrespect and make fun of me" results from disrespecting or being critical of others. When we make choices consciously from a posture of what we have to give and not from what we have to gain, miracles begin to occur in the form of good fortune, lucky breaks, spontaneous creative inspiration, and random acts of kindness shown to us.

Part of the exquisite torture of turning within is getting past our own BS, learning how to differentiate truth from ego. As we become more practiced at aligning with God-consciousness, we're better able to discern between the two. Because intuition is funneled from the universal mind through our individual brains, higher insights can feel like our own thought patterns—which is why a regular practice of getting out of the mind is so necessary. (The ego-self is an impressively complex structure that feeds our doubts and distracts us from our center.) The very good news is that with training, we begin to naturally recognize when we're divinely connected and what that feels like, versus when we're being tripped up by our egos and minds. I'm not spending much time on this point here, but it's a big, big thing to GET and something that everyone has to work through on the journey.

Feedback from like-minded individuals you trust goes a

long way in testing our BS-Truth meter. Early in my creative and intuitive awakening, I was given free rein to fine-tune this ability with SFF Nancy—and she with me. We'd bounce insights off one another and play with the process. Sometimes, when one of us already knew the outcome or answer to a situation, we'd quiz the other in a sort of psychic Jeopardy, drawing out the questions and filling in the details. Flexing our intuitive muscles in this way has made them stronger over time.

By contrast, I've noticed others who tend to hide behind Spirit at times. I've heard some people say "Spirit told me to do this or that" when it's really just wish fulfillment being given a spiritual moniker. When we do this, we're only fooling ourselves. The effectiveness of turning within to derive our own best answers depends upon the clarity and purity of our connection to the Divine. In other words, we must learn to cut the crap, get real and really listen to higher intelligence with an open heart. Gradually, we stop looking to external sources for confirmation because we realize this is not necessary.

The Point of Past Lives and Karma

Another aspect of turning within is re-turning to our past . . . and former iterations of ourselves. Living through our intuition allows us to perceive ourselves as soul beings, and our souls have lived a multitude of lives. But what is the value of remembering prior lifetimes? In a nutshell, our past lives have played a significant role in helping us grow into who we are here and now (as with my connection to Scribe). Past life information can uncover and demystify our motivations, desires, relationships, health conditions and many other aspects of ourselves. Personal patterns and circumstances begin to make greater sense when viewed from a soul level.

Most dedicated spiritual enthusiasts reach a point where they discover some recurring theme or pattern in their current lives that cannot be explained any other way than its being something that originated in a past life. (Likewise, parents of child prodigies or kids with stellar talents at an unusually young age begin to suspect that their child "came in" with this ability. *Children's Past Lives* by Carol Bowman is a good place to begin research on this topic.)

If you want to know more about your past lives, start by looking at your present life. Are there certain geographic areas that you're drawn to? You may have lived there in a prior life. What professions intrigue you? If you're fascinated with medicine or mathematics, perhaps you were a doctor or scientist at one time. What type of art attracts you? If you love French Impressionism, for instance, you could simply be like many others who appreciate the works of Monet and other masters; or, you may have lived in France during that time period and even known the artists. Certain books, clothing, architecture, languages or furniture can spark past life memories. Do you have an unexplainable phobia? Again, it could be related to a former life.

Some individuals who are completely unaware of their past lives have said to me, "Hey, it hasn't hindered me or hurt me in any way." While knowing such intimate knowledge about one's former incarnations is certainly not necessary, it sure does come in handy for those of us who are interested in living with the fullest self-knowledge and universal understanding possible. It also increases the joy factor in our lives because we can discern by delving into past-self histories that many circumstances that happen to us are not "personal" (read *The Four Agreements*, by Don Miguel Ruiz, for more commentary on this). From the aerial view of Everything Matters, Nothing Matters, life can be seen neutrally as a graduate school for "spiritual beings learning how to be human beings."

The concepts of reincarnation and karma are intertwined.

Many people who aren't aware of the deeper meaning of spiritual cause and effect use karma as a simplistic explanation for painful events—even to the extent of deciding that a "victim" deserves no compassion because he (karmically) brought it on himself. In *I: Reality and Subjectivity*, Hawkins explains the higher meaning of karma: "The world can be viewed as a spiritual workshop wherein the consequences of past mistakes can be reworked so that, hopefully, one will 'choose differently this time' . . . One does not get punished by some arbitrary God for past errors; instead, one merely follows them through to their consequences and learns that what is depicted as 'sin' is essentially error based on ignorance."

When I interviewed bestselling author Joan Borysenko, PhD, I wanted to ask her opinion about how we commonly understand the concept of karma. "In certain spiritual circles," I began, "it's a word that is tossed around and even used to explain why horrible things happen to good people. What has your research borne out about the emotional or psychological impact of ascribing karma as cause?"

Joan responded: "It's not a universally easy thing to look at because [often] people who believe in karma hold that belief in the same way that someone does who believes in a punitive god. It's extremely disempowering." In her book *Guilt is the Teacher, Love is the Lesson*, Joan discusses how people attribute the cause of trauma. In short, she concludes that the psychology of karma is complex; one way to cut through it is to look at our beliefs—whether religious, spiritual or psychological— and see how such beliefs can be cast in a more positive way. (Another of Joan's books, *Fire in the Soul: the New Psychology of Spiritual Optimism*, was written specifically for people who've gone through a difficult, traumatic experience; it was used by many support groups around the country in the aftermath of 9/11.)

OF HUMAN BONDING:
CREATIVE PEAKS AND DIVERGENT PATHS

What happens as we spelunk into the crevices of our own psyche or scale new heights toward our spiritual summit? Our relationships morph and twist and cling and whine and basically make toast of anything that resembles stagnation. Expect your relationships to be tested. Prepare to be shaken to your core. Realize that aligning with your passion and allowing your inner flame to fully glow is going to unnerve and even unglue some people. Evolve, but know that not everyone in your present life is going into the caverns or up the mountain with you.

And, yes . . . brace yourself for criticism of your most precious creative expressions. (*This paragraph is really important so please read it several times.*) There is a specific page in David Whyte's *Crossing the Unknown Sea* that I had him autograph, as the words on it literally kept me going in my creative life when the critical voices around me threatened to drown out my own heartsong. Speaking of his decision to become a full-time poet, David "had an intuition that when you really annunciate what you want in the world you will always be greeted, in the first place, with some species of silence. It may be that the silence is there so that you can hear exactly what you have asked for, and hear it more clearly so that you can get it right. If the goal is real and intensely personal, as it should be, others naturally should not be able to understand it the first time it finds its own voice. It means in a way, in a very difficult way, that you are on to something." Indeed, when we've finally strained through the chlorophyll that blinds us to our true colors, and we summon just enough boldness to share this essential part of ourselves, we want—even expect—others to feel the preciousness of it, as well. Be careful with whom you choose to share your creative gems, especially if they are still unpolished and mined from a very deep place or very high source.

As I worked on strengthening my inner fortitude and solidifying my link to higher realities, my creative side found increasing ways to reveal itself. (By this time, in addition to full-time writing and inspired event planning, I'd returned to practicing another lifelong love: classical dance.) Along the way, curious things happened in my interactions with others— from casual acquaintances to my most cherished loves. I have felt the splendorous ahhh of divine love-radiance (sometimes from unexpected sources) and, on the other end of the spectrum, the painful falling away of relationships that I assumed would always be a part of my life. It gives me solace to recognize from an Everything Matters, Nothing Matters perspective that people come in and out of our lives for specific reasons and with great purpose.

My dear SFF Jennifer is an *anam čara*, one of those special people with whom I've felt safe and free to be me through various stages of my spiritual progression. Early on in our soul-sisterhood, she and I had this glorious gift of time to luxuriate in the details of each other's awakening. We were side by side, parallel on the path, walking closely together in cadence. Doing so catapulted us both forward, as we were able to be splendid mirrors for each other through all the profound experiences we encountered. Looking back, this was quite necessary at the time because we were advancing so rapidly that if we didn't have each other, we probably would have thought we were going insane—with all the otherworldly things that were happening to us—or perhaps gotten frightened and wanted to close it down completely. Through our companionship, we realized that we weren't alone and that similar experiences were happening to other people, as well.

Then, as divine perfection would have it, our paths

diverged for a short while. Uneasy feelings simmered between us, causing us to step away from each other's light. While painful, this too was necessary because as we progressed, we didn't need the same level of reliance on each other (or anyone). In fact, it would have held us back to continue to spend time analyzing our experiences together. Speaking for myself, it became more important to put the knowledge we'd gained into action, to bring it into material form somehow. Doing so required a transference of my attention away from the two of us exploring together, and towards how I could and should bring it into the world through my independent creations. I'm happy to say that Jen and I were quick studies in this particular course, probably because we wanted to get the lesson and move past this shadowy phase in our friendship.

In the end, it bonded us more deeply. In fact, one of the most poignant experiences of my spiritual life occurred when Jen and I, and my other dearest SFF Lee Ann, recently traveled to Mexico for a retreat in the land of the Mayans. One of the many revelations that I had during that trip is, I think, important to share here . . . then I will tell what happened with the three of us.

The revelation: During a meditation leading up to the retreat, Spirit gave me a three-point hierarchy and told me to bear this in mind.

Self

Soul Friends

Healers/Teachers

The retreat was to be focused around the work of several spiritual teachers, but I was encouraged by my inner guidance to deemphasize the notion of anyone "leading" me, and that I was my own best healer—hence, "self" is top on the list. Second (also above healers/teachers) is soul friends. ("Our feelings towards our friends reflect our feelings towards ourselves," Aristotle once said.) Towards the end of our week in San Miguel de Allende, our retreat group visited a sacred site, La Gruta Hot Springs. Lee Ann, Jennifer and I went off on our own and swam our way through the tepid mineral water into a cavernous tunnel that then led into a snug, mystical, womblike space no bigger than an igloo. Once there, Jen spoke a powerful extemporaneous prayer that suffused the womb, drawing forth its ancient feminine energy.

Half-entranced by the profundity of her words, the heat and the pulsation of my breath—which echoed off the walls and back into my body—I waded in this magical space quietly and alone for some time. Then I heard Lee Ann speak my name and, spontaneously, the three of us joined together in a sublime embrace, a tiny circle of *anam ċara* remembrance and belonging. In that timeless sacramental moment, sweat and tears streaming from our faces, we came home to ourselves, each other and Divine Mother. I will forever hold the warmth of that sisterly love in my heart.

MY FATHER'S FINAL TRIUMPH

But, ultimately, we all have to go it alone. This is something I began to appreciate at an early age. From the time I was a girl, I remember feeling that I had only myself to rely upon, and that whatever happened in my life was going to be contingent upon my own choices, not the result of fate or some outer happenstance. Perhaps this characteristic was partly nature, partly nurture.

Integral to my own story of turning within is that of my father. Dad was, at times, a force (not) to be reckoned with, a man with a sharp mind and many talents who commanded, and deserved, respect. Under it all, he had a feeling heart and emotions that ran deep. To be sure, my father has been a major influence on my life. In my younger years, he was actually my deepest wound, but I see now that everything that happened between us was a crucial part of bringing forth who I am today.

Not all relationships that are right for us are peaceful; in fact, they can be our most valuable learning tools. For this reason alone, I'm in gratitude to my father. What a tremendous teacher he has been, whether intentional or not. (And I might add that my mom, a deeply religious and compassionate woman, is very intentionally one of my life's great teachers of unconditional love, among many other things.) My relationship with Dad improved as the years went on in our adult lives and then, when he was around 80, we began to notice that something was happening with Dad's mind. As many of you with older parents can attest, it's devastating to watch someone you've always looked upon as strong and vital deteriorate before your eyes.

Because Everything Matters, the fact that my father's health condition reached a critical turning point the day after I arrived home from meeting Edemir for the first time—and had just begun the process of releasing ingrained patterns from my childhood—was not lost on me. Not so ironically, the start of my most intensive inner quest to unburden myself of all outworn patterns marked the first day of the end of Dad's life as he had known it.

Early that morning, I received the phone call that I'd been at once dreading and hoping my mom would make. My father was spiraling down with psychosis and dementia, and I encouraged Mom to tell me when she felt that taking care of him had become too much to handle. That day had arrived.

"I can't take anymore," she said. And that's all she needed to say.

She'd been single-handedly caring for my dad in their home 24/7 during the frightening years when he was slowly losing his mind. For Mom, it was a living hell but she bore her cross with unfaltering love and dignity. With statistics showing that long-term caregivers oftentimes die before the person they're caring for due to stress, I was afraid that Dad's worsening condition and the trauma it involved on a daily basis would overcome her. But Mom has an incredible ironclad faith in Jesus and a quiet inner strength that surpasses practically anyone I've ever met. She would continue to need to draw on her tremendous reserve of physical and emotional fortitude to endure the coming years of Dad's illness. (Later, when the caseworker in the psych ward discovered that my mom was Dad's sole caregiver, his response was, "My God, Sarah, how did you survive that? You know, we have a team of people working round the clock taking care of your husband.")

The day of Mom's phone call was one of the most devastating days of my life, and hers. Dad was violent and so mentally gone that we were forced to make a heart wrenching choice—commit him against his will. The look in his eyes in those moments lives with me still. The whole ordeal was surreal, a nightmare, and if I ever needed inner calm, a quick, clear head and the ability to witness a situation (Chapter 6 will be all about Witnessing), it was that day. I thank God that I was available to help Mom. If it had been a day earlier, I would have been out of town.

Jump ahead one year to May 2004. Due to his worsening condition, Dad was not allowed to continue residing at the assisted living facility where he'd lived for less than a year. The coming summer was a cruel one. Dad was shuttled in and out of various hospitals, rehab centers and psychiatric wards. Eventually, we needed to find a suitable longer-term facility with an available bed. After reviewing his case history, no one would take him. His behavior made him a danger to other residents. In early August, we learned of another place that specialized in dementia patients. Mom and I spent yet another long day filling out paperwork and reiterating Dad's medical history to the staff. We were candid about Dad's behavioral issues but the caseworker reassured us that they had the best specialists to handle this. Later that evening, we left Dad in their hands, hoping for the best.

Five days later, he acted up with another patient and was shipped out quicker than you can read this page. They admitted him to the geriatric/psych ward of a hospital south of the city. Mom and I were at our wits' end. Our options were running out.

Along with the practical legwork of calling his former caseworkers for suggestions and doing research online to locate another facility, I made a conscious decision to intensify my efforts to connect with Dad on a subconscious level. I wanted to understand, underneath the illness, why he was being so aggressive, so agitated. Of course, it was the progression of the dementia. Perhaps by communicating with him on a soul level, I could better comprehend what he was going through. And, yes, Alzheimer's has no cure (yet). Still, I sensed that some essential healing needed to take place on deeper psychic and psychological levels—why else would Dad still be on earth with us?

For the duration of Dad's illness, I'd been asking for advice from my own guides on how to manage things. I had stopped short of connecting directly to Dad's subconscious. For whatever reason, I was intimidated by the thought of "going there," not knowing what I would find, or how I'd feel. For many years in my younger life, Dad was my nemesis. Perhaps I had residual fear that linking with his essence would over- whelm me. Still, the desperateness of the situation gave me an awkward courage with which to proceed, and I viewed it as another way to help Dad.

All trepidation disappeared when I awoke the next morning from a vivid dream: Dad and I are sitting together on a park bench. He is loving and sweet towards me. I hold his hand and he's able to speak. I want to tell him that there's this whole world beyond the physical, that his earthly life is not the end. Just then, he starts to talk and communicates to me all of the things I was getting ready to tell him. He knew.

Finally, that Monday morning, I was emotionally ready to connect with Dad's heart and soul. During this same week, Mom was praying a novena to the Blessed Mother, and so I proceeded with confidence that I was bolstering her intent in my own way—through focused meditation. I was instructed by my guides to do a series of five meditations, one hour each morning that week.

DAY 1: Figuring that Mom had the Blessed Mother covered on her end, I ask, "Who else is here now to help with Dad?" Immediately, I sense a male presence coming through. I ask who it is, and St. Joseph appears (the first time I'd ever seen him clairvoyantly). He tells me that he is a guide to my father now. He has dark, wavy hair, like my Dad in his 20s. Funny, he looks like Dad, or Dad like him. (Interestingly, my father's name is Guiseppe, or Joseph.) In my mind's eye, I watch as St. Joseph walks towards Dad and places his essence into Dad's body, as if the two are merging. They become one. With this, he/Dad stands up and begins to walk.

"What are you doing?" I ask St. Joseph.

"I'm walking in your father's shoes, and he in mine," he conveys. "I'm teaching him about the great sacrifices we make for our loved ones. As my earthly son demonstrated, death is the ultimate sacrifice."

Surprised by this, I ask for further clarification. "Do you

mean that you are helping Dad to accept death?

"Yes, death offers the hope of rising again."

I send unconditional love to Dad's heart and close the meditation.

DAY 2: St. Joseph informs me that he will be guiding my father through a phase that will last several months or longer, during which he will penetrate the source of Dad's agitation and help him come to a state of inner calm. The vision begins with Dad "in the dark." St. Joseph stands behind his wheelchair and gives it a gentle push. The wheelchair rolls forward and is transformed into a chariot. Dad resists and attempts to put on the brakes.

Again, I send unconditional love to Dad's heart and end with a prayer.

DAY 3: Before I close my eyes and sink into the deepness, I draw a card from the Osho Zen Tarot deck. As I'm shuffling, the Miser card falls to the floor. It says: *Whatever you are clinging to, whatever you feel you have to protect, let go.*

St. Joseph's presence is here again. This time, he is clothed in a white robe. He pushes back his left sleeve, leans forward and moves his outstretched arm, palm upward, from left to right. A throng of nameless, faceless people emerge from the shadows. They file past St. Joseph, each placing gold coins in his hand. I sense that this represents earthly possessions, as well as those in the shadows who dwell on the trappings of the material world. St. Joseph tells me that he is conveying to Dad that worldly belongings mean nothing once you cross over. He encourages Dad to release attachment to these things so that he is "freer to go."

I close the work by once more sending unconditional love to Dad's heart.

DAY 4: "Can you help my father see the beauty of the light?" I ask St. Joseph. He suggests that I do this. Reticent, I tune into Dad through his eyes, which are intense, deep and dark. I literally feel emotional pain throughout my body. I speak aloud through tears:

"Dad, no matter what, you are my father and I love you. I want the best for you. If you wish, you can end this earthly struggle and choose to go with Jesus and St. Joseph. With them, you will have every abundance that you sought on earth and more, only you will not have to lock it in a safe in the basement. There will be an infinite supply of riches, wealth and health."

I'm sobbing, partly from the recent memory of opening a large safe that my father kept in his basement, a remnant from his years as owner of a jewelry store. During his remaining months at home, he'd taken to storing items in that safe, almost a daily obsession, as if struggling to put a value on his life.

After this meditation, I draw the Breakthrough card. Then, a miracle occurs. The phone rings. A very reputable, private facility located within 15 minutes of my house calls to say that they're willing to take Dad as a resident. I phone Mom. We are elated, and patiently await word of when Dad will be transferred.

DAY 5: I begin the day by sitting in deep gratitude for the immensity of what my father has brought into my life— the heartache and the joy. The phone rings, interrupting the silence, and the day lurches forward with Mercury retrograde in full regalia. Dad is being transferred within the hour but the facility can't reach my mom to approve the transfer. The previous evening's storm had disrupted her phone service—but neither of us realizes this until hours later. I'm concerned that Mom isn't answering the phone. Is she okay? I try to call her neighbor—no answer. I call her priest—he's out of town for the week. The driver is on his way to Mom's house—with Dad in the van—and she doesn't know. What should I do? Leery of sending anyone to Mom's home that she doesn't recognize, I call the police, explain the situation, and instruct them to tell her I sent them. Luckily, they arrive before the driver. Mom calls me from the patrol car and I tell her to get ready (physically and emotionally) because the driver is en route with Dad to pick her up.

I meet Mom at the facility and begin the process of paperwork—again. As I walk into the meeting room, Dad's new caregiver, Pam, says excitedly: "You must be Gina!" I nod. "Oh, your dad talked about you the whole way up in the van. Gina, Gina, Gina! Did you know that he thinks the world of you? He told me that he would do ANYTHING for you. He is so proud of you!"

I'm startled to hear this and ponder why Dad would say these things, and why today. Dad was always emotionally reserved with us kids and wasn't one to give us praise or say "I love you." I knew full well that his illness caused him to say strange things but, oddly, what had been coming from his mouth in the last year of his life was truth, without pretense— similar to how children speak.

I talk with Pam further about the van ride. "He was completely lucid," she says, and I'm amazed. He remembers an astonishing array of details from his life: Mom's brasciole, songs from childhood in Italy, how long it takes to get into the city from his house. He looks at Pam's ring and knows the type of stone and grade of gold. He tells her that King's Restaurant is his favorite. As Pam and I speak, Dad is in the dining room finishing his third plate of food, and asking for another slice of that delicious pie. I walk in and he gives me an enormous smile that is both innocent and all knowing. He makes me laugh when I leave by saying "I'm okay, you go. You might as well have fun and make some money!" It was a random, quirky comment like so many others I'd heard him say, only this time, it came with a sense of relief. Something had shifted and I knew Dad would be okay at his new home.

Reflecting back on that day, it was all confirmation that the energy I was sending to Dad that week had reached him. It made perfect sense. I'd been sending unconditional love to Dad every morning in meditation. Then to hear from his caregiver that he had words of praise for me, well, I can't express how astounding this was, since my dad never directly articulated this sentiment to me during his lifetime. I took it as a sign that the energy work I'd done that week on his behalf did something tangible to change his situation for the better. Just as St. Joseph had told me, my father had the most peaceful period of his illness during the next four months. He seemed happy at his new home, the staff loved him, and he had no incidents while he was there.

As my father's story illustrates, we're able to connect with loved ones on a soul level. This is especially important with individuals who are not cognitively responsive. Some souls linger on earth with pain and disease in their minds and bodies because they are fearful of the transition of death or because they mistakenly believe the family cannot carry on without them. Letting Dad know that it was fine to go, if he chose, was a good thing to do.

While I will continue my father's story in a later chapter, I'd like to emphasize at the close of this one that turning within obviously isn't just for our individual benefit. When we tap the rich inner world of the Divine to investigate and arrive at answers to whatever challenges occur in our lives, miracles happen—for ourselves and everyone who is energetically connected to us. Considering that we're all one, that includes everybody on the planet.

five

WORKING WITH A MENTOR

Masters don't teach the truth; there is no way to teach it. It is a
transmission beyond words. It's energy provoking energy in you . . .
Truth is a radical, personal realization. You have to come to it.

—OSHO

"*There* are two kinds of teachers: those who take your
power, and those who give your power back to you,"
says author Alan Cohen. "The inferior teacher tells you that
something is wrong with you and offers to fix it. The superior
teacher tells you that something is right with you and helps
you bring it forth. . . A real teacher makes him or herself progressively more unnecessary." This is what having a spiritual
mentor means to me, someone who can take my hand, walk
me through my own walls of doubt and assist me in bringing
my creative self into fullest expression.

These past five years, the significance of having a spiritual teacher has not been lost on me. I've typically thought
of myself as someone who goes it alone, but have wised to
the fact that yielding a heavy sickle and slicing a solitary trail
is not the only way to traverse through life. Others can help
us "cut tall grass" and clear a path to reveal higher, broader

perspectives. Yes, we must ultimately find our own answers by Turning Within, yet I've come to realize that being in holy company every so often can catapult us faster and farther. Meeting someone who is at a higher level of mastery shows us that such a state is possible.

I've heard it said that enlightened teachers are really just survivors of the death of the ego. From this pure, high frequency state, the benefit of being in the presence of an advanced teacher—either in silence or through their words of encouragement—can serve to raise us up, as well. There are plenty of authentic and very studied teachers out there who provide a great service to many people. Yet, to know about something and to BE it are totally different. In the presence of a master, words are superfluous. In fact, some of my most powerful healings have come cloaked in utter silence.

IN HOLY COMPANY:
THE PRESENCE OF A TEACHER

Is a mentor necessary? Eventually, yes. If you wish to learn advanced calculus, you find a professor. If you aspire to be in the Olympics, you seek out coaches and trainers who've been there. True, some people have crushing experiences such as illness or deep grief that crack them open and lead to illumination—instantaneously, in some cases. For the many of us who are on this journey for the long term, glimmerings of higher consciousness come from being with those who are at a place of higher mastery than we are.

"A frequent problem of the relentless spiritual seeker," Hawkins says, "is that they have not had the personal presence of a teacher with a high enough level of consciousness, that is, one whose aura has the power to catalyze the transformation of information into subjective awareness/experience. A truly enlightened teacher provides, via the aura, a high-energy context that illuminates and activates the student's content from the mental body into the higher spiritual bodies."

I'd never had a mentor of any sort and wasn't seeking one on a conscious level—although it is an ancient truth that when the student is ready, the teacher appears. I never quite understood devotees to a guru; this didn't seem to be me. Why would anyone wish to give their power to someone else or change their lifestyle to follow someone else's lead? Now, I somewhat understand the allure. I further understand that many so called larger-than-life individuals differ from the rest of us chiefly because they are profoundly present to the stuff in their lives, to what is happening within themselves and around them. And I know that my "path of yoga" in this lifetime is one of right action and service (karma yoga), not devotion (bhakti yoga). So, for me, working with a master is not about worship. It's about scrutiny. It's about certainty through the empirical, being able to observe and deduce for myself using all my human powers of discrimination alongside my belief that anything is possible with God.

What has aligning with a mentor done for me? In the beginning, he and I worked on multi-dimensional levels to raise my energy vibration, which in turn opened my third eye, expanded my consciousness of higher realms and unshackled the wounded parts of my creative soul. A tall order, but it happened fairly quickly. This is partly what is referred to as the "grace of the guru," because while I could have done it on my own, it probably would have taken a heck of a lot longer. (And if you really want to know God, there's a yearning to get on with it as soon as possible!) To be sure, blowing the lid off my own limited thinking—about my creative self, humanity and the cosmos—has transformed my life. This isn't metaphysical mind candy, I'm talking practicality. Very simply, having expanded awareness, and thus the freedom to meet the muses where they live, has graced me with the abiding faith that *anything* is attainable, that we're constrained only by our own beliefs. Experiencing the realm of infinite potentiality has given me a fresh, bold, almost fearless confidence in my life. When we have the understanding of why we're here and what it all means, it's much easier to make decisions instead of spinning our wheels out of indecisiveness about what's best for us.

A Master Arrives

Jen and some other friends had convinced me to take a girls-only weekend to Washington, for two reasons: R&R away from kids, house and work, and to meet Edemir, the energy healer from Brazil. Having turned within for many years, determined to find my own answers through reading and experimenting on my own, I didn't have a big expectation but I'd heard good things about his work. While Edemir had gathered his healing acumen across many cultural and religious traditions—including shamanism, Zen Buddhism and Brazilian Umbanda—I liked the fact that he was raised in the Catholic tradition and most closely followed the teachings and spiritual guidance of Jesus and Mother Mary.

Edemir's healing work primarily takes place in a private residence in northwest DC when he is in the United States (he works in Curitiba and São Paolo most of the time). From the first moment I entered this home, the atmosphere inside it felt welcoming, reassuring. Edemir walked into the sitting room, greeted me with a warm smile and grasped both my hands. Small in stature and tanned from the subtropic sun, he looked into my eyes with a tranquil, unwavering gaze. Something in my soul responded. A calm sensation had filled the room when he entered and I felt viscerally that this was a person who is present in the fullest sense, loving in the purest way.

In that first round of four sessions that I had with Edemir, he seemed patient, kind and very humble. I saw great strength in that. Before beginning the energy work (which is done while the client lies on a massage table), Edemir asked only a few simple, direct questions: "How are you? Why are you here today? What would you like to work on?" He listened to my answers with such completeness. Even though he'd just met me, he seemed to know where my soul wanted me to go, yet he never told me what to do. Rather, he showed me, through example, that higher consciousness is ordinary, tangible and contingent upon the amount of work I was willing to put into my self-development.

I've heard it said that a person assimilates spiritual truths on many levels—the most important of which is nonverbal, formless and beyond the mind. This silent transmission often occurs in the presence of a teacher whose level of consciousness is more highly energized than our own. The assimilation is nothing short of our personal metamorphosis from chrysalis state to butterfly. A dramatic internal change occurs, and all of the spiritual learning we've accumulated—everything we've read, been taught and mentally know—suddenly reorganizes. Our very being is transformed and we emerge from the experience with wings full tilt, able to soar like never before. This is similar to what happened to me upon meeting and working with Edemir that weekend. Everything I had reasoned through in my mind about unseen realities rushed to the fore. Quite unexpectedly, I was experiencing what I'd only read about, and I could glimpse my potential to become a beautiful creature with a greater sense of freedom in my own life.

When I first met Edemir, I couldn't adequately articulate the exact reason for the small yet deep well of sadness that I felt at my core. It had to do with a lot of things—unresolved experiences, unrealized potential (especially creatively) and emotions locked far inside, coupled with an undefined yearning to live larger, with daily surety of purpose and a dollop of wild abandon. With ER's encouragement, I ventured across my own abyss like a circus acrobat who trains to swing skillfully from one trapeze to another, confident in her timing, concentration and grip. As I let go of one bar to fly towards the next, Edemir told me, in so many words, "You'll make it, you'll make it." I knew that soaring sky-high between trapezes would be frightening and exhilarating, and I was so ready to take that first step up the ladder to new heights.

Meeting Myself

"I have this great life," I tell Edemir during my first-ever healing session with him. "I've got two beautiful children, a wonderful husband, family, good friends, I'm healthy and I've chosen work that I'm passionate about . . . BUT I can't help feeling that there's so much more. I feel ungrateful! I know my dharma is to write and I'm working ferociously at it. Still, something is impeding me from making real progress. It almost feels like something is blocking me."

"So let's ask God what's blocking you," Edemir says. "Close your eyes."

It takes a while for a message to filter into my mind, as I'm new at this. Edemir is patient. Finally, inwardly, I hear, *I'm blocking myself!* I can't believe it. "How is this possible, for all of my initiative?" I ask aloud.

"Let's ask God," ER repeats, making me tune in while he focuses energy towards me.

"It's related to patterns remaining from my upbringing," I hear myself saying. "I was discouraged from expressing my exuberant self. When I did something good like get straight A's, my father didn't acknowledge it. I just wanted to please him, to be noticed by him." At this point, I'm thinking, *not this same old crap!* as I'd already worked through forgiveness issues related to my father years ago. "I'm sick of talking about that. Can we just be done with it?"

Edemir knows I'm not "done with it." On a cellular level, remnants of this pattern still needed to be cleared if I was to begin unbinding my creative potential. Sure, my dad and I were cool, but I never forgave myself.

Edemir asks me to go to a time in my childhood. Against the background of my inner vision, I see myself as eight years old—knobby kneed, summery dress, a cascade of brown curls, holding a bunch of yellow flowers. Wow, I'm so pure, innocent, shy, quiet but happy. I tune into this little girl. ER tells me to tell her she is loved, appreciated. I draw her close to my heart, hug her with my essence, and tell her this.

Now, this inner child starts talking to me, teaching ME. She says: "There is a distinction between feeling self-confident and feeling worthy." Yes, I feel confident in my creative ability but do I feel worthy? "You're an open, loving person but a part of you is closed," the girl continues. "It's a defense mechanism you've built around your emotional self to get you through to adulthood."

The girl doesn't have this because she hasn't needed it yet. She is aware that I've carried this through life for too long. "You don't need it anymore!" she tells me.

Just then, I'm struck with the revelation that this girl is me before I turned cynical. She is me in pure form—untainted, trusting and very sweet. When I realize this, the girl extends her arms and offers me the bouquet of flowers, as if to say, "I am now returning this part of yourself to you."

In the months following this first round of sessions, the universe conspired to arrange situations in which I could test the possibility of removing this ingrained pattern of undeservedness. Light bulbs began to turn on about ways in which I'd self-sabotaged. In one such instance (pre-sessions), I'd recommended another journalist for a plum assignment that was offered to me. *Why did I do that?* I asked myself, incredulously. The assignment was given to me because I had the exact right experience and knowledge of the subject matter. The journalist I recommended had less experience and little knowledge of the topic. The biggest difference, however, is that this colleague boldly stepped up with self-assuredness, even though he suspected that he might be in over his head. Riding his enthusiasm, he couldn't believe his good fortune at being handed this assignment—I even provided him with necessary background research. As it turned out, he botched the piece so badly that he asked me to bail him out by assisting with the rewrites. I even spent two hours on a phone conference instructing him how to finesse the language and present the topic in the fairest, most comprehensive manner. Naturally, Everything Matters: he learned valuable lessons from this experience, as did I. When the piece was finally published (post-sessions) and he received accolades for the work, his work, a wave of emotional bile backed up in my energy field: jealousy, resentment, frustration, anger—it wasn't pretty. Mainly, I was PO-ed at myself. It was the jolt I needed to ask myself some hard questions: *If he can do it, why can't you? If you can do it better, then why aren't you?* Sure enough, as my inner child had lovingly told me, I had plenty of confidence in my ability, I just hadn't felt worthy.

*   *   *

After four initial healing sessions over that spring weekend in DC, during which I work through energetic attachments related to childhood patterns of unworthiness, my creative spirit feels freer, and for the next six months or so it continues to soar upwards. During the next round of sessions with Edemir that take place in Pittsburgh, the peaks are dramatic. In one, a quicksilver energy penetrates my skull (I could feel this), as if my brain is being recalibrated. "What the heck was that?" I ask Edemir afterwards. "I was guided to work on your mental process," he answers. "Come again?" I say. "We opened more parts of your brain so you can handle the higher vibrations coming in," he explains. In another session, the boundary between my physical body and the space beyond it utterly dissolves. When I sit up on the healing table, I feel both more luminous and (no other word for it) voluminous. "What did you do?" I query Edemir. "I expanded your energy field, that's it," he says as a matter of fact.

A third session sends me to the heavens, unfettered and exquisitely light. Afterwards, it's like someone has taken Windex and swiped my world clean. No more smears, streaks and bug splats. As I leave the healing room and walk down the corridor towards several friends, colors and shapes pop. My mind is dazed and sharply honed at the same time; both witticisms and wisdom flash through it. I'm laughing aloud and I'm dead calm. I can hear better, too—not decibel-wise, just that I don't miss a trick. I slouch onto a sofa like a marionette with too much slack. "How ARE you?" my friends ask. "I . . . have . . . just . . . begun . . . to live," is all I manage to say.

From that second round of sessions forward, with many internal blocks substantially resolved, I worked on extending the reach of both my writing/editing practice and event planning work, spanning out geographically and aligning with people of greater influence. I told ER that I wanted the emphasis to be on "spiraling up and out." Of course, during the six-month intervals between my sessions I continued to set specific intentions with this open-ended objective. By now, I understood that goals were not something to be achieved through wantonness, by just throwing energy at them, but rather by simple decision, commitment and choosing right action as an outcome of knowing myself and what moves me. Slowly, my writing and editing assignments began migrating from the suburbs where I live to the city, outward into other areas of the North and Southeast. I continued to let go of any internal and external resistances—everything from "am I up to the task" to "are the children going to be okay while I'm traveling"—and before I knew it, I was garnering assignments from Texas, Washington State, Oregon, Florida and various parts of California.

Funny thing is, these projects arrived in varied—and very serendipitous—ways. I noticed an undeniable trend: I wasn't marketing my services any longer (other than my website). Instead of promoting, I was *attracting*. In some cases, there was no other rational explanation for how some clients found me. And while the work was stretching geographically, it was evolving in other ways, as well. I began to effortlessly meet and be granted interviews with people whom I most admired and whose work I wanted to support. This success continued to beget more success, and continues to this day. At one point, it happily dawned on me that I could no longer say or even think the phrase, "my dreams will come true" (as Edemir said to me early on). I had to edit my speech to reflect my new-found reality: "my dreams ARE coming true." It was a pivotal moment in which I realized that all of the concepts I have outlined so far in this book—Intention, Daily Practice, Paying Attention, Turning Within and Working with a Mentor—were paying tangible dividends in the form of creating the sacred, fascinating and fulfilling work life that I could only dream of having years earlier. I still have a long, long way to go because there are many more dreams I wish to realize and many stories I would like to share. Remember what the Zen teacher Suzuki Roshi said about how we hobble ourselves by carrying a second horse on top of the one we're one? Well, at least I could now say that I'd gotten rid of the second horse!

THE DARK HAS WORK TO DO

The renowned psychiatrist Elisabeth Kübler-Ross, whose work I've always admired (her groundbreaking book, *On Death and Dying*, was the subject of my high school term paper, for goodness sakes!) once said: "People are like stained-glass windows. They sparkle and shine when the sun is out but when the darkness sets in, their true beauty is revealed only if there is a light from within." Working with integrity-based healers—as well as discussing matters of deep inquiry with New Thought leaders and others who live in a state of refined awareness—has taught me that we are capable of so much more than we give ourselves credit for. It has also revealed to me that spiritual evolution is incremental and not without hazard. Along with the elation of hearing more clearly the divine echo inside me, I've discovered that there is great strangeness in the shadowed light of our soul world, and it's just as important, even desirable, to become conversant with that shrouded portion of our soul-light.

"It is not possible to get the blessing without the madness," writes Norman O. Brown in *Apocalypse and/or Metamorphosis*. "It is not possible to get the illuminations without the derangement." In other words, as we open to other dimensions, we open to everything, the light and the dark. So, it's important to be aware of what we're doing when we begin spiritual work in earnest; hence, the value of having a proper teacher to assist along the way. The goal, I've learned, is to encounter the darkness, when necessary, without having a negative experience. Actually, nothing is a negative experience; it is there to teach us, to show us what's missing. This polarity is how we come to really know ourselves. ". . . darkness holds

it all: the shape and the flame, the animal and myself . . ."
Rilke penned.

As we move deeper and deeper into the subconscious aspects of things—the cobwebby corners of our psyche—we can bring up longer-term issues we have with certain individuals who are closest to our hearts or have done things to us that are difficult to forgive. (Most difficult for me has been to bless those who have smote me creatively—this is how I know that helping others connect with their creative souls is my dharma. As Julia Cameron wrote, "Anger points the way, not just the finger.") At the same time, we're reaching the understanding more quickly that Everything Matters—and Nothing Matters. We're able to step outside ourselves, see things in a more compassionate light and understand the relevance of why situations are in our life at a particular time. This process is really quite astonishing. Salvation can actually be found in the center of a so-called negative experience because, as conscious beings, we can feel it softening us and enhancing our capacity to live through our hearts. Author Roger Housden offers this analogy: "The heart, like a grape, is prone to delivering its harvest in the same moment that it appears to be crushed."

It's reassuring to know that love overcomes all things in the end. "The dark and light are not equal energies," the widely studied channeled writings of Kryon explain. "If you have a dark place and light comes in, darkness does not creep away into another dark place. Instead, it is transformed. Of the two, light is the only one that has an active component and a physical presence. You cannot 'beam darkness' into a light place. It can only be the other way around. This is because they aren't equal. One is the absence of the other."

As I see it, we can use the light that we gather along the way to go a little farther into the darkness. (This is partly what I mean when I say the journey is vertical in nature.) And when we process "unhealthy" experiences with assistance from mentors and SFFs, we don't risk getting sucked into the abyss of our own darkness—we are able to shine light down on it and examine the darkness from above.

According to Edemir, the light and the dark work together in accordance with God's will. "There are those in the dark who work for the light," he said to me one day while explaining his model for understanding the energetic workings of the cosmos. "But there is a third kind of energy that is outside of the laws of God: the shadow energy. This energy wants to BE God. It is pure evil and works against God's will. As with the dark, we should not run from the shadow. We should acknowledge it, respect it, then work to transmute it." Sooner than expected, I would be testing his theory.

From Inner Child to Outer Space

I may be stretching credulity with this next story, but I must tell it exactly as it transpired. I include it here as an example of several things: 1) how we open to everything as we advance, not just the light; 2) how working with a mentor prompted me get to the root of a situation that had caused me emotional and physical unease for years; and 3) how shadow energy differs from the dark.

This story involves deep healing from a longstanding situation with one of my siblings (as I said, my lessons have gotten increasingly personal). I am blessed to have two wonderful brothers who would do anything for me, and I for them. We have a third brother who, sadly, has managed to single-handedly ostracize himself from his siblings and parents, his ex-wife and even his children. For years, I was distraught over this brother's actions towards me, thinking that I had done something to offend him. Because Everything Matters, I spent quite a bit of time reflecting on why this was all happening with a family member, whom I couldn't just dismiss from my life. Looking back, I didn't realize the severity of what I was dealing with. For years, I tried to "kill him with kindness," rationalizing that it's possible to heal all things with love. True, but the other party has to be willing to respond to that love. For several more years, I shunned him from my life completely, afraid that his contentious attitude would deplete me, as it had on various occasions. It was Edemir who taught me to neither heal him against his will nor ignore the situation, but accept and co-exist with it. That would be some feat.

I hadn't mentioned anything about this situation to Edemir in my first few rounds of healing sessions with him. As usually happens with energy work, what is most in need of healing rises to the surface to be cleared before deeper work can take place. While on the healing table in a state of meditation, I see a flash of black bugs with red, glowing wings scattering in various directions. I can't make sense of this and don't tell Edemir about it. The next morning, he asks out of the blue: "What's going on with your brother?" I briefly convey how he's the only person in my life from whom I can't seem to energetically shield myself. "When I'm around him, or even when I feel him thinking about me," I explain, "it hits me in the solar plexus and turns me nauseous and freezing cold from the inside out. I visibly shake in his presence!" I describe how this feels different from other negative energies I'd experienced that were projections of someone's ego. Instead, this felt evil, like it had no conscience. I struggled to accept that this could be my sibling's true nature. Being raised in the same household as the rest of us, how could he turn out like this? Over the years, he seemed to dwell increasingly on the lower emotions (jealousy, pride, paranoia), as if some external negative force was slowly overtaking him.

Edemir tells me that in my session the previous day he

had sensed something, but hasn't yet figured out where it's coming from. "There's a foreign object, a disc, in your solar plexus that's weakening you, splicing your energy in half," he says. While this may sound "out there," looking back, it was the most rational explanation I'd heard to date for why I literally felt cut in half. He explains that this isn't a pattern within myself that needs to be reframed as with my earlier inner child encounter; rather, the origin of this energy is outside me—in fact, is a shadow energy attached to my brother, and because I was in the vulnerable position of extending myself to him, this force saw an easy in through my weakened solar plexus. ER suggests tracing the energy back to its origin to eradicate it from my energy field.

We enter meditation. Jennifer is there too, lending energetic support. I'm feeling nauseous already. ER tells me to tune into my solar plexus and report what I see. "A hole," I say. "I see a cave with a dark energy lurking inside." After that, I see a void that extends beyond the back of the cave, which connects to a black vortex in space, a wormhole. I follow the energy. It takes me far, far away, to another planetary realm.

"What do you see there?" ER asks.

"It feels extraterrestrial, insect-like," I say, feeling a bit foolish. ER encourages me to go on, so I describe what I see: insects with red wings. Suddenly, my meditation vision from the previous day makes sense.

"What happened there?" ER asks. I realize that I must enter the insect planet to answer this question. I stare into the nothingness but my intuitive eye seems to have closed; I still feel queasy and frigid to the marrow. On the one hand, I'm thinking that my reality check has just bounced in a major way; on the other, I feel that I'm onto something and must proceed.

I tune into this alien landscape and begin to see the form

of the dominant leader insect. It is massive in comparison to the tiny planetary drones that it's controlling. The leader achieves his power through the use of energy, clicking laser-like currents into each lesser insect with a device that looks like a TV remote (or are these currents shooting from one of his tentacles?). This energy disturbance puts the inhabitants into a catatonic state. "The inhabitants have lost their sense of what they are, they're empty inside, shells of themselves," I report.

Edemir, Jennifer and I ask God to send a healing presence to heal this planet. I wait. Out of nothingness comes a holy being—an avatar, who carries with him immeasurable spiritual power. He is adorned in a suit of armor, riding on something like a horse (although I can't see the animal). He is wearing an ornate metal headdress and holding a sheath or sword of some sort, which could just as well be a beam of light. With my mind, I ask the avatar to heal the insect planet. I don't know what will happen in response to this. A war? Suffering? Alien nation uprising? Annihilation? Instantly, the avatar's mere presence effects enormous change on this planet. The leader insect is diminished energetically, as it realizes its delusion of being the most omnipotent force in the universe. As this occurs, the avatar infuses the lesser insects with light and energy; they are empowered. The leader is not killed; rather, it is minimized to the same size as the other inhabitants. "Everyone is equal," I realize, "as it should be." ER adds: "The era of domination over others is gone." I know this is all about my brother and his controlling personality, presented to me in this strange imagery.

I want to know if the avatar has a name. "Ask him," ER suggests. So I do. Right away, I get "Bruce Almighty" and laugh out loud. Edemir hasn't heard of this movie starring Jim Carrey so I explain that the main character inherits God's power for a day. "Ah, very interesting," Edemir says, grinning. I am amused at both the humor and significance of this moniker. Spirit brought levity to those moments, which I needed. That week, Edemir and I continue to work on the situation with my brother. Gradually, I feel the nausea begin to leave me.

The following month, I have a chance to test whether the energy work had bolstered my solar plexus and given me courage to co-exist with this sibling. I see him at a holiday gathering. Things seem "altered" between us. He is less hostile towards me; I feel more neutral towards him. We are cordial and interact for several hours without pretense. On the drive home, I have a revelation: no nausea—the first time in years when I didn't feel kicked in the gut in his presence, a true miracle for me.

There is much more to this story, which is ongoing. While my brother has chosen to remain estranged, I've come to feel compassion for him in spite of the suffering he's caused our family, especially my dear mom, who is now 85. When I start to feel angry that he hasn't spoken to Mom in several years, I tune in and, in effect, can see that the forces guiding him are beyond his own comprehension—he has truly lost himself, like those drone-insects—and until he is willing to do his own internal work, until he finds the strength, he won't be entirely free of it. I cannot rescue a brother who needs to save himself. In the meantime, I have derived much learning from the situation—how to energetically protect myself, how to detach from the emotional pain and observe impartially (more on this soon) and, perhaps most importantly, to realize that I cannot make someone wake up any more than they could make me devolve from my spiritual growth.

* * *

By the time ER came to Pittsburgh that fall, I'd become

curious and interested in learning more about energy work—
not just as a client but as the healer experiences it. Edemir
sensed the potential in both Jennifer and me to be of service
and encouraged us to join him in the work. In most cases,
the client knew we were in the healing room for part of the
time; some weren't aware of it but had no objection when
they learned this later. In every case, the unspoken modus
operandi amongst the three of us was like the slogan for Las
Vegas: what happens in the healing room stays in the healing room. ER never formally talked to us about healer-client
confidentiality; I learned this by observing him and from my
own moral code. I wouldn't dream of breaching the trust of
someone who was choosing to work through the most vulnerable parts of themselves, whether physical, emotional, mental
or spiritual. Frankly, I was in awe of each person who had the
courage to face himself more fully. More often than not, the
client opened up to me after the session about whatever was on
their mind or in their heart and, as a result, I've forged many
gratifying friendships.

THE CONSCIOUS RESOLUTION:
REFRAMING EXPERIENCES

"To resolve any situation, we need just three things: the problem, ourselves and God," ER said to Jennifer and me one day.
The simplicity of his explanation seemed to bring so-called
insurmountable situations down to scale, along with a confidence that any shadow or darkness in life can fade in the light
of awareness. As we rise to the highest truth that Everything
Matters and Nothing Matters, we're able to lessen potentially
painful dilemmas by not taking them personally, and can even
eliminate past suffering by reframing it from a place of broader
understanding. Throughout these pages, I offer personal anec-

dotes that speak to the value of reframing. I have often participated in healing sessions when Spirit will instruct me to reframe an experience on behalf of another individual. Here is what happened on one such occasion.

Atlantis Revisited

When ER invited me to participate in the following session early on in my training, I was still a bit unsure of the veracity and value of the intuitive knowledge I was receiving. (Since then, I've learned to go with what I get and not question it.) I asked him every so often to confirm what I was getting during the session, which helped build my confidence. The client in this case was a teenage boy I'd met for the first time that day. I knew nothing about this quiet, mannerly young man or why he had come for a healing appointment. As the session began, Edemir instructed me to sit in a chair near the healing table, meditate and "wait for knowledge."

I close my eyes and—suddenly and fantastically—am on my way to another time and place. In my inner vision, I see an underground pipe with water flowing through it. Water spills out the right end of the pipe and splashes down into what looks like the ocean. I notice tall buildings beneath the ocean water, and these buildings begin to rise out of the water. The phrase "crystal city" enters my consciousness. As I follow the spires of the buildings downward, I realize these structures "live" at the bottom of the ocean. So I take a deep breath and tell myself to dive into the indigo water. I find an elaborate metropolis, an entire civilization, in this place under the ocean.

Because I'm fairly new at this, Edemir momentarily steps away from the client, comes to my side and asks what I see. "I think it's Atlantis, a past life?" I whisper hesitantly. He tells me to go deeper into the meditation to learn what happened to the boy during that lifetime. Very soon, I see the boy. He is down inside one of the buildings, perhaps a basement area. It is dark, he is alone.

"Nothing 'happened' to him, rather he was born with an affliction," I report quietly to ER as this knowledge comes. I go into the boy's essence and discover that he is disfigured on his left side and blind in his left eye. I can't help but notice that I can physically feel the blindness, as though my left eye is gouged out (I feel a pressure in that area). When I open my eyes for a few seconds, I literally cannot see out of my left eye. I am amazed by this sensation. At this moment, I am the boy, the boy is me.

Minutes pass. ER approaches again. Careful to not break the quietude in the room, I whisper to him what I intuit: the parents are ashamed of the boy. He has what looks like leprosy and they confine him to a dark room in their house. This worsens his condition and keeps him isolated from everything. He doesn't know that just beyond the walls of his home, great things are happening. In this city, much is being accomplished in the way of energy healing and crystal therapy. This work could easily cure him but he remains disconnected from it.

Eventually, I see the boy as a young man. He has survived to adulthood, miraculously, and he is out on the streets, leaning into a cane on his left side. He is mesmerized by what is going on around him, all the activity on the streets—people alive and healthy, bustling about.

I tell Edemir this. "Send him a healer," he instructs.

I settle back into this vision. Next, I see the young man leaning against a slightly inclined "healing slab" in the middle of a healing arc that I can only describe as a circular, domed-and-pillared temple of quartz crystal. It is out in the open, like a piazza in Italy or Greece. A healer comes towards him, dressed in white. A swirl of white energy encircles the young man, creating an aseptic space around him, like in an operating room. The healer directs kaleidoscopic beams of light to rain down into the space. It contains all the colors of a prism; this slowly begins to balance the young man. I feel his (my) left side becoming stronger. Eventually, it feels equal to my (his) right side. All sores and scars heal and fade away. I feel what the young man feels: I can see out of both eyes for the first time in my life! I am balanced, whole and elated. The work is done.

Right on cue, ER tells me to "close the work" and he does the same. (Before and after each session, we silently recite a prayer, each in our own words, to give thanks for the presence of God and all energies from the highest realms working with us. Also at the end of each session, Edemir speaks a closing prayer that concludes the work and helps the client to come fully back into their physical body.) After the session, I learn some facts about this boy. His health condition is something he was born with and is rare; this is partly why he sought energy healing—his medical doctors had done all they could. This congenital illness had affected the left side of his body, including his eyesight. It all made perfect sense based on what I saw but I still questioned the value of being able to tune into this boy's past life. As I've learned since then, there's a lot of healing value in this, since there seem to be so many layers to the healing process—many of which are subconscious or on a cellular, subatomic level. Individuals aren't always able to access these more subtle levels on their own, either because they are unaware or unable to do so. I felt peaceful knowing that the level I worked on that day may have, in some way, aided in this young man's multi-layered healing. Edemir continued to work with him, and the boy's health improved significantly to the point where he was able to hold down a full course load in college. As far as I know, he is feeling stronger and leading an active life.

Now, let's time-warp to the Middle Ages for another example of a client situation that was reframed—with tangible results in this lifetime. Edward looks healthy enough when I meet him before his session. I don't learn until afterwards that he came to Edemir seeking relief from chronic conditions related to his lungs and chest—asthma, acid reflux and a susceptibility to every cold and flu virus that came in on the wind. As I connect with his energy and follow my mind's eye, Edward is lying on a stone slab altar, outside, with a crowd looking on. Lit candles are everywhere, symbolic of a fire ritual of some kind. The time period is during the Crusades, the Holy Wars.

I'm given the knowledge that Edward is being sacrificed. I'm a bit intimidated by this and "pause the DVD" for a minute. I center myself, tune in further and realize that, yes, Edward is one of many people being sacrificed in the name of many that they have killed—a revenge of sorts. Only, Edward is WILLINGLY sacrificing himself for God, much like today's jihads impel Muslims to become suicide bombers for Allah. Fire blazes around the stone altar, illuminating skulls on the ground in its red-orange glow. With a sword, his executioner cuts the shape of a large cross across his chest, mocking Edward's faith. Then he delivers a massive stab wound to the heart. Edward is left to die. (If I hadn't been able to stay in an energetic space of observation during this session, I probably would have flung peaches.) I begin to call in God's light to clear Edward from this past-life situation and return him to wholeness now—not that I'm demanding an outcome, but asking for whatever relief is possible and karmically correct for him.

I wasn't able to share any of this with Edward, since the session took place on his lunch hour and he needed to get back to his office—but I'm not sure I would have anyway, or that it was even necessary. After continued sessions of energy work, Edward's overall immunity grew stronger; in particular, his chest and lung region. I never did tell him of the horrific vision because it seemed to have done its work simply by allowing me to witness it.

THE MANY FACES OF GOD-GODDESS-CREATOR

Alongside consciousness expansion, working with those who are further along the path has also given me a refined system for connecting with higher realms—an ability to call on ascended masters, holy entities and inspired muses to help solve situations for myself and others. What that leads to is not feeling alone; instead, knowing we're always being guided and supported. Again, this isn't just a salve to make myself feel better. This works tremendously well and with irrefutable results. In many cases, answers arrive that are so much more effectual than anything I could think through on my own. Creatively speaking, once we "unfasten the heavens" in this manner, to quote Pablo Neruda, we begin to realize that our imagination, no matter how vivid, is but a road on the freeway to our own homecoming.

I'm continually amazed at the complexity of the unseen worlds I tap into. It's truly a feeling of "the more I learn, the more I don't know." There are so many manifestations of the Source—from mythological archetypes and religious icons to past civilizations and futuristic worlds. Even other types of beings from the stars. I've found that it always comes through in ways that are precisely relevant for the person in need of healing. We ALL need healing of some sort, and whatever energy or information presents itself is generally advantageous in bettering our lives in some way or offering answers to things that plague us.

To somewhat simplify matters here, I'm choosing to

categorize the complexity of this higher intelligence into three fundamental groups: Past Lives, Divine Guides, and Archetypes and Symbols. All three can tap you into an infinite surplus of creative inspiration. Speaking just for myself, I couldn't make all this stuff up, and I'm willing to give credit where it's due!

Past Lives (Revisited)

Most of us can reflect on our childhoods and pinpoint incidents, relationships or learned behaviors that could benefit from some form of healing or forgiveness. As our consciousness expands, we realize that the patterns and memories we acquire don't necessarily begin on the day our mothers gave birth to us—but rather, are accumulated over many incarnations. When we consider the possibility that we entered this lifetime with certain propensities or soul memories of glory and suffering, we're not only that much closer to healing things in our lives that otherwise have no rational explanation or obvious origin point, but also to reclaiming capabilities and confidences that we may have had "before." As previously mentioned, reconnecting with our former selves can unblock, reframe or serve to remind us of some past life thread and, in doing so, bring greater wholeness to our experiences in this lifetime. I realized this to greater degrees in my subsequent years of apprenticeship in the healing room when Edemir was in the States—an occasional few weeks each spring, summer and fall in DC and Pittsburgh. (I had also begun to work gratis with individuals who sought me out through word of mouth).

Jeffrey. Jeffrey first came to see Edemir because he was distraught over a situation with a partner in his company. A lot was at stake—money, status, livelihoods of the employees' families, the company's reputation—and this partner had basically lied flat-out to Jeffrey about several key issues that could make or break the company. "What irritates me the most,"

Jeffrey said, "is that he didn't keep his word!" Jeffrey was so blinded by bitterness towards this man that it was costing him not just his company but his career and marriage. When I meet Jeffery for the first time before his session, I don't know anything about him except what his energetic presence is screaming at me: he'd done something in his past that caused a lot of people great suffering, and that's the psychological vein I need to scope out in his session. Wow, he seemed like a gentleman, I couldn't imagine what had happened. The answer came as soon as he lay down on the healing table.

As I tune in, I'm whisked back to what feels like one of Jeffrey's recent former lives. He is on horseback, leading his army into battle. They reach the crest of a hill, only to be met by the opposing army's head-on attack. Jeffrey's horse rears up and takes off down the hill to *join* the enemy. The word "turncoat" appears in my mind's eye. That's it! He purposely led his men into battle knowing he would betray them. Many men died for his personal gain. Now, in this lifetime, he is experiencing the flip-side of this action: what it feels like to be betrayed.

After this session, without my getting into the details of this intuitive vision, Jeffrey and I speak about the value of atonement for past actions. I simply explain that I believe he might have brought the theme of betrayal into this lifetime. Several years later, I encountered Jeffrey again. While it had taken him this long to work through the financial and emotional carnage this partner left in his wake, he said in retrospect that something in our energy work had made it easier for him to see the bigger picture—to see how he himself might actually have *created* the betrayal scenario in his life. Now, from a less personal space, he had eventually been able to forgive his former partner for what he'd done, at least enough so that Jeffrey could move beyond ill feelings about the situation and get on with rebuilding his life.

Carrie. My immediate intuitive image of Carrie is as a clever, creative girl during the Italian Renaissance. Wearing a burgundy velvet dress, she is happily sitting by an easel, painting. Her creative expression is in full flower in that lifetime and I get a clear sense that she has carried this inspiration into her current life. When I mentioned this, Carrie replied that she felt it was confirmation of her deepest dreams for herself. Her true essence (in this lifetime), she said, is that of a Renaissance woman, expressing herself freely in the creative arts (and she has, in fact, participated in Renaissance Faires). "I want so badly to live that kind of life, the life of an artist!" she confided, adding that she felt stifled working in the IT industry. To keep from "losing her identity," she painted self-portraits on weekends.

About a year later, I received an invitation to an art gallery showing that featured her paintings—not only self-portraits, but paintings that showed her to be a gifted artist. "Thanks for coming!" Carrie said in greeting. "Yes, m'lady!" I responded with a curtsy, and we both smiled brightly. Carrie then revealed that she had resigned her IT position and had gone full-time artist. She certainly seemed much happier, more herself. And I was so happy for her.

A child in darkness. I once had the privilege of participating in a healing session with a 15-month-old baby boy who'd been having seizures since birth. His parents had sought every possible medical explanation for his condition but the seizures continued. As I ask for Spirit to shed light on the situation, what comes to me is this little soul's former incarnation in which he was held captive in a dark, eerily silent place (a closet? very unsettling!). The intense fear that he experienced in that lifetime (in particular, a fear of the dark) is still trapped in his emotional body/cellular memory and is manifesting as "impulses of energy" wanting to escape—thus, seizures. I ask for guidance and am instructed to work on severing the boy's etheric ties to that lifetime and to remind his higher self that he no longer needs to hold this memory. In talking briefly with the parents after the session, I was interested to learn that the baby's seizures were most severe at nighttime—when it's dark and quiet. I haven't had contact with the family since that day; we reside thousands of miles apart. As I write this, I hope that little guy is healthy and well. Whether what I saw and did helped him, I may never know. I do know that I felt honored to be able to offer my earnest intent in support of his healing.

Divine Guides and Archetypes

Whether or not we can sense their presence, we have personal aspects of the Creator around us all the time. As we progress through various stages and situations in our lives, different ethereal guides step in to help us. These guides can be loved ones who have passed over (including pets/animals), souls we've known in prior lives, archangels and angels, ancients, ascended masters, disciples, teachers or healers who choose to help us (and whose help we accept). Call on any of these mystical colleagues for assistance just as you would pray to God for ultimate guidance. They can provide many of the missing pieces in this complex jigsaw puzzle called life.

These manifestations of Spirit seem to come to us in ways that we feel most comfortable and familiar with (and that is partly contingent upon how open minded we are). As a Christian, I'm most awed by the energetic presence of Jesus, Mother Mary, the Holy Spirit, Mary Magdalene and the archangels (particularly Michael and Metatron) and various saints—yet I've drawn great inspiration at times from Buddha, Lord Krishna, Kuan Yin, Kali, Babaji and Yogananda, as well as masters and avatars from other cosmic realms. I've also learned a lot from my deceased grandmothers, aunts and other ancestors. In most instances, I didn't originally call in these forms of Spirit (I didn't even know some of them existed! I had to ask, "Who are you?"). They seemed to arrive when most needed, even though their ability to fill a particular need was unbeknownst to me at the time. Now, after aligning with certain higher energies, I'm able to draw them close just by asking for their presence—and now I know what to call on them for (we'll get to that in a minute).

Guides give us concrete proof of their presence . . . if we're Paying Attention. One day I was driving with several friends. One was feeling despondent that her life commitments were preventing her from fully developing her spirituality and "soaring with the angels." Another friend was consoling her, telling her that the angels are always with her and that SHE is an angel—to us and many people. At that moment, a car passed on our right. I couldn't help but notice its vanity plate. "Hey, look at that!" I chimed in. The license plate was: BNANGEL. We had a good laugh at that one.

While I tend to think of spirit guides as inspiration that I draw upon from beyond myself, archetypes seem to arise from within, more like reconnecting with some long-lost part of myself. They are truly an expression of in-sight. When I met with mythologist, futurist and prolific author Jean Houston, PhD, we had a lively chat about archetypes (she is brilliant on this subject) and the fact that as we evolve, we gain understanding that everything we need is already inside of us.

"We have such complexity going on beneath the surface of our consciousness," Jean said. "Of the psychological genres we have within us, the ego is but one image of multiple images of the psyche. We have many, many personas. And we can expand who we are so we have more of a crew to draw upon when we need it." To illustrate, Jean gave this example: "I have 22 published books and about 70,000 unpublished pages mouldering on my shelves," she explained. "But the thing is, I can't write. I can't write at all. When I begin to write a book, I call on my muse, which happens to be a chef. I'm a VERY good cook."

Archetypes encourage our individuality to emerge. I resonate with certain mythological figures such as the Greek muses, goddesses Athena and Aphrodite, as well as Isis, Osiris, Thoth and others from ancient Egypt and Mesopotamia. Wearing the Isis necklace that SFF Nancy gave me as a birthday gift, however, doesn't mean that I idolize Isis; rather, she is a representation of my own self writ large. So, in a sense, I am an "Isis-type character," as Jean would say. This archetype allows me to live my larger story through symbol and metaphor. Once I'm able to both visually see and experience symbolically this aspect of myself, then I can begin to actualize it. (I will talk in a later chapter about how my connection to Isis empowered me to live more fully.)

I've seen how such tales can be great templates upon which individuals can weave a more centered, stronger version of themselves and open to a greater creative force. In one healing session, I intuitively saw the young woman on the table walking out among the masses with a lion, and I got the feeling that this woman would be very effective and in her element if she went out into her community to begin what felt like a grassroots effort of some sort. When I explained this to her, she shared with me that she indeed had a vision of something she wanted to create in her community, but she didn't have the confidence to begin. I noticed that she recoiled at the word "grassroots." To her, it meant being lowest on the pecking order with no funding and no support. When I mentioned the king-of-the-jungle power beside her, she was able to view this possible role from another perspective—one of influence and abundance. When she got up from the healing table, I was struck by her long, golden hair, like a lion's mane! "You carry the power of the lion within you," I said in no uncertain terms, as I felt this about her so strongly. I hope that she took that energy into her project and is implementing her vision for her community. (I should have asked if she is a Leo.)

The energy of archetypes is real and powerful, even if the person doesn't consciously connect a feeling with a specific image. I worked one day with a musician who asked for my help because he was feeling uninspired and disconnected from his music. As we spoke in his living room, one of the nine Muses appeared (Calliope, I believe). She laid her body over him and pressed her heart against his, as if emboldening his heart. Just then, his posture straightened and he took a slow, calming breath. I could see his aura change, the colors brighten. He sat up, and after a moment in silence said, "I know what I need to do. I need to begin today writing my own style of music, not the kind my band members have been forcing me to write." I knew that the presence of this muse was nudging him to come into his own and that his music going forward would be from his own higher inspiration, and not someone else's.

I've noticed that manifestations of higher guidance often have a theme or area of specialty. For example, Scribe has appeared many times to inspire me with my writing; he has a straightforward, clear energy and helps me buckle down to work. While traveling in Mexico in 2007, I connected immediately with the essence of Frida Kahlo—not so difficult to do, as her image is everywhere you turn. The pain and passion in Frida's art has always inspired me, but at the time of my passage through her native country, she encouraged me to NOT suffer for my art, as she did—emotionally and physically.

The Hindu deity Ganesh appears when I need to surmount a critical obstacle. Archangel Michael swoops in with his sword when I need extra protection in some form. He is strong and formidable and, at times, I've felt like his energy secures me in a makeshift suit of armor. The Blessed Mother comes immediately when I'm dealing with anything related to mothering or parenting. Her energy nearly always brings me to tears. Have you felt her? What a breathtaking combo: a complete embrace of motherly love in all its purity and humility with an underlying, uncompromising firmness based on that highest form of love. Mother Mary has encouraged me to stand strong in matters regarding my children, especially where their safety is concerned. She understands to the highest degree that suffering serves to test and ultimately strengthen our capacity to love, and that our capacity to love is the truest measure of the value of our time here on earth.

The guide that I fondly call Sage came to me at a time when I was taking on greater challenges in my life and I needed a steady, strong energy to give me courage and confidence. When I first saw Sage with my inner sight, he looked like a Native elder but as his image became clearer, I could see that he looked more like an elder statesman, dressed in an all-white suit, white hair and beard. His presence was rock solid, almost like he was a column of white granite, enduring and mighty. "You will need this energy now as you go further out into the world," he communicated to me. "Others will notice this in you without being able to put their finger on what it is. Men will see you as competent, and will be drawn to work with you—women, too."

This is precisely what happened. I entered into a phase in which I connected with many people, forged new work relationships and even developed a few close male friendships to balance out the wonderful female companionship around me. Then, exactly two years after Sage came into my life, he left. His departure was indisputable. As I stood in the same place where I had met him, on a beach in the Gulf of Florida, he told me, lovingly but definitively, that I no longer needed him. A sadness washed over me like a wave at high tide. I was losing an ally, someone who loved me non-judgmentally and stood by me no matter what. "You can call on me whenever you need me and I'll come," he said, "but it's no longer necessary for me to stay by your side. You have reached higher energies, and that is where you will go from here." Sage was right. New guides moved in for the next phase of my life and while I still remember Sage with gratitude, I never felt the need to call upon him again.

Guides and archetypes can take on countless forms. You can find them described in spiritual literature throughout the ages, and in the memoirs of some of the great artists, writers and musicians. Perhaps these divine manifestations are infinite because the guidance is meant to come through in ways specific to each individual. And perhaps we need them to come to us in these subjective, personal forms so that we can better grasp their meaning and utilize the energies for some positive outcome.

Symbols

This is one way I would describe intuition and how it works for us: God sends us signs of His love and our minds ascribe form to it, thereby making it real in our lives. In order for higher insight to be processed by our minds, it must take some shape that we can comprehend (even if it's just a thought form). Scientists might dismiss these forms—whether thoughts, feelings, inner visions or even spirit guides, as just described—as merely outpicturings of our mental process, but call it what you will, the divine impetus behind them is pure and true.

Many times when we ask for higher guidance (especially if we're new to the process), we don't receive complete stories or specific deities who step in and instruct us on what to do. More often, we glean bits of knowledge in the form of symbols. When working on behalf of others, it's usually not necessary to know the whole story, anyway. In my experience, the symbols that arise typically complete whatever healing message needs to be conveyed—like the appearance of a Ferris Wheel that turned out to symbolize a client's problem with "spinning his wheels," or a black aboriginal mask that guided me to help another client's desire to "lighten up." In those cases, it hadn't been necessary to see more than that in order to be led to the heart of the issue. Healing intuition goes where it's most needed, in whatever way is best for the person requiring help.

While I would never claim to have medical expertise, it's fascinating when symbols come through that point the way to a diagnosis of sorts. I believe that medical intuitives such as Carolyn Myss and Christiane Northrup provide a valuable service of working in tandem with physicians to help uncover causes of health issues that are difficult or impossible to identify. In many cases, individuals work with energy healers to accomplish just that.

Such was the case with Eve, who had various symptoms, including fatigue, indigestion, muscle weakness and decreased immunity to colds and flu. After a series of tests, her doctor had diagnosed her with fibromyalgia and said it's "just something you'll have to live with." When I tune in during her session, curiously, I see an old-fashioned glass milk bottle hovering over her body. "Does this represent dairy products?" I silently ask. Confirmation comes in the form of another symbol: GOT MILK? I see in my mind's eye. *Is she lactose intolerant?* No. *Is it something IN the milk?* Yes. Now, I see cows grazing on grass with pesticides and I know she has ingested traces of toxins.

I'm told that she should eat organic but first must purge these toxins from her body. After the session, I lightly suggest that she consult with a dietician. A month later, Eve emails to say that she took my suggestion and is working through her health problem. "The dietician recommended that I go off all dairy products. I'm already feeling much better."

Years ago, I took part in two amazing healings (as different as night and day) with a petite, perky woman from the mid-West who was recovering from cancer. The work was filled with many symbols which, when pieced together, helped me to understand how to best serve her at that point in her healing journey. The first session was in the evening, which made the healing room seem more solemn than usual. As I closed my eyes, I immediately traveled inside her body, where I saw complex patterns of green and black. I knew the green signified where healing had taken place, and black indicated vulnerable areas where the chemo had ravaged her down to the cellular level. The best way to describe what I envisioned is to say that her cells looked confused and chaotic, like strangers had just invaded their space, leaving them bewildered. I also sensed that the blackness indicated she wasn't out of the woods yet —there was a potential for her to relapse.

What happened next was strange, at least for me. My mind traveled to the cosmos, where I saw beings pulling strands of larvae out of the woman's body. Sounds grotesque, I know, but I perceived that these beings meant well. They were there to help her, yet what they were doing wasn't strong enough to heal her. As I witnessed this, I didn't understand how this energy came to be associated with the woman. It didn't seem "right" for her. For this reason, I put her in God's light and focused on that for the duration of the session. I sensed that if she didn't receive a big healing soon to strengthen her immune system, her dazed cells would possibly mutate into cancer again.

After the session, I told Edemir what I saw. He explained to me that on the astral level, cancer looks like larvae. As we compared mental notes, we realized that the (human) healer she'd been working with back home had brought the alien energy in with him, which is why it felt wrong for her. This healer had every intention to help her but wasn't working at a high enough vibration to sufficiently boost her energy field. ER confirmed that my decision to disconnect her from this energy and put her in God's light was good.

Edemir did another healing with her the next morning, then called Jennifer and me into her afternoon session. The weather outside was sunny, the healing room was bright and upbeat instrumental music was on the CD player. As I tuned in, I saw the client under a pristine healing dome of light. Large, regular-shaped pink cells slowly flowed in unison around the rim of this dome. Just then, a row of light beings appeared and surrounded the healing table, creating a radiant, glowing circle around the woman. As the session went on, ER, Jen and I became so filled with the joyful energy that we found ourselves swaying to the music. Without words, we glanced at each other and knew she was out of the woods. Now, years later, she is healthy and grateful for what she calls her "second chance to get life right." Did *we* heal her? No. Did we join our energies with hers in healing intention? That's what we were there for.

* * *

Spirit has a tremendous sense of humor. So it stands to reason that we're given humorous symbols and archetypes to help us "get the point." In 2006, I needed to decide about attending a large book expo for the publishing trade. As usual, a series of coincidences pointed towards the right decision, which was, in this case, to go: for one thing, it was being held on the East Coast, within driving distance from where I reside. A friend offered her home for me to stay in, conveniently located near the conference hall. Editors and publishers whom I'd been working with but hadn't had a chance to yet meet in person would all be at the event, making it easy to connect with everyone at one time and place. Even a magazine editor I'd once worked with was going to be in town that weekend; it would be nice to visit with him.

The day that I went online to register was one of those days that I'm sure we all have from time to time. I felt temporarily overwhelmed by all the work assignments that I had intended and therefore created for myself—complete with looming due dates. And in less than six weeks, my children would be out of school for the summer. *This is too difficult, I'm only one person and I don't have enough hours in the day!* I thought. (Sound familiar?) How could I take a week off for this conference and, besides, who would even care if I was there or not? I'm nobody!

I observed myself being this way, knowing in my higher mind that attending that event would bring me up to speed on publishing trends, probably lead to valuable professional connections, and much more. On some level, though, I was feeling fatigued and defeated. Wanting to clear this feeling, I took it into my meditation the next morning.

"Should I stay or should I go?" I asked. Just then, an image formed in my inner vision. It looked like a female in a long, white dress—an angel? a queen? a spirit guide of some sort? I couldn't tell. Then I realized who it was. "What is Cinderella doing inside my third eye?" I laughed. "Okay, guys, you're going to have to help me out with this one, why are you showing me Cinderella?"

I got my intuitive answer: "Think about it, she went from scrubbing out the hearth, covered in soot and rags, to being the belle of the ball. She was a 'nobody,' too. And her own family forbade her to go! But she mustered the courage and followed her instincts. Not only did she have a transformational evening, everyone wanted to know 'Who is that girl? Is she a princess?' She made quite a splash.

"Go to the ball, Gina! Scrub up and walk in with the attitude that you have much to offer. Just wear something more comfortable than glass slippers when walking around that convention hall."

"Oh, that's a fairy tale," I said right back. "Why should I believe in something that's not even real?"

"Did you hear what you just thought?" this higher voice asked.

"Okay, I get it. But it's still a fairy tale."

Just then, I was shown another image: the Wicked Witch of the East, slumping over her cauldron, green skin, warty nose and all. "What is this, classic movie week?" I said, knowing all the while that this whimsical image, too, had meaning.

From on high: "Think about how quick you are to believe that some force, some evil presence, has the power to thwart your progress, to cause difficulty on your journey and even prevent you from reaching your personal Oz."

"I guess that's true," I admitted. I had been acting that week like some outside force was tripping me up. If this was possible then I should give at least equal weight to a magical force that had the power to elevate me from kitchen drudge to belle-of-the-ball status. As it turned out, this meditation insight filled me with a sense of purpose and lightness, and I had a great experience at the conference—no witches in sight.

*   *   *

A couple of caveats before leaving this section: First, as

your intuition expands, you'll find (or may have found already) that there's a fine line between sharing with others what you intuit and keeping it to yourself. It's not always appropriate to tell a person what you're tuning into. Most people don't like to be revealed! How do you know when it's right to do so? Use your instincts, of course. Keep the ego's need to prove anything out of it, and go with your heart and gut. I felt that Carrie would be inspired by her Renaissance past life. With the teenager (who seemed shy and reserved), I kept silent, feeling confident that spoken words were superfluous to the healing work. Same with the parents of the baby boy; peace came over me after the session, confirmation that I helped on some level. What further good would it have done to relate the images I saw of their son's tragic past life? It probably would have upset them . . . it upset me! In some cases, I get that adding a verbal element is part of the healing, and so I share what I intuit about the person; but please be advised that not everyone has a happy, open-minded reaction to hearing what they may not expect or want to hear—especially about themselves. I can relate . . . I've been there! In other cases, people want to know all they can, so they'll ask for the information. Again, be aware of when to talk and where to stop. Sometimes, it's about the hole, not the doughnut—meaning, there are times when the best thing to do is nothing at all, except hold a space for the person to do their own processing.

FINDING THE MENTOR YOU ARE MEANT FOR

It's a million-dollar question: How does one find the right teacher? Of course, it isn't something you search for on Yellowpages.com. But you have the tools at hand. You can apply the philosophies outlined thus far:

Have the Intention to manifest an appropriate mentor when the time is ripe.

Continue to convene with the Divine through Daily Practice.

Pay Attention so that you will recognize this individual (or group) when they show up.

And when challenges cause you to feel alone in the process, find the clarity you need by Turning Within with a faithful posture.

The early phases of our spiritual progress are more educational in nature. This is a fertile time to acquire knowledge through reading books, attending public talks, joining groups that focus on consciousness studies, or even revisiting our religious roots to behold with fresh eyes the beauty inherent in its doctrines and ceremony. If we search for a mentor too early in the expedition, we run the risk of encountering individuals who may not be integrity-based or have our best interests at heart. (We are, in a sense, more susceptible to this, so it is good to be aware.) Let's say you hear about a particular teacher and want to know more. You cannot necessarily gauge the rightness of that individual for you based on others' experiences because the relationship he has with each student may be different. What's more, the same teacher can play varied roles within each of his student's spiritual quests. The bond between seeker and spiritual teacher can be, at times, emotionally delicate and psychologically complex—we may view our mentor as a best friend, parent, enemy, lover, demi-god and antichrist, all within an hour's time.

As we become more spiritually sophisticated, we're better able to intuit who is authentic and working for the highest good. When we team up with a suitable mentor during a period of time in which we are also maturing, our relationship with that person progressively deepens. In the final analysis, the only real barometer is our own intuitive reaction to the person—do we resonate with their philosophies? How do we feel in their presence? How do they treat those closest to them? None of us is perfect but now more than ever, I believe, those who do Spirit's work need to be impeccable in their motivations and serious about the responsibility inherent in the work.

Here's another caveat that I'd like to share: As you ascend intuitively and your vibration becomes more refined, be careful who you have work on you. I've seen people say yes without hesitation when an energy healer, practitioner or bodyworker offers them reiki, deeksha or other forms of subtle body work or transference of spiritual energy. Check with your internal guidance first! It's not the modality that's at issue here or even the intention of the person, which is probably based in love—it's about how your energy field resonates at that time with whatever new energy you are introducing it to. This is definitely something to consider. Unbalanced healers may still be at a level of greater wholeness than many clients who come to them but, as mass consciousness evolves and we become purer in mind-body-spirit, we should seek only the healthiest of healers.

Over the years, I've established an inner circle of practitioners and doctors whom I know and trust; even with those individuals, I tune in to discern how clear they are on the day I go for a chiropractic adjustment or other treatment. In some cases, I've respectfully declined healing work—especially in settings where the physical space has not been adequately prepared for sacred work. In a few other cases, I've gone against my instincts and allowed healers into my energy field, with damaging results to my psychic health. I don't mean to make you paranoid, just cautious. Have faith in others but trust your gut above all else.

Which brings me to this point: Our mentors, and the impact they have on us, are relative to where we are on the path. I'm thinking now of the person whom I consider to be not quite a mentor, but my first metaphysical teacher. She was extremely gifted as a healer and seemed to have the whole package: physical beauty, intelligence, warm heart, a loving family. I admired her natural gifts although, in retrospect, I can see that I relied a great deal on what she told me. In fact, I remember how fascinated I was that I could walk into a room and have her "read" my life so fluently. How amazed I was by that is a reflection of where I was, consciousness-wise, at the time. I suppose that I needed someone like her then to give me direct feedback, as she did. I hadn't yet considered that I could sharpen my own abilities to that refined a level. If I'd met Edemir in those days, we may not have clicked, as he is someone who has expected nothing less than for me to develop my own abilities with an eye towards self-reliance. In essence, by doing his job well, he has also made himself progressively obsolete in my life, as Cohen said. I'm thinking now of a simple yet profound comment made by the indigenous Peruvian/Mexican/Ramuri healer Maria Teresa Valenzuela, a very humble yet powerful medicine woman I had a chance to meet in 2007. She said, "The day of the teacher is over. We are all teachers. We are all students. We teach each other and learn from each other."

That says it all. Once we attune to our inner voice, we depend less and less on others to tell us about ourselves or give us answers. It becomes more about getting confirmation of what we intuitively know by aligning with those who are parallel on the path with us. Over time (and after years of Turning Within), we become primed from the inside out for a far more advanced level of learning. Ultimately we realize, yes, we are our own best healers.

As it seems, I was ready to work (at least for a while) with a mentor who could train me, the intuitive high-wire student, on two apparatuses. The first was my personal development, honing my capacity to leap from the flying trapeze into higher levels of consciousness, while knowing an All-Powerful Net was there to catch me, no matter what. The second was unexpected: being placed in an apprentice-type role of participating in client healing sessions, as well as enjoying the bounty of this teacher's wisdom outside the healing room. Working so closely with a mentor has been revelatory, a spiritual Cirque de Soleil of fascinating adventures that has propelled me into increasingly expanded realizations of what's possible.

That first year, in particular, flipped me upside down and inside out in ways that no single chapter of a book could even begin to describe, except to offer up a few examples in hopes that they would at least point in the general direction of my trajectory. What a trip! At times, I've felt like Lucy in the Sky with Diamonds—in other moments, a contortionist, a fire walker, a sword swallower, even a sideshow freak (projections of my inner archetypes, perhaps?). But when I received comments from these clients expressing how profoundly the healing work has impacted their lives, it's really gratifying. That's what spiritual work is all about, helping each other understand and interpret the contents of our lives so we can move more joyfully and completely towards our personal potential—physically, spiritually, emotionally and creatively. With that destination in mind, why would we ever want to scale back down the ladder to the three-ring circus that was once our daily existence?

six

WITNESSING

Jai guru deva, nothing's gonna change my world.

—JOHN LENNON

I first experienced Witnessing in a big way during a trip to Boston in 2000, which I now describe as the flight I could have taken without an airplane. At the time, I couldn't put my finger on what was happening to me, I only knew it was unprecedented and astonishing. Witnessing is the tipping point into Everything Matters, Nothing Matters—the phenomenon through which we transcend ordinary consciousness and can maintain a strong, broad connection to God-consciousness. We're able to split the mind and live in an aware-state and mind-state simultaneously. We are in our bodies living our human experiences and, at the same time, able to step outside of ego and observe still frames of life with objectivity.

We begin to see, truly, that everything *does* matter—and truly, everything does *not* matter! While witnessing enables us to be outside of our minds, it also helps us be of more sound mind because we're able to circumvent the human emotions that so often take hold of us and lead us down a path that may not be the best for us.

Of course, everything happens for a reason. Yet with witnessing, we get to the core of an issue much quicker because we're able to see it with more clarity, neutrality and egolessness. We understand not just what's best for us but for everyone involved in a situation—and everyone who is NOT involved; in other words, the highest outcome for all concerned, long term.

Leading up to that trip to Boston, circumstances conspired to lift me to a higher level of consciousness but, as usually happens with such transitions, I first had to hit bottom. That year, I had self-published a book and had been working nearly non-stop for six months on promotion—giving talks and book signings, meeting with booksellers, and doing everything I could think of to get media coverage and boost sales. In the midst of all this (as if my attempt to go from total literary obscurity to partial literary obscurity wasn't challenging enough) my co-author basically decided to bail on the project, for personal reasons over which I had no control. In retrospect, I see the perfection in why our work partnership played out the way it did. At the time, of course, I was devastated that she wasn't following through on our co-author contract. I felt abandoned and bitter.

For me, everything came to a head two days before I was to leave for a holistic expo in Boston. Nothing seemed to be going right. Proverbial doors were slamming left and right but I pressed on, readying for the weekend conference. At the last minute, SFF Nancy, who owned a bookstore, offered to come along to help me set up at the conference and sell books. I was humbled by her generous expression of friendship and it lifted my mood. Still, I could feel frustration, resentment and pressure building behind my eyes like a levee about to crack open.

I awoke the next morning feeling emotional but got right to work. Sifting through a stack of mail, I noticed a rejection letter from a book contest I'd entered—a miniscule detail that morphed into the final straw. Not able to reach my husband at work, I made an impromptu call to a colleague who works as a life coach.

"Something's really wrong," I told Tom, feeling foolish. "It's only 10 o'clock in the morning and I think I'm going to burst into tears."

"Tell me everything," he said, and the levee broke. For two hours, I wept and raged in such dramatic fashion (Tom was my rock, so loving and nonjudgmental) that I ended my diatribe feeling like a lake after a summer storm, refreshed from above and cleansed of former impurities. The sadness—even though it continued to pass through me that day—took on a poignant, sensual quality, and by the next morning, I awoke feeling light and strangely sublime. And ready to board the plane to Boston.

For the next three days of my "trip," I was living in a state of grace, beyond reproach and above the world, able to simply watch with humor and wonder everything that transpired around me. All was perfect and complete. No anxiety, regret or rage. And while things happened to *me*, Nothing Mattered. I listened objectively when the person at Logan Airport baggage claim informed me that my box of books hadn't made the flight for some reason. I simply observed the downpour of rain on our way to the convention hall. At dinner that evening I chuckled with childlike innocence when several drunken sailors fell across and actually broke our table. I didn't get upset the next day when housekeeping cleaned out my room 15 minutes before my talk and couldn't find which closet they stored my belongings in—including my handouts, easel and speaker's notes. Nothing fazed me, not even when the elastic decided to leave my dress slacks the following morning while I was on my way to the exhibit hall (bizarre, as it was a fairly new, fine quality suit). Nancy safety-pinned me in and I floated blithely to my vendor booth.

The paradox, of course, is that Everything Mattered that weekend: the architectural intricacies of Faneuil Hall, our Irish cabbie's brogue, the fluff of the pillows as I finally lay down to sleep each night—every detail swirled into one big, miraculous pastiche of sensations. It was my freshman experience in grasping lessons I'd been attempting to learn for some time about centeredness, patience, not being knocked off-kilter by external circumstances. After my weekend in Beantown, I understood with greater emphasis that it's not what happens to us—it's our response to what happens to us (and, more importantly, who we *are* going through those experiences) that sets the tone for our daily existence.

MAKE ME A WITNESS: THE PHENOMENON OF EXTERNAL OBSERVATION

When we become practiced at contemplation, we organically begin to move into a space where we can impartially survey, as if from a distance, what is happening around us and to us. In Zen Buddhism, this state is called *kensho* or *satori*—a non-dual, non-personal experience where there is no difference between, nor separation of, "experiencer" and "experience." In Hinduism, the Sanskrit term for this shift from ordinary, sense-dominated perception into an awakened state of clarity is *anubhava*—the direct experiencing of who we really are. In ancient Greek and to the earliest Christians, the term was *gnosis*—realizing direct knowledge. Such realizations come not through the intellect or senses, not even through emotions or intuition. It is a mysterious opening that is not fully describable in words. Deepak Chopra says it succinctly: It's the observer being the observed.

Eckhart Tolle explains the concept in *The Power of Now*: "When we become conscious of Being, what is really happening is that Being becomes conscious of itself. When Being becomes conscious of itself—that's presence. Since Being, consciousness, and life are synonymous, we could say that presence means consciousness becoming conscious of itself, or life attaining self-consciousness. But don't get attached to the words, and don't make an effort to understand this. There is nothing that you need to understand before you can become present."

After the experience in Boston, I kept trying to find a way to "get back there." I would return only in snippets. Over time, as I continued with my intuitive studies and expanding my creative channel, these flying-without-an-airplane moments came with greater frequency and in a more grounded way. After a while, it became "dual nature"—meaning, I could watch the aircraft flying overhead AND be in that plane, looking down at the total landscape of a situation. I was HERE and yet could be THERE, watching HERE. At first, this seemed to happen outside of my will. Now, I can effortlessly delineate and be both, just by quieting my own mind and tuning into the cosmic mind. (What's next? Astral travel? Teleporting? Sure, why not?) From this impersonal space in which there really is no "me," the confluent interaction and spontaneous perfection of All That Is reveals itself of its own accord. All I have to do is kick back and watch the parade.

Recently, a kind and pleasant woman I know, Alice, called to confide in me that she was ashamed of the way she had reacted to a stranger that morning. When this stranger very rudely accused Alice of doing something she didn't do—right in the middle of a grocery store—Alice angrily grabbed the back of the woman's shirt and pulled her. Alice was shocked at her own behavior. But she's a tuned-in person, so, almost on the spot, she asked herself: *Why did that incense me? What is in myself that drew that out and caused me react that way?* With a tinge of remorse Alice said to me, "I was not in a place of observing myself in that situation because, if I had been, I would have had a very different reaction to that woman. Maybe I would have chosen to have NO reaction to her accusations."

Because Everything Matters, Alice was able to surmise why this incident erupted in the first place: she was subconsciously working through larger issues related to tolerance, and along came a perfect object lesson, right in her face. Or so it seemed. By the end of our phone conversation, we concluded that, hey, we're only human. As an aware person, Alice knows that events are inherently neutral, and that at the same time we create events and draw lessons to ourselves. Even knowing this, we can slip out of higher awareness into "human" mode. In the substrate of our humanity lurks the inevitability that we won't always choose the wisest, most loving course—which is why the phenomenon of Witnessing is so magnificent. It reduces and even obliterates that margin of human error. From the apex of witnessing, nothing causes anything . . . it just is.

The Trinity of Witnessing

Paramahansa Yogananda writes in his *Autobiography of a Yogi*, ". . . the divine eye is center everywhere, circumference nowhere." This phrase, I think, offers the utmost description of witnessing. The ability to witness has unlimited practical applications in our lives. I can't begin to recall how many times this has aided me, especially in relationships and matters involving the safety and security of myself and others. I'd like to add my personal spin on several ways in which this ability to observe from all perspectives has shown up in my life.

Remember my experience at Zeus' Temple in Chapter 4? Even though I was going through a profound psychic shift, I was completely aware of where I was and what I was doing. Part of myself watched me walk up the monument steps. In fact, in those moments, I had become the steps, the monument, the tourists, the sunlight, the whispering breeze—and they, me. Add to that: I was also conscious that I was in a sort-of trance state—or, entranced state. Another part of me perceived that I was touching another realm (in this case, a past life remembrance)—which I simultaneously witnessed, as well. So, the hallmark of this daydream-like foray into witnessing is that we are the "observer and observed" on more than one level. Said another way, we are HERE and THERE, watching ourselves being HERE and THERE.

Something different happens when I work in healing sessions or focus on a situation in everyday life that concerns someone else. In those instances, I'm observing someone else's story, not my own. I connect, step outside the mind and allow the universal intelligence to funnel in. In most cases, it's like watching a movie or documentary being played about that individual. I simply have to wait for the film to roll. I'm not a character in the movie. I have no vested interest in which way the plot unfolds. I'm a silent viewer sitting in the audience waiting to see what the characters will do.

Again, this doesn't only happen during energy work; it can occur at any time based on circumstances that arise from day to day. For instance, I recently witnessed three car accidents in a month's time—up close. In each case, I was driving on the interstate directly behind the car that wiped out. Also in each case, I was given a few seconds of advance notice (intuitively) and was able to slow down not only my car but time itself . . . as if in slow motion. If I hadn't been in observation mode, I may have panicked and caused a chain reaction on the road. As it was, I simply pulled over, called 911 and assisted the accident victims. And because Everything Matters, you better believe that I wanted to know the meaning behind my witnessing this triad of accidents. (Let's just say I was getting a little careless with cell phone calls while commuting!)

To be sure, the most useful variety of witnessing is observing ourselves. During a period when I was ruminating on the distinction between the soul and the ego, a circumstance arose that provided not only an amusing confirmation of what I was studying, but forced me to make a choice—preferably from an observer-being-observed perspective. I got a call one day from the managing editor of a highly regarded lifestyle magazine in my city. He informed me that one of their upcoming issues was going to debut an annual feature profiling the "25 Most Beautiful People" in the region—not just outward beauty but people who were doing heart-based things in the community. "Your name came up in our editorial meeting," he informed me. "You've been nominated and we'd like to send our photographer out to your home for a photo shoot." What a surprise! What an honor! The shoot was so much fun. I felt glamorous and pampered and special. That's the "ego" part.

Here's the "soul" part. For years, I had wanted to join the masthead of this same magazine as a contributing writer. When the managing editor, Stephen, called to interview me for a write-up to accompany the photo spread, we got to talking. By the end of the conversation, we'd mapped out a strategy for bringing me on board. What a surprise! What an honor! Thinking about that first assignment was so much fun. I felt purposeful and dedicated and lucky. Here's the rub: Being part of the editorial staff was now a conflict of interest for the "25 People" piece. "It would be like we're tooting our own horn," Stephen later said. "What do you want to do? If you come on board, we'll have to nix the photo." From a witnessing perspective, it was a classic ego versus soul battle. In the long run, if I had to choose between ego (glamorous photo spread) and soul (furthering my dharma by writing for one of the city's premier publications), I would choose soul. So I did.

Witnessing Versus Apathy

Witnessing allows us to be in a state of nonattachment, which means that we take a neutral stance towards what is happening around us and can see the divine play, or Lila, in all things. The flow of life is neither sought nor resisted, as the Tao teaches. When we can stand squarely in our truth, we often don't feel a need to react, refute or prove anything. It's very freeing, and extremely useful to us as creative beings. Yet spiritual progression entails much more than learning to speak our truth or depict it through our art—that is only the beginning. The greater challenge, I believe, is being nonattached to others' reactions (or non-reaction) to our truth. Not an easy task, but the more we live in the moment, the less room there is to anticipate or expect anything.

This is not to say that we remain *detached* (which is different from nonattachment). With detachment, the tendency is to avoid, refuse or devalue what is happening. The goal certainly isn't to become uncaring, indifferent or joyless—quite the contrary.

Stress is so prevalent today, but what is stress but trying to control what we cannot control? Stress originates in the mind. If we have an expectation about another's actions or opinions, we are attached. And when things don't go our way, we become frustrated, angry or hurt . . . and stressed. Learning to release expectations may be a harder pill to swallow than something we take by prescription, but long term, it's the only real healing solution.

I'm making the distinction here between nonattachment and detachment because, as I've inched my way into the light of awareness, I've noticed that sometimes my neutral witnessing demeanor has been mistaken for lack of interest or concern. And that's not it at all. With nonattachment, you care, but you can stop short of falling into the patterns, projections and drama that others may bring to the interaction—consciously or subconsciously. When you are nonattached, your well being isn't dependent upon other people or situations, so others' choices are just that—their choices, which don't add or subtract anything from you. This is a gift that results from devotion to Spirit. We can intend or even desire a certain outcome and, at the same time, be completely willing to do without it.

Someone (I don't recall who) said, perceptively, that we human beings are the only species privileged enough to refuse our own blossoming. I don't believe that flowers fear their own blooming or doubt their beauty; they simply open to their glad, lush, reckless, trembling selves, in "their eagerness to be wild and perfect for a moment, before they are nothing, forever," as Mary Oliver wrote in her poem, "Peonies." In other words, flowers do that being-in-the-moment thing exceptionally well. It doesn't mean they're aloof or unsympathetic. They're just being flowers in bloom. They are remarkably present, the opposite of apathy. And look what they are able to give!

I've also noticed something within myself that I never imagined would change. I've always had a self-propelled, determined, ambitious and somewhat perfectionistic nature—at least towards myself. As we gain the healthy, whole perspective that Nothing Matters, the push to achieve, to prove—and sometimes even do anything at all—begins to fade away. Not to say that we renounce all goals and become couch potatoes. In fact, connecting with our soul's desire affords us a greater sense of purpose. It's just that that inner drive becomes less useful to us once we realize that action happens of its own accord as a result of our intentions. "Needing" anything (outside of creature comforts) is less crucial; same with having something to "gain." Whatever is truly necessary is provided, and then some. Anxiousness melts away and enjoyment (emphasis on the joy) replaces it. Everything seems as it should be. Without doing anything, we can be powerful. We can feel the stirrings of yet-to-be-actualized potential and sense the shape of coming events.

On the other hand, there is danger in spiritual posturing, pretending to be less attached than one is. Sometimes, when I can't get to that place of nonattachment, I consciously decide to be broken and messy and weepy and anal. It sure beats pretending that something hasn't affected me deeply when it has. Even then, I allow myself to go completely into the messiness, the weepiness, the brokenness. Being fully present in it enables me to move through it more quickly.

A GOOD DEATH:
WITNESSING UP CLOSE AND PERSONAL

When we become practiced at witnessing, something remarkable happens. We become eagle-like, able to see the big picture with acute clarity—AND, at the same time, can derive answers for situations as we observe them. I will now return to my father's story as an example of how I was granted the mercy of witnessing during his final days on earth.

Holiday festivities were over, relatives had returned home, and I could at last get back to my regular routine of morning meditations. It was the first Monday of the new year. I was alone and quiet. I began thinking of my dad and was inspired to draw three cards representing his immediate past, present and future. The cards were Comparison, Letting Go, and Rebirth. I interpret the first card to mean that, for some time, he's been comparing earth vs. heaven, deciding between staying and leaving. The rebirth card is obvious—at some point in the future he is going to meet with death, which signals rebirth. The Letting Go card was no surprise, either. Dad was certainly in the long process of letting go, whether it took months or even years. I didn't realize until I got a call from the nursing home on Friday how literal that card was about the "present."

Dad has taken a turn for the worse, I'm told. It sounds grave, so I phone my out-of-town siblings. One flies in that evening; the other drives up early the next morning. I'm numb and don't know what to do next. I tune in and ask. I hear, "There is nothing you need to do at the moment." I have about 20 minutes before my children arrive home from school. So I decide to light a stick of incense and sit quietly in my meditation space to calm myself. The incense smoke splits in two and forms what looks like the pulse line on an EKG machine. I'm consumed with a feeling of inevitability—this is it, he is slowing down and will pass very soon. I close my eyes and quickly go deep. St. Joseph is there, only this time, his arms are outstretched, his gaze downward, as if waiting to receive my father's spirit.

My husband arrives home to stay with the kids, and I leave for the nursing home. Before rushing out the door, I fumble through my Bible for a picture of St. Joseph. I find a yellowed prayer card of an Italian saint named Guiseppe. (Giuseppe means Joseph in Italian, but it's another saint, not Dad's Joseph.) The writing is in Italian and I'm in a hurry, so I slide the card in my wallet and leave. I'm disappointed that I couldn't find the one item that I feel might have significance, but I trust that it will appear. Later, in Dad's room, I show the card to Mom. "Do you know who this is?" I say. She doesn't recognize the saint and asks me why I'm asking. "I was looking for a picture of St. Joseph," I tell her.

We stay with Dad until about 9 p.m. When I get home,

I ask "What's going to happen with Dad during the night?" I pull the Traveling card. I get the overwhelming sense that he has made the decision to transition and has begun to leave the body.

I pull two more cards before going to bed, one for Saturday and one for Sunday. I get Intensity and Patience. I take Intensity to mean that it would be an emotionally draining day for us, then we'd have a period of waiting on Sunday. For sure, Saturday becomes the most intense day, and as it progresses, it is evident that Dad won't last much longer. During the few moments that Dad opens his eyes, I can see that he is no longer there.

The hospice nurse, Isabel, talks to my brothers Joe and Jerome about the spiritual side of death, and they listen attentively. While they may not put an emphasis on metaphysics in their lives as I do, they instinctually get this stuff and I am happy that a professional caregiver is conversing with them about such matters. Jerome surprises me by listening to my St. Joseph story and being open to it. It feels good to share this with or without validation. My confidence that I'm fulfilling a specific part of the end process for Dad is so strong that I'm guided to stay on task and even risk looking foolish in my family's eyes. This turns out to be a non-issue. In these hours, everyone is a believer.

Around 3 p.m., we all go out for a bite to eat. Mom wants to stay with Dad, so we say goodbye and head to a nearby restaurant. Afterwards, Don takes our son, Carlin, to hockey practice and the rest of us return to Dad's room. I sit next to Mom and she says, "Gina, I have a little surprise for you." She hands me a small prayer book and explains that it was in the bottom of her purse for who knows how long. Smack in the middle is a prayer to St. Joseph and a picture of him holding Baby Jesus. I simply say, "I knew it would appear, thank you for finding it." I quietly place it upright on the dresser at the foot of Dad's bed. Though it is just printed paper, I know this picture of St. Joseph will help hold the energetic bond between Dad and this saint, who had become his guardian angel and was waiting to usher him in.

Isabel explains to us that many times a dying patient will "wait" for loved ones before passing. She asks if there's anyone my dad was close with who wasn't there. No, I tell her. Still, I feel there's a missing element. Around this time, Joe asks if Dad's priest is coming to visit. He seems urgent about this, and I immediately connect that this is the missing piece. Dad will not go without last rites. I kick into gear and get on the phone. I leave a voice message for my parents' priest, then call two other churches in proximity to the nursing home. Both say they're busy with Saturday evening masses and confessions. Meanwhile, I'm wondering where Don and Carlin are; they should have been back here by now. Then Don calls to say that Carlin accidentally stepped into a big puddle and is covered in mud. He wants to go home and change his clothes and shoes. I have a knot in my stomach. "Just get here as soon as you can," I say. "Dad is waiting for you."

Still, I have a profound sense of calm, as if Dad is calling the shots, and I'm able to interpret what he needs and wants in his death process. I'm certain that he wants to say goodbye to my husband and son, and to have last rites.

Everyone in my immediate family plays a role in helping Dad make the transition. Throughout the day, we each speak to Dad individually, in our own time. My message to Dad is that he is in control, and we are there to "carry out his orders." I tell him we are patient and can wait for however long it takes. I show him the photo of St. Joseph, and remind him that he's been working with Dad for months now, so Dad is familiar with him.

Isabel tells me to open the window to "let the spirits out." I smile privately at the thought that mere glass would impede them. I know it couldn't.

5:30 p.m. Dad's vitals are dropping but we still have no word from the hospice nurses how long this will go on. Around 5:45, I am inwardly called to stand at the foot of Dad's bed, beside the window and in between Dad and the picture of St. Joseph.

5:45 p.m. Our priest, Father Don (who also married my Don and me), phones to say he's rescheduling his evening to come see Dad.

6:30 p.m. Father Don arrives and administers last rites.

6:45 p.m. As Father is leaving, my Don and Carlin finally return. One at a time, they talk to Dad and say their goodbyes, which my daughter and I have already done.

7:00 p.m. Through deep sobs, Mom tells Dad that it's okay to go. She consoles him, saying she will always love him. Then suddenly, she stands up and says," It's time to leave." We are hesitant, but we can see that Mom clearly wants to go home. She is emotionally spent. Joe offers to drive her. She plans on returning in the morning, but I know Dad will be gone by then. I realize afterward that Dad did not want his beloved to be there when he passed. It would have been too much for her.

7:15 p.m. The hospice nurse checks Dad's vitals, says it won't be long now. They give him a final morphine dose. He is in no pain, he looks calm and peaceful.

7:30 p.m. Dad takes his last breath. It was a very good death, completely on his own terms.

On the way home, I ask for a sign that Dad is okay. I hear, "Turn on the radio." *Oh, that's too cliché*, I think. "No, turn on the radio." I hit the scan button. It goes to a station I've never heard before: 91.7 FM out of Morgantown—a station from "almost heaven," West Virginia. Through mostly static, I hear a song. I turn it up. The signal becomes clearer. It's a choir singing a rousing hymn: "All you need is the love of Jesus." In my mind's eye, I see Dad ascending like Jesus on Easter morning. The beauty of the song fills me with gladness. I know Dad is in bliss.

I was struck by how divinely interrelated everything had been: my Dad's passing, the feast of the Epiphany (January 6, the day he took a turn for the worse) and the story of Jesus' birth—particularly regarding the earthly father of Jesus, St. Joseph. Just as St. Joseph had told me the prior August, I believe he had been working with Dad on his life review and acceptance of death. As promised, he delivered my father to the Almighty Father.

Dad's passing would have been a totally different experience for me—and I'm certain, not as positive an experience as it was—had I not been in a place of witnessing, able to get outside of my own emotion of sorrow and loss. As it was, I felt purposeful in being able to assist in his death process. Under the circumstances, there is nothing higher that I could have been graced with. By staying connected and deriving intuitive answers in the moment about what I felt Dad needed, I'm confident that he left his earthly life with maximum peace and closure, fully equipped and ready to go onto his next life in pure spirit.

WITNESSING UNIVERSAL FLOW:
MAKING SENSE OF WORLD EVENTS

I have already mentioned that when we expand our consciousness to a high degree, we open to everything in the cosmos and beyond. The same applies to the phenomenon of Witnessing. Sometimes, during meditation or contemplation, energies will show up that I recognize as the impending actualization of world events. I believe this happens simply because of the interconnectedness of all things. Universal witnessing doesn't operate in time and place, so it's not really any more unusual to tune into something happening on the other side of the globe as opposed to your own neighborhood—especially when the situation involves a large-scale energy fluctuation of some sort. I offer the following anecdote as an example of this, as well as to make the point that being a conscious person in this 21st century is about action and inclusion, not passivity and separateness. Being more aware is only one side of the coin; being of compassionate service (for whomever and wherever it's needed most) is the other. This is what could be called our spiritual "response-ability."

The week before Christmas 2004, a presence came forth in my morning prayers that I couldn't identify. It felt ancient, Old Testament. So I asked, "Who is here?" and was given the name Ezekiel. The energy felt somewhat ominous, as if he wanted to foretell something that was about to happen. I remember the name Ezekiel from the Bible, but I'm no Bible scholar so I went online and did some research. I (re)learned that Ezekiel represents "faithfulness in the midst of trials." He is the prophet who foretold the complete destruction of the kingdom of Judah and annihilation of the city and temple. Ezekiel had revelations through amazing visions of what was to come.

I pondered what all this meant. Was some trial going to happen to me or someone I know? Was I zeroing in on something about to occur elsewhere? It wasn't a sense of doom and gloom, just an uneasy feeling. I went further into this sensation. No, it wasn't about anyone I know personally. Oh yes, it was about a vast number of people somewhere on the planet. With holiday travel in full swing, international terrorism crossed my mind. No, it wasn't that. Then what? Even though I couldn't get a clear read on this future event, I didn't dismiss it; it had hit my radar screen for some reason and thus I felt somehow connected to it. Because of this and because it was the season of Jesus' birth, I took this seriously and spent extra focused time in my meditation that evening and the next morning sending out compassionate intent around the world for the highest and best outcome to this situation.

The day after Christmas, I was pouring myself a morning cup of coffee when Don greeted me with: "There's been a terrible tsunami in Asia. It's all over the news." Out of my mouth flew this: "Yes, I heard about that. Isn't it so tragic?" To which he replied, "When did you hear? It just happened." I had no answer to give him, because I couldn't explain why I had this "reverse déjà vu." What I *could* finally explain, however, was Ezekiel's message of faithfulness in the midst of trials and the accompanying uneasy feeling I'd had. Being ultra-connected isn't always comfortable, but I'd rather feel and know what's going on around me and in the world at large than be disconnected and comfortably numb.

The fall of that same year, SFF Jennifer arranged for her, me and our other SFF and business partner Lee Ann to fly to New York City. Our company, Epiphany Works, had been offered an opportunity to possibly help produce an interactive theatre show that would debut in Manhattan. This could put our company on a national stage. While we were excited to be considered for this, we were concerned that it would require a lot more time, focus and attention than we could give to the project. Nevertheless, while Jennifer tended to another business matter uptown, Lee Ann and I cabbed over to the Yamaha Center for a meeting to learn more about what the project would involve.

It was November 2, Election Day, Bush versus Kerry. As

we started our downwind into Kennedy Airport, I had a vision of Bette Midler singing "From a Distance" in Yankee Stadium after 9/11, a poignant performance by a masterful songstress about world unity. On our final descent, I closed my eyes and asked about the significance of flying to NYC on Election Day for this particular meeting. Here's what came: "Democracy is one of the greatest demonstrations in mankind's history of the power of choice. With opportunity comes responsibility. Choose thoughtfully. Why NYC? It's an epicenter. Great things happen at the epicenter; also, not so great things happen (9/11). Being at the epicenter can make you feel vulnerable, a target—for good or bad." In this instance, two international events (9/11 and the election of an American president) were juxtaposed against our comparatively small business decision. From a witnessing vantage point, I understood that we are the sum total of our choices (individually, societally and as a species), and putting ourselves at the center of things can bring with it a sense of apprehension. Witnessing can help us decipher if that apprehension is our gut telling us, "No, don't do it," or if it's our fear holding us back from our own greatness. (By the way, before we landed, just for fun, I asked, "Who will win the election today?" Answer: "Bush. For better or worse!")

Shortly after Pope John Paul II died in early 2005, our Intuitive Dialogue group gathered for our monthly meeting. As we stood holding hands and opened the space, I spontaneously started to recite the Our Father—something we've never done in our group. As I prayed, I pushed back tears at the passing of this great man who was not only a munificent leader of the Catholic Church but a spiritual role model for all humanity. Immediately, the room filled with the energy of the many, many souls around the world who were at the same time mourning the Pope. My energy field brimmed from the outpouring of emotion that I felt around us in the room, as if we had crossed a threshold into grief. Later in the evening as we did a guided meditation, SFF Nancy instructed us to envision a circle of light in the ground, so I did this. Out of it came a statue of the Blessed Mother followed by a vertical "reel" of all the Christian apostles, saints and martyrs from the beginning of time to the present day. This went on for about 15 minutes! At the end of the reel was a rosary with a crucifix, showing one of the greatest examples of all: Jesus. I was given the message: "Look at how many people have been devoted to God!" It awed me and, at the same time, put into witnessing perspective that Pope John Paul II is one of a multitude of holy men and women who have gifted us with extraordinary examples of how to live with faith, devotion and unconditional love. By the close of the meditation, I felt only peace and gratitude.

* * *

I sit on my garden swing, thinking about the gifts of illumination that our great teachers have been trying to impart to us since the beginning. My mind drifts to a story from ancient India, an allegory about how we can be divine beings and still keep ourselves planted on earthly ground.

It's the story in the *Bhagavad Gita* about Prince Arjuna. Arjuna is in his war chariot on a hill, looking out on two great armies arrayed for battle—two powerful clans in a struggle for control of the kingdom. Arjuna belongs to one clan (the good guys), but also has beloved relatives in the other, even though there are many dark souls among them too; and so he is torn, not wanting to do battle at all.

Beside him in the chariot is his divine mentor and guide, Lord Krishna. "The business of existence is action," the great god advises him, saying that non-action is not an option for someone who aspires to full realization. Krishna tells him that he must do his moral duty in the world. The supreme goal, he says, is to experience one's material form and at the same time consciously be in union with the Divine. He then grants Arjuna a stunning vision of that cosmic paradox—the reality beyond imagining—and Arjuna finally "gets it." He is now able to accept his duty, take the necessary action and unify his kingdom.

The story is one of the most revered in Hindu culture. Symbolically, Arjuna is facing the warring forces within himself, many of them beloved, many of them treacherous, and he takes the action necessary to unify his own kingdom. But success wouldn't have been his if he had not been given the vision of himself as simultaneously a cosmic and a physical being. Now, *that's* the power of Witnessing.

seven

INTEGRATION

Spiritual enlightenment is not about getting high.
It's not about leaving and how often you leave.
It's about coming back.

— KRISHNA DAS

I had the pleasure of meeting musician Krishna Das at one of his concerts—a delightful soul who lives his earthly mission with humor and grace. What he said that evening about leaving and coming back was the exact right message for me at the exact right time, as I had been experiencing many peak states that year. Like a moth to a flame, I was becoming seduced by the intensity of the light—to the possible exclusion of other things.

And so we reach the final step in our process: Integration.

As it turns out, being out of your mind is a glorious place to be. There is great peace, harmony and sweetness in this outer space (beyond the mind). It's magical to live in a world where all things, no matter how trivial, have meaning, and the universe seems to be scheming on my behalf, only for me. Its intelligent design mesmerizes and incites me. I float on Cloud

10, sublimely contented. Come down? Don't think so.

Yet as KD said, the true splendor of consciousness expansion is not in getting hooked on these peaks but in bringing the brilliance of higher realms into everyday life. This is the second coming of Christ that revered yogi Paramahansa Yogananda spoke about in his teachings. He wasn't referring to a literal return of Jesus to earth but rather our reward for purifying and expanding our inner being through meditation, to prepare the way for an inflow of Christ consciousness. "The real second coming of Christ," he said, "will take place right in the devotee's own consciousness." In other words, heaven-on-earth is us, baby.

Yes, it's tricky to integrate this without being overcome by it at times. I'm reminded of a scene in *American Beauty* (Best Picture of 2000). The introspective voyeur teen-ager, Ricky Fitts, is transfixed by an image he caught on video: an ordinary plastic bag dancing on the wind in a parking lot. "It was one of those days when it's a minute away from snowing and there's this electricity in the air," Ricky emotes to his girlfriend, Jane. "You can almost hear it, right? This bag was, like, dancing with me. That's the day I knew there was this entire life behind things. Sometimes, I see so much beauty in the world, I can barely stand it."

Bliss states bring with them a poignant sense of joy, of being in love with everyone, everything (plastic bags included) and with life. We Intend, Practice, Pay Attention and Witness divine perfection all around. Everything oozes beauty and sanctity, even the seemingly mundane, ugly or obscene. Childlike delight seeps from our pores and we randomly gush at flowers, kitties, trash cans, the sidewalk, this sign, that symbol, these words being spoken by those people. It all converges and spreads like a delectable soup into and through every crack and seam of our existence. How else can I describe the ecstasy of it? Feel with your heart these words from the 16th century Indian poet-saint Mirabai:

One sip from the cup of that sweetness,
The world starts to spin.
Now I'm a drunk for life. Unsoberable.
Tell them it's useless to try.

To speak frankly, I've had moments when the rapture gave me pause, caused me to consider renouncing everything in my life in utter surrender, become a devotee of sorts, or get on with ascension to the nth-degree—leaving entirely. In those moments, I've wondered, "How can I return to the people and things that constitute my 'normal' life?" I've questioned, is this real? Or am I like an actor immersed so voraciously in a role so she can BE that character and play her well? (It's the existential quandary I refer to in the Introduction—which reality is really real?) When I'm on fire with a yearning for meta-phenomenal experiences, a desire to go deep, I want to live in that intensity, that deepness. I want to run towards God with my whole life. It's a quest that can never be sated because there is always more to investigate, more to master.

Even in such moments, however, I've always known it wasn't my course to take. I realized that, like most of us, I have to be amphibious—able to breathe in the vast ocean of emotional waves of divine love but also stay grounded and "live on land." And so, after fervid periods (a week or less) of spiritual work, I go back to my regularly scheduled programming: family, housekeeping, writing. Early on, the energy work was so transformational that returning to ordinary life was like the Microsoft Word prompt that you get when attempting to overwrite a file: "Normal already exists, do you want to create a new normal?"

My re-entries have gradually become more seamless but it hasn't always been pleasant returning to the denser energies of the 3-D world. Part of that return is the inevitability that we'll be faced with the next round of lessons necessary to our growth—unless, of course, we decide to stop the bullet train and get off for a while. I actually said to a friend after a recent crazy ride of challenges that hit one after the other, "I could use a little mediocrity right now, a little status quo." Then I reminded myself of a few truths: I intended this ride, I invented this train, I've set the destination and, come what may, I'm the conductor on this trip. So after a few days of idling, it was back to *here we grow again*.

Dr. Hawkins has an interesting term for why facing the initial set of challenges of our next higher level is no picnic. He calls it "being above your karma" and explained it to me this way: "When you're above your karma—meaning, when you've successfully resolved or reframed the events that have happened in your prior life up to that moment—you're feeling beatific until the next thing comes up; then you feel like you've crashed. Well, you haven't really crashed, it's just that you're not above your karma anymore. You've brought up the next layer to be worked on. It actually means you're making progress, that's why it's coming up.

"When you're working on deep issues and feeling the pain of them, you're far from blissful," he continued. "You have definitely moved ahead, although psychologically and emotionally you're not feeling high. You're still better than before when you were in denial. So you come out of denial, you go through the pain of facing what you're facing and work out the guilt about it, the self-recrimination, and forgive yourself, then life gets beautiful again until the next thing comes up. This is characteristic of the entire spiritual pathway."

So, given the choice (which we all have) between coasting and accelerated personal growth, I will probably always ask God to bring it on—because even when the going gets really tough, the only way out is through.

Once a Facet, Now the Diamond

We are in human bodies on Planet Earth and, as such, our imperative is to assimilate into our material-world existence the spiritual wisdom we acquire within a lifetime. As Hawkins says, every time we crash through an old paradigm and break the mold of our former, smaller selves, we eventually adjust to the next higher plane of vibration and reshape ourselves into that new way of being—until the next level of attainable proficiency, our next mountain, becomes apparent on the horizon. This is what being spiritual means—not seeing the Divine as just one facet of life, but realizing that it is the entire diamond, the vibrant foundation that gives all aspects of our existence greater sparkle. SFF Dan calls this *spiritual marbling*, the sacred richness that ripples through everything, giving life its juice and complex flavor.

A successful businesswoman once expressed to me: "I fear that I have to give up my family and walk away from my career in order to embrace spirituality." Not! Spirituality isn't something to be compartmentalized, something we pull out of a box when we meditate or retrieve from a shelf whenever we have a crisis. We don't give up a certain lifestyle in order to gain a spiritual lifestyle; it's a matter of keeping our ordinary life and making it extraordinary by spiritualizing everything in it.

If we're working long-term on expanding our consciousness and our creative potential, then integration becomes a necessity—at least if we're going to be of any real use to the world. I mentioned in an earlier chapter about a shaman gifting me with a rare Night Whitehawk feather—a symbol of those who work in other realms. I didn't know before that evening event that we were going to construct a medicine wheel, and that everyone was to bring an offering to place on it. Luckily, in my sweater pocket, I rediscovered a piece of tree bark that a friend had brought back for me from a national forest in Oregon. So I made this my offering to the medicine wheel. After receiving the feather, the "reason" for the bark made sense. The Night Whitehawk—a true light in the dark—soars to other realms, transmitting spirit messages beyond the stratosphere; but in between flights, it safely returns to the tree and perches on the bark. The tree is deep rooted, secure, intransient. And so the medicine wheel's personal message for me was this: both soaring and landing are essential. I've seen what happens to those who fly but don't come to ground—especially individuals who work in the healing arts. They crash and burn eventually because they're not able to integrate ego-soul, human-spiritual, light-dark, vertical-horizontal.

INTERNAL INTEGRATION: FINDING YOUR POWER CENTER

The process of Integration is ongoing. I can attest that it does get easier over time, but the need to align, balance and assimilate never totally goes away, because we are not static snapshots—and we make our choices within a multi-dimensional matrix. We're more like holographic images, continuously in motion and ever-changing from all angles. Eventually, as we leave and come back, leave and come back, leave, come back, leave, come back, a sense of our own power constructs itself in the center of our being and sets up permanent residence. We feel more solid, more self-assured, less and less destructible.

By the summer of 2004, some aspects of my life were coming to completion and others were just being initiated. Those balmy months were consumed with my children's activities, my father's illness, writing work and the startup of my new business venture, Epiphany Works. (This inspired event planning company is my answer to bringing alive what I write about, since consciousness is something that must ultimately be *experienced*. So, we plan one-of-a-kind public events that stir the creativity, spirit and will of participants to live their best lives.) The summer before, I'd set the intention to further expand my work to include collaborating more with others of like mind. With Epiphany Works, I didn't want to go it alone. Not surprisingly, a series of synchronicities lined up like geese flying in formation, pointing the way across the great sky to the answer I was seeking. Before long, I had gathered a team of accomplished women with a powerful mix of business talent and spiritual determination. Among us, we had all the skills we'd need to run a small company. In short order, we took off with our first original event idea, to be held that fall. In the midst of it all, Jennifer and I (along with Lee Ann and Nancy, by this time) found time to work for a week that September with Edemir—hosting him in Pittsburgh and continuing our apprenticeship in the healing room, then culminating with a weekend of personal sessions in DC.

As we get more in touch with our vertical lives, we learn that our only real restriction is a lack of fully imagining what our reality could be. Said another way, it became increasingly clear to me around that time how important it is for us to know what we want—because once we become practiced at the use of intention, we have every possibility of getting it. If our intentions (conscious or subconscious) are meager, convoluted, self-serving or unclear, that's what boomerangs back to us—not always in a comfortable way.

That fall, I was ready to take an aerial view of everything I was doing, everything I had to offer, and reposition it into a much larger framework. With David Whyte's poetic phrase as my mantra—*Anything that does not bring you alive is too small for you*—I entered into my personal energy healing sessions with a mission: replace self with Self. Dissolve resistances, release expectations, envision greatness, embrace immensity. Live as if the Divine has climbed into my breast pocket. Others will know this secret by the light in my eyes.

Isis Rising

"Gina, you are a powerful, brave woman," ER said after my first session that week. (He says encouraging things like this to almost everyone, not just me.) "Your dreams WILL come true." And I thought, hmmmm, what IS my ultimate dream? What IS it? I knew in that instant that I hadn't yet imagined it. I knew it was much bigger than what I'd been focusing on, that there were some dots I hadn't yet connected. And I thought, *What am I choosing to do with my personal power? Am I really brave or am I holding back? What good is bravery and power if we don't utilize it in some meaningful way?* Spirit understood that I needed something to encourage me to raise the bar higher once more.

In the next session, the dots begin to connect themselves. I let go and relax, not feeling a need to tune in. But I sense that some information is coming to ER, something important. Afterwards, he tells me that Isis came to me by way of the moon, symbolizing that I'm ready to take the next step towards unlocking greater mysteries. He relates that Isis was shining down a tremendous light upon me. Intellectually, I get what he's saying and think it's great that this Egyptian diety took time out of her busy mythological life to pay me a visit in real time. On a soul level, this makes perfect sense, given my karmic history with Egypt. But I don't feel the truth of it in my bones, so I remain detached from the message.

The next morning, I have another session. Edemir also

sees a woman warrior guide with a shield of armor, holding an arrow. He says she is not there to do battle but is needed now in my life to go further with my endeavors. "Now you have everything you need," Edemir imparts. Again, the information sits pleasantly well with me, but I don't FEEL it. I don't like that! *I'm* the one who should be getting these messages for me. I don't like feeling disconnected from what is being told to me, even if it's by a person I respect.

After the session, I meander down to Madelaine's on M Street for coffee then cross the street to Barnes & Noble to buy a *Washington Post*. As I enter the bookstore, I can't help but notice glances in my direction. I wonder if I have latte foam on my face. The sales clerk flashes a smile as I browse a table of books about politics, the Beltway and the upcoming November elections. "Finding everything okay?" he asks then strikes up a conversation about Rod Stewart's gilded living room on the latest cover of *Architectural Digest*.

He's dark-haired and cute, energetic and expressive, a beautiful Columbian accent. He tells me his name is Javier. His teeth are perfect. He's obviously well read. We speak for all of five minutes about a multitude of things—the architecture of Frank Lloyd Wright, the Tuscany region of Italy, his friend's villa in Montego Bay that barely escaped Hurricane Ivan that week, the fact that his secret passion is handcrafting jewelry— even his next career move to the Library of Congress or one of the university libraries. I'm eons removed from the dating scene so I'm actually oblivious to the fact that this sweet, young Latin man with the perfect smile is casually attempting a pick-up right in the middle of his workday—in fact, I assumed I was impervious to such things, due to the rings on my left hand, which is clutching that *Washington Post*.

"Well, I have to run!" I announce, glancing at the time on my cell phone. Javier jots his personal email on a business card and slides it inside my newspaper. I graciously accept it, pay for my paper, exit through the security pillars and toss the card in the nearest trash receptacle. I re-emerge into the brightness and blare of M Street and snicker to myself. There I was, no makeup, not showered, hair barely brushed, dressed in old jeans and sneakers, eyes puffy from lack of sleep. Hmmm . . . What just happened?

About an hour later, I begin the drive home from DC and, as usual, "shift happens." Tuning in while cruising I-270, I delight in the landscape, the glimmering mirrored buildings, the road signs, the sky, other cars whizzing by. Suddenly, a luminous ball of white light begins to coalesce in my solar plexus. It warms and calms me. Then slowly, the whiteness surges outward through my pores and radiates around me. I'm inundated with a flood of inner strength. I know at once that Isis is with me. I drive for a good 10 miles, savoring this power surge. Then I ask, "Are you my guide?" She promptly corrects me: "I am not a guide, I AM A GODDESS." I think, *Oh sure, now I'm supposed to act like a goddess?* She assumes my misinterpretation of the word—"not a diva, a goddess", she clarifies—then further infuses me with what I would describe as absolute feminine power, what I imagine it must feel like to be the ideal woman, a divine mother, a woman who is worshipped and revered yet completely serene and humble. In fact, that's partly WHY she is so loved. Isis conveys to me that I'm once again elevating to the next level of my spiritual-creative development and "this is what is required" of me, how I am to be, when I get there. "It's not how you look or what you say," she explains, "it's your inner power that's important."

So . . . Be It

As I meditate the following morning at home, Isis is still with me—and so is the luminosity she brought with her. She instructs me to create an image of myself based on this empowered inner feeling, then stick with it: "This is living authentically but with a higher twist—your highest ideal, the most perfect image of yourself. Not perfectionism, but an unwavering belief in your potential so internally powerful that nothing can thwart you, no disappointment is too great. You keep going because of your belief in the infinite possibility of the universe. There is no lack. Make choices based on the outward expression of that inner power. Create ways to express it. There are countless forms. You decide. See how I am . . . calm, confident, beautiful from the inside out. I travel through time to greet you with a feeling of empowerment that will resonate with you from now on. You must *feel* this, not think it. You are as powerful as your image of me, as you are part of me." The significance of what happened the day before in the bookstore struck me, and I remembered Isis' words to me on the drive home: "It's not your outward physical appearance . . . it's not what you say . . . it's your internal essence that's important." That week, Isis integrated me, period. The essence of Mother-God climbed into the center of my being and put a light in my eyes. Going forward, it prompted me to create a new benchmark for how I want to be and feel in my life and in my own body. Now, I just needed my outward actions to completely reflect that.

Remember: Keep Your Power Center Clear and Protected

On this autobahn towards inner growth, I've discovered that as we expand our intuitive capabilities and refine our vibration, we become more sensitive to *all* energy—not just the kind we come in direct contact with, but energies everywhere around the globe (as mentioned in Chapter 6). For this reason, we should remain vigilant. External forces (for lack of a better word) may or may not be compatible with our newly acquired level of consciousness. As I said earlier, I've learned that I have to carefully choose the individuals who do any type of health care, healing or bodywork on me—whether conventional or integrative medicine. Once, I had a massage by a woman who was not balanced and completely healthy. She was interested in spiritual matters; however, her level of awareness did not resonate with mine. As she worked on me, I inadvertently took on her anxieties and minor pains. Needless to say, what was supposed to be a relaxing day turned out the opposite—I was a mess! That night, I had to clear her energy from my field— lesson learned.

Another time, I was reminded of the importance of clearing away energetic influences that are incongruous with my field when an out-of-town friend came to visit. I was aware that she had an impending divorce and was carrying a lot of emotional scars. Before she arrived at my home, I told myself that I was simply going to hold a space for her to open up and share whatever she wanted to get off her chest, which she freely did. It was a loving but teary conversation and while I didn't agree with everything she said about her husband, who was also a friend of mine, I kept sending love and acceptance to her on a subconscious level. By the time she left that evening, she had energetically purged a lot of stuff, to the point that I said to Don later on, "I should smudge the chair she was sitting in!" (And Don agreed, as he could feel the depressed tone in the room, as well.) I didn't heed my own advice, and I didn't close the visit with a prayer to cleanse the energetic "trash" she left behind (it sounds mean to say this but that's what it was, really).

For the next few days, I felt off-kilter. While I went about my normal work and family activities, I felt unmotivated, drained, heavy, sad and, well, *alone*. I observed myself feeling this way, knowing that it wasn't originating from a core issue inside me, but rather, precipitated from an outside source (an important distinction to make when tracing back the cause of something that is creating an imbalance in your energy field). I could feel these emotions and recognize them as "not mine." Mid-week, I had an encounter with a centipede in my kitchen sink—it scared the bejeebers out of me for a few seconds until I thought, *Okay, why?* I watched that poor insect, a hundred legs running in place, desperate to climb the side of my sink to no avail—then paralyzed with fear. The entire week had a spinning-my-wheels kind of feel but, again, I couldn't claim it as my own.

By Friday, there was no denying that something was up with me. So, I finally took time to tune in and ask what's going on. No wonder I felt the way I just described—I was walking around with my friend's feelings! This was confirmed for me later that day when Edemir called to specifically ask what I had been doing last Monday evening, because he'd etherically connected with me that week and seen a block behind my solar plexus chakra, along my spine, as if someone had drained away my energy.

"Why did this happen to me?" I asked him.

"Because you're a healer, my friend," he said, explaining that my heart was open to her and by holding a loving space as I did, I had effectually given her a healing. "But you forgot to transmute and clear the energy."

"I knew that, I knew that, but I didn't do it," I admitted.

"And so next time, you will," he said in that firm yet loving tone of his.

Gender Neutral: Integration of Masculine and Feminine

Living as an intuitionist and experimenting with various aspects of our human nature—mental, emotional, psychic, spiritual, physical, metaphysical—has made me aware of the importance of having male-female symmetry within ourselves. In my young life, perhaps due in part to my father's sway, I felt more masculine than feminine, with a desire to assert, control, lead, be bold. As I struck out on my own and was able to have more control over my life, I leaned the other way: I became a wife, mother, homemaker, caretaker in many ways. Compassion, forgiveness, acceptance, stillness and softness were the attributes I most wanted to attain. Around that same time I began to delve into consciousness studies. No surprise, I discovered that my mentors in spirit were women—the Blessed Mother, Grandmothers Philomena and Carmella, Aunt Rose. As my children grew and I put more emphasis towards my vocation, male guides stepped up—Scribe, Sage, Native elders, Aristotle, Socrates, the Archangels, Ashtar and, best of all, Jesus. Once I had firm footing in my work, female energy returned—Athena, Isis, Kali, Mataji, Magdelene, St. Teresa of Avila. And so goes the divine dance of balancing the masculine and feminine aspects within us, a delicate choreography of integration.

Edemir and I were talking one day in DC on the subject of masculine-feminine and after much discussion, we came to a simple revelation: God is not God, God is a Goddess. The feminine, after all, is creation energy, the womb of All That Is. "Goddess was so lonely that she created God to be with her!" Edemir said with an impish laugh. "Goddess energy is pure love beyond consciousness. To be in touch with the feminine is to be in touch with creative energy, and to be in touch with a sweet way of being in the world—a state of being 'in love'."

Male energy has dominated civilization for the past 2,000 years or so, and now the pendulum is swinging in the other direction. No doubt, more women will continue to enter positions of power in business and commerce, politics and policymaking, environmental affairs and other formerly male bastions. It may not happen immediately but eventually, things will come to center. This isn't a gender issue. We don't necessarily need more women to run the world. It's more about balancing the masculine-feminine in everyone. As the primary feminine attributes of compassion, creativity, intuition, stillness, nurturance and love become more of a presence in society at large, a natural shift will occur, making it more normal for ALL individuals—male and female—to see situations from an integrated perspective. As this happens, we will find ourselves making more informed choices than we've made in the past.

For all you dudes out there who think I'm asking you to become more womanish, I offer words from Tim Ward, author of *Savage Breast: One Man's Search for the Goddess*. He laughs when others say this, because "It's just the opposite. It's my masculinity, the darkest part of it, that yearns for [the feminine], like a lost lover, like an orphaned child." He describes his personal search for the goddess as a "shadow that lured me deeper into the unknown than the gods of my fathers ever did. Jesus and Buddha, they urged me away from the world, taught me to resist the ways of the flesh and seek a Kingdom of God, heaven, a higher consciousness. It's different with her. It's visceral, immediate, and a matter of heart, balls and belly." There's no risk of turning into what Ward's sister calls a SNAG (Sensitive New Age Guy). The reward for embracing the feminine, Ward says, is finding your own center as a man.

SFF Dan has this to say: "The Great Feminine is something deeply embedded in me. I started thinking one day that all the male stuff that I do—the 'going after, hunter-gatherer, survive and thrive' energy—may not be right. I was discounting the importance of my intuition, my ability to feel. As I re-explored this feminine side of me, allowed it to live and not choke it off or ridicule it, what rose to the surface was a renewed masculine energy. I still want to provide for my family but now I have a context for it, an ability to connect with others' hearts and souls, a greater love for all things in my life. Now, both sides are a must for me."

Coming Soon: The Integral Couple

I arrive at this point in the book with some trepidation, because I know that to be fully open with you, I need to speak about the effects of my "inward going" on the primary male in my own life. If I'm offering insights into every dimension of life, and leave out what is arguably the most intimate, I'm not serving you (or my purpose) well.

Most of us are in, have been in, or hope to be in, a close, committed relationship. Relationships (not only marriage) succeed by a combination of respect for differences and an awareness that there are times when we feel it's best to step up and offer a new energy to the partnership as a whole. Times when we shouldn't stay quiet and let it be, but instead verbalize that we see a way in which it can be deeper, closer, better for both partners—in effect, more integrated. If we're fortunate in our partners, as I have been, we can work at this together. Even then it's never a cakewalk, but so worth the effort—as I think you will see in the pages that follow. My hubby, Don, has the masculine aspects of his being down pat. He takes pride in his ability to provide for our family—to be the hunter-gatherer—and to protect his clan. In fact, I've heard Don speak of this role as the most important one in his life, above all else. He is, without a doubt, a dedicated husband and father. As we've grown together through our married years (and as I've simultaneously grown in Spirit), I have felt an increasing yearning for my chosen other to ease into equal fullness with his feminine aspects—that is, matters of the heart such as compassion, sweetness, patience, stillness and deep listening—which is entirely possible for a man to do without emasculating himself (just as it's possible for a woman to address her own masculine/feminine without defeminizing herself).

A while ago, with the thought that another man's words of wisdom would help open the door for us to be more comfortable speaking of these things, I gifted Don with a book that offers an enlightened perspective on this topic. In *The Way of the Superior Man*, author David Deida, a renowned teacher on sacred intimacy, talks candidly to his male readers about mastering the challenges of work, career, sex, women, love and life purpose. The superior man, he says, has discovered that "it's time to evolve beyond the macho jerk ideal, all spine and no heart" and, at the same time, "it is also time to evolve beyond the sensitive and caring wimp ideal, all heart and no spine." A fully actualized male, he explains, is only able to step into the completeness of his being—focused, powerful, clear, purposeful—by directly connecting to his heart.

Before giving the book to Don, I read it first and, oh boy, did it resonate with me. (Ladies, buy a copy for your guy.) For some time, I had been encouraging Don—pushing him, perhaps—to begin his own strictly internal journey into the obscured areas of his heart, as I could sense that he had suppressed painful experiences from his young life and sequestered vital parts of himself in his efforts to fulfill his husband-father role—to the point that he could no longer find, or define, what was missing in his life. (It took him years to admit there *was* something missing, or to even talk to me about it.) I recognized the disquiet in him because I, too, had once been in that desolate space, if only in the privacy of my own conscience. And I know that Don is just like me in a fundamental way: he wants to be the best person he can be, to live with passion, gratitude and much laughter, and to be of service to some greater good. In short, he has a terrific heart; I simply wish for him to reveal it more. To Don's credit, I can understand how sharing life with me could be a lot of work. I'm not interested in just drifting along, staying only on the surface of things. Don has often said to me, "Gina, not everything has to be deep. Not everything has to *mean* something. Sometimes, it is what it is." But to me, everything is profound (even levity); everything *does* have meaning. This is the world that I inhabit.

As I say in the beginning of this book, sepia-tone living (in which we rein back our greatness) holds no contest to the prismatic bliss of ravishing life with full abandon—which requires an open mind and a trusting heart. On some level, I've wanted my significant other to join me in experiencing the wild and wide-open freedom of higher consciousness living, though in his own time and his own way. I wanted this for him, for myself, and for us as a couple. Was I wanting too much? For years, I felt (and heard) Don's resistance to my own spiritual quest. More often than I care to admit, it has been a bone of contention in our home, something that has been looked upon as weird, self-indulgent, suspicious, and divisive to our family—as opposed to (perfect phrase) the truth of what it really is: a blessing that has added untold richness, wonder, insight and, I hope, ultimately, peace to our lives.

I had been mentally preparing to pull back entirely from encouraging Don towards his own quest around the time I discovered Deida's book. As I paged through it before giving it to Don, I came across this passage: "The most loving women are the women who will test you the most. She wants you to be your fullest, most magnificent self . . . she knows in your deepest heart you are free, you are Shiva. Anything less than that she will torment . . . Yet, if your purpose is to be free, you wouldn't have it any other way . . . Her gift, if she is a good woman, is to test you . . . over and over and over, until your consciousness is unperturbed by feminine challenge, and you are able to pervade her with your love . . . In response to your fearless consciousness, she will drench your world in love and light."

Dieda's words read to me like a description of an integrated, spiritualized male-female bond between two people who choose—in the full recognition of enduring karmic union, not the illusory force of carnal attraction—to be together and, when necessary for one's growth, to arouse in that person the fortitude to unmask one's truest self. I intuitively know, as does Don, that we are together in this lifetime for reasons that reach down to our souls. And yet, it's the day-to-day—where the rubber meets the road—that repeatedly tests our commitment. (You know what I'm talking about, right?) Some days, the road can be treacherous because, in any committed relationship, there is no escaping the dark corners of another person, no canvas thick enough to mute the shadow that another casts on your own vulnerabilities. Add to that one or both partners being in the throes of spiritual growth, and the road becomes all the more perilous. We can feel insulted, angry, even estranged from our partner but are still bound by promise to join mind and body with that person. Again, add to that one or both of you being ultra-sensitive to energy vibration and nonverbal cues—well, it can sure make coming together in union with the very person who wounded you a skittish affair, at best.

It seems to me that if two people are to stay together and honor the choice they made in their vows to one another, each must, at some point, take on the courageous work of forging a deeper intimacy—or else an impasse is reached, and the relationship stagnates. I just don't see how deeper intimacy is possible without the conscious consideration that Everything Matters—every glance, every word, every assumption, every broken promise, every unspoken apology—and a willingness, when the moment calls for it, to drop all affectation and simply say to your chosen other: "Nothing Matters except my devotion to you. I don't need to be right, I don't need to control, I don't need you to be perfect, I don't need you to meet my needs, I don't even need you to need me . . . I am simply going to give love to you right here, right now, just for the sake of giving love, wanting nothing in return."

Granted, there are many levels at which couples can exist. The highest level, I imagine, requires a balance of the essential aspects of the masculine and feminine—in the man and the woman—with both hearts leading the way. Maybe such a partnership could be called "the integral couple." It's going to take some doing but I believe it's possible (anything is possible) for my relationship with Don to reach the exalted plane of loving for the sake of loving—no suppression, total dissolve, unblemished clarity on why we are re-choosing daily to be together. I have faith that this is doable—especially since, in recent months, Don has made a firm commitment to what he calls (using his own unique metaphor) his personal Corps of Discovery. Taking inspiration from the writings and legend of Lewis and Clark, he has begun his own undaunted expedition into the bravery of his heart—his compass being that the journey itself provides the richest gifts.

So, we'll see what happens from here. For the first time in a long while, I actually felt Don's heart opening when he shared with me that he'd like us to renew our vows for our 20th anniversary next year. "To me, that would be like reaching the Pacific Ocean," he said. You can see why I'm optimistic. He's a good man. And I want to be around when he crosses the great divide and discovers his own uncharted West Territory.

(After I finished writing this section, I showed it to Don and he approved, to my great relief. I asked if he would like to add some words of his own about what prompted him to begin his Corps of Discovery. Here is what he wrote.)

"I wanted to reconnect with someone I no longer recognized—myself. My over-weighted focus on providing for my family and what I had perceived to be their needs resulted in my putting the things that were meaningful and inspirational to me several levels down the totem pole of priorities. Years of this mindset accumulated until I realized one day that the best of myself had disappeared. I was well aware of the saying, 'one cannot truly love someone else until they love themselves.' I had not been at that place for a long time.

"I had watched Gina become immersed in her journey of spiritual expansion, but my attempts to seek similar inspiration as a means of creating a parallel path with hers simply resulted in my frustration. I finally read something—Deida's book—that shattered most of my preconceptions of what a person's path is supposed to look like. I concluded that Gina's inspiration does not have to be my inspiration. That was very liberating. So far, my personal Corps of Discovery has yielded unexpected gifts of self-rediscovery. As I peel back the onion, I see more and more clearly that Gina's gift to me is an awareness of the life splendor that we can all have."

EXTERNAL INTEGRATION:
OUTWARD EXPRESSIONS OF OUR POWER

As we choose our unique destination, face what we once denied, grow stronger through personal adversities and absorb radiance from the Divine along the way, the inner tranquility and confidence we've acquired becomes outwardly noticeable. A person who is well-connected (gives new meaning to the term) emits an inner light, an exceedingly attractive calmness. The skin is clear, the aura is bright and the person appears to be light-in-body, light-in-spirit. (In-light-ened.) Every word, every action, every gesture—and even the way this person is while doing nothing at all—is like spiritual pollen that fertilizes all she comes in contact with. This is the soul's essence shining forth, the core star of that individual shimmering out through her energy field and beyond. To people who are not open and aware, this phenomenon is inexplicable. They may not understand why a person is so attractive. They only know that this individual has a natural beauty. Others are drawn to that person, regardless of how they look externally. Because real beauty emanates from the soul and a connection to the Divine, becoming beautiful and becoming spiritually enlightened are synonymous.

No doubt, the pursuit of internal beauty is much more useful. External beauty is fleeting; internal beauty becomes more attractive as it is nourished. Kahlil Gibran wrote, "Beauty is not in the face; beauty is a light in the heart." We only need to watch E! News to know that there are plenty of physically gorgeous people who are tormented inside, who feel ugly or flawed. But from an Everything Matters, Nothing Matters intelligence, a person (let's say a woman) who has fully experienced her inner divinity would never consider herself to be ugly or imperfect. Those who have successfully tapped their inner source know that all is perfection.

Our Work in the World
Here's my definition of inspired higher creativity: it's the outward expression of our internal beauty, revealed through our

chosen endeavors. Of course we can decide to create some-thing with an eye on the external (perhaps mimicking others' inventions) and whip up some pretty good stuff, but all work that is truly inspired emanates from a pure, clear connection to two things: the deepest truth that your soul yearns to express and the highest devotion to rebirthing Creation through your Self. That is what the seven concepts in this book lead us towards—shining forth our truest nature in some form that is practical and useful in the world.

"Our work is to make ourselves visible in the world"—another of my favorite lines from David Whyte's *Crossing the Unknown Sea*. "This is the soul's individual journey, and the soul would much rather fail at its own life than succeed at someone else's." At a Vermont writers retreat a few years ago, I listened as David spoke movingly about the importance of having "the courageous interior conversation" with ourselves—and how if we don't, everything else is leaden in our hands. "The courageous conversation is the one in which you don't know who you'd be if you had it," he articulated. "The great thing about conversation is you don't know what it will be. Just begin. If you can stop telling yourself all the things you say that dominate your psyche, you'll actually be in the proper conversation."

For me, the proper conversation is the one in which I'm able to uncloak some as-of-yet unspoken truth—some-thing about this human life or myself that has mystified even me—and offer it to up as a prayer. Every time I've been brave enough to do this, I've received a gift in return: creative inspi-ration of the highest measure. When we say that certain artists, athletes or CEOs are gifted, who is doing the gifting? Some of us may have more natural ability than others but we are all born through and with a creative spark. We all have some-thing to express, or a pull towards something that wants to be expressed. Sure, we may not know what it is or what shape it will take in the material world. That's no problem, really. Just begin. Along the way, you will find that the soul recognizes it, intuition captures it, the heart feels it, the mind shapes it and hands birth it. We keep the conversation alive among all these aspects—we integrate ourselves. And we, as creator, become one with Creator.

CONSCIOUS PARENTING

As the outward expression of our integration takes shape, it positively impacts everything in our lives—especially our relationships. For me, a major earthly priority for becoming more aware is to be the best mother possible. I have a superb role model. Anyone who's ever met my mother would agree that my brothers and I have been blessed with (as I tell her) "the best mom ever invented"—truly, a consummate example of love, kindness, generosity, poise, grace, faith and complete devotion to Jesus. She is like Divine Mother, a woman who makes you a better, happier person just by being around her. I heard one of her cousins say to her recently, "Sally, I light up when I see you!" She has that impact on just about everyone.

There are so many ways to grow spiritually through relationships other than your own children, but for all of you whose path includes parenthood, I offer the following thoughts. I'm convinced that we cannot be parents (or, for that matter, sons or daughters) on a spiritual path and disregard the importance of the parental role, especially maternal. (The very wise Buddhist teacher Thich Nhat Hahn said, "Your child is your continuation . . . Who is your mother? Your mother is you.") I think about my female SFFs and the beautiful relationships they have with their children. All of us feel like corporeal goddesses who have birthed these beings from our own blessed

wombs. My children are me, I am them (and we are all together). Being their mother is something that I live for in addition
to God. As such, my imperative is to nurture and nourish these
souls who have come from the Source, who incarnate to learn
and grow—and to suffer, because we cannot learn without this
part of life. I write these words knowing that there are many
ways to embrace the fullest meaning of parenting—to include
those who nurture not only their own children, but the world's
children and all its creatures . . . and even those who nurture
a spark of a divine creative idea as their "child."

It's emotionally challenging at times, knowing that our
job is not to save our children from all pain. Yes, we protect
their health, safety and well being but we cannot deny them
the experience of the completeness of the circle of life, which
includes joy and sadness, highs and lows. As spiritual stew-
ards, we're not interested in trying to manage, control or mold
our kids to fit our expectations of how they should be. And
we wouldn't dream of ever abandoning them, because we're
conscious that Everything Matters and Nothing Matters (we
may not always approve of their choices but we know that
they have their own destiny to follow). The most we can do
is support, guide and love them to no end. No matter how old
or smart or successful we become, we always need our mother.
And as spiritual beings, we always have an urge (whether
defined or undefined) to know that Divine Mother is available to us—regardless of whether our earthly mothers are or
are not.

"[Conscious] parenting begins not so much with your connection to your child but with your connection to yourself,"
notes author Arjuna Ardagh in *The Translucent Revolution*.
"When we feel fully connected to who we are, deeper than
concepts, we are also connected to reality as it is, and this
allows us to really connect with our children as they are in

this moment . . . we can feel them as living mysteries."

As my children have grown, and I have, too, I've come to certain realizations about what it means to be a conscious parent. When I took the time to ponder this while writing these pages, the following overarching insights came to me about how I want to (continue to) "raise" my children.

1. Assume their intelligence.

From the time my children were toddlers, I've always thought of them as whole beings with their own hearts, minds, personalities, affinities and inherent senses of integrity and goodness. In fact, when they were very young, I often referred to them as my "little people." (Now that they're into their teen years, I've had to switch to "young adults." Sigh!)

"As translucent [conscious] parents," Ardagh continues, "we see the wholeness in our children. When we meet them in our own sense of wholeness, symptoms that might be interpreted as 'problems' through [a filter of distrust and separation] seem healthy and natural from clear seeing. Translucent parents speak of their children with gratitude, admiration, appreciation and with deep trust of their unique trajectory. When we see our children as whole, they will also see themselves as whole."

Many times, my children have been my teachers. I allow myself to learn from them. On occasion, wisdom pours from their mouths like young sages, so pure and clear—and I pay attention. When they ask for my advice, I start with the belief that they can grasp a complex topic or handle a difficult situation; then, based on their feedback, I break it down from there and offer possible resolutions, as needed. Intuitively, I don't feel that I should solve their problems for them. Childhood is their beta site, their personal laboratory. I don't expect them to "prove the hypothesis" before they've had opportunities to "do the experiment." Sure, there are going to be some meltdowns, broken beakers, random explosions—that's to be expected (or not). And sometimes, honoring their intelligence is simply a languaging thing—for example, instead of saying "you're too young to know about this" I might say, "when the time is right for you to experience this, you will."

I also assume their spiritual intelligence—something that I believe all children are born with but that gets censored out (by parents, schools, society, the media) in their maturation process. In subtle, casual ways, I encourage my son and daughter to experiment with the seven concepts in this book. At first, they may have thought that some of my suggestions were odd or unusual but at least they've been given opportunities to view intuition, intentionality and the possibility of unseen worlds as a natural extension of other things they're learning as they grow.

Of course, they understand that not everyone adheres to such an open-minded approach to such matters. One day when my daughter Gianne was about seven, she was in our living room with a friend. They were reading a children's book I'd bought her about mind-body-spirit topics. As I walked into the room, the girls giggled and put their hands behind their backs as if hiding something.

"What do you have?" I asked. They had teaspoons. "What are you trying to do?" I asked.

"We're trying to bend them with our minds," Gianne said. I smiled at their sense of adventure and curiosity. Her friend looked at me with apprehension and said, sheepishly, "My mother doesn't believe in any of that." To which my daughter replied: "Ha! My Mom IS that." It wasn't until that moment that I realized my subtle expressions about expanded consciousness were even being noticed!

2. Show them the way but not the where.

As my son and daughter mature, I continue to encourage them to listen to their inner voice, use intention setting, pay attention and observe things from various perspectives. Another example: Gianne is close friends with a girl named Bethany, who lived two doors down from us. When the family relocated to St. Louis, both girls were sad but vowed to continue their friendship—which they did. One day during summer break, Gianne couldn't find her address book with Bethany's contact information. We researched online and called directory assistance but there was no listing (we later found out that they had moved to another community). "What should I do?" Gianne asked.

"Why don't you write her a letter and send it to her old address," I suggested. "It will reach her eventually. And one more thing: say a bedtime prayer and ask to connect with her mind so she will know you're trying to get in touch with her. I'll do the same." (She and her BFFs have had fun practicing what they call mentelapy—short for mental telepathy).

"I really want to visit her this summer," Gianne said.

When I came home from an appointment the next day, Gianne ran downstairs to greet me. "Guess who called today?" she said, excitedly. "Bethany!" It was the first time they'd connected since the winter holiday.

"How cool is that?" I exclaimed and gave her a happy hug.

"And guess what else? Bethany is coming here to visit next week with her family. I get to see her! Her mom said she could hang with us for a couple of days—is that okay?" It was more than okay. When things flow together that beautifully, you can't deny the blessing.

3. Accept that they are not yours.

Later that summer, I was challenged to walk my talk about raising my children to be capable, confident, independent adults—and realizing that they are only in my care for a brief moment in time. Gianne was invited to visit Bethany at her new home in St. Louis. Could I bring myself to let Gianne fly on a plane by herself for the first time? Nearly 14 and already well traveled, she wasn't a bit nervous and, secretly, I think, couldn't wait to feel the freedom of going hundreds of miles away on her own. I kicked into witnessing mode. Once I did, several things occurred to calm me.

Before we left for the airport, I pulled a guidance card from the Saints & Angels deck on my altar. The card was: Be Brave. "Is this for me or her?" I asked. "For you!" I heard. "There's no need to get emotional. This is life. Just go with it. She's going to be fine." Then I tuned in further: I got that her flight would be a nonevent, that all would go smoothly and she would be with Bethany's family before I knew it (which, it would turn out, is what happened; she was already with them before I arrived home from the airport).

While waiting in line at the ticket counter, I slipped out of witnessing mode for a few moments. *Gosh, my mother would have never risked putting me on a plane at Gianne's age, am I crazy?* I thought. Just then, I noticed that the woman in line behind me was putting TWO of her daughters (younger than mine) on the plane.

Back in witnessing mode, I picked up that Gianne needed a reminder to always have her wits about her, never leave her bag unattended, use her highly trained karate techniques when necessary, blah, blah, blah. "Mom, I *know*," she said in a tone of exasperation. "It's just common sense." After they pre-boarded her, a woman came up to me with Gianne's purse—she had left it on the seat (she later said it fell out of her carry-on bag).

I'm sure that when she saw the flight attendant walking down the plane aisle with her purse, it was the tiny wake-up call she needed to heed Mom's common sense words.

But the most beautiful message was delivered after I'd watched the plane push off and I went into a retail store at the air mall. The salesperson left for a moment to retrieve an item from the stockroom that I wanted to purchase. As I waited, slightly dazed, still residually questioning the rightness of my decision to allow Gianne to go alone on this trip, I noticed in front of me a display of plaques. I paid attention! My eyes zoomed in on one of them. It read:

> **You may see her some night silhouetted against the moon and ask who taught her to fly. My mother, she'll say. She was a good teacher. As far as my wings carry me, my heart always knows its way home.**

A surge of emotion passed through me—equal parts peacefulness that I made the correct choice and gratitude that I was given so clear a confirmation precisely when I needed it most.

4. Encourage their intuition and creativity . . . and respect your own.

As a conscious parent, I believe that we have to offer our children chances to embrace or reject spiritual philosophies, religious traditions, cultural beliefs, world issues and other knowledge that speaks to the fact that were are one humanity sharing Planet Earth. In addition to attending Catholic Mass, I've taken them to various spiritually-themed events over the years. Sometimes they have great experiences; other times, they're bored and disinterested. The important thing is to include them because, as this chapter reminds us, it's all about Integration.

A small example: I brought them with me to a summer solstice celebration at the home of a husband and wife who have long been spiritual role models for me. On the way, Gianne said, "I hope we're not the only kids because one time we got looks from other adults." I informed her and my son, quite eruditely I thought, but with a humorous twist, that they have the power to set a new trend with adults and other kids, to share that they have really cool parents who include them in all kinds of grown-up stuff, and act so nonchalant about having such open minds . . . and thank goodness their mom and dad aren't intolerant, old-fashioned, maniacally conservative paranoid lunatics who tell them to lock the doors and go to bed early (not my exact words but you get the point). The evening was lovely. We learned about nature and Native traditions. "That wasn't so bad!" they said afterwards.

By the same token, Don and I have made it a priority to nurture our children's creative lives. We let them take the lead on pursuits that call to them and, when time and budget permit, support their trying new things. Now, as young teens, they have settled on certain passions. With Gianne, I believe, the performing arts gods had a line on her from the word go. She is musician, singer, songwriter, lyricist, performer and dancer all in one. I am amazed by her creative flow and realize the importance of giving her space to commune with the Sweet Muse of Music that she is literally tune-ing into. Carlin, too, is a terrific drummer and singer but his real passion—obsession, I might say—is ice hockey. (A t-shirt he owns says it all: *Eat, breathe, sleep and bleed hockey...then repeat.*) In my eyes, he is beautiful on the ice—a mix of power, speed and grace. Both Gianne and Carlin have also earned black belts in Tang Soo Do Karate and continue to learn so much about life through their martial arts training. As conscious parents, we teach by example, so it's equally important that our children see us continuing to nurture our own creativity. I still train every week in classical and modern dance, and perform occasionally. Don has picked up a musical instrument that he's always wanted to learn: the Scottish bagpipes. It sure is noisy around our house but at least we're not creatively challenged!

5. Clean your own basement before you ask them to clean their rooms.

In *Embracing Our True Self*, Paul Ferrini writes that there are two types of people: those who are aware of their pain and those who are in denial about it. As a parent, I believe that we cannot raise healthy children if we are, ourselves, wounded. I don't mean to say that we must get in touch and heal through all our core traumas before we decide to start a family. But I am saying that we should be aware of and not in denial about what makes us less than our best selves. Turning Within and Witnessing sure come in handy here. Since I've worked at becoming familiar with my deep trigger points, I can look back and see instances where I might have risked putting my own "stuff" onto my children. That's the last thing I wanted to do! This tendency to project falls away in the wisdom of awareness and the willingness to step back, face our own fears, and break our reactive behavior patterns. I'm far from expert at this. I live and learn, and there have been times when I've been frustrated with myself. I can also pinpoint times when guiding my children through their difficulties has helped me correct erroneous beliefs I've held about myself. From an Everything Matters, Nothing Matters stance, it's all good.

I feel strongly that we do our children a disservice when we don't have our act together—emotionally, spiritually and psychologically—or aren't, at least, actively working on this. When we live our parental lives from a victim stance of guilt or sacrifice, we are only betraying ourselves...our children don't require this! As Carl Jung noted, "Nothing has a stronger influence psychologically on their environment and especially on their children than the unlived life of the parent." This is where the integration of our many selves—with spirituality and creativity at the axis—is crucial. So long as you're not hurting your children and are in your integrity, live your life the way you want to! Clean your basement and be free! It's so much easier and more joyful than living only in the vicarious sense.

SPIRITUAL MATURITY: WITH GREAT KNOWLEDGE COMES GREAT RESPONSIBILITY

In our lifetime, an increasing percentage of the population has become interested in higher-consciousness values of tolerance, equality, reverence for life and an appreciation for ancient philosophies and mysticism. In fact, the work of futurist and cultural anthropologist Jennifer James, PhD, finds that civilization is undergoing "a gradual increase in kindness." According to her extensive research, we're essentially becoming more civilized over time as we endure the long process of learning to be kind. I agree that our tendency towards love rather than hate (although we don't see this reflected in our media) isn't a passing fad, but rather an evolutionary phenomenon; it is moving us slowly away from a cultural mindset of hierarchical authority and towards one of personal responsibility—far more powerful and effective than any system of imposed rules. What is driving this shift? Our increasing spiritual maturity . . . and maybe a sense of what could happen if we ignore the imperative to make fundamental changes, and soon.

It's finally dawning on a lot of us (think global warming,) that we're all in this together. We can't afford to think in terms of "us" and "them." There is only "we" and "one." For many people, this isn't a normal or even a desirable way to think, but the impetus for us to grow spiritually is going to continue—because integration is inevitable, and it's happening. For this integration to occur on all levels, we will have to do away with views that even remotely resemble spiritual snobbery—the attitude that any one person is any better than anyone else in any way. We are all exactly where we need to be . . . and where we are is, in fact, of our own choosing.

Imagine what can happen when enough of us bring spiritual maturity to bear on issues ranging from warfare, economic disparity, consumerism, destruction of the planet, freedom of the press, education of our youth, the way we transact business and how we care for the indigent—to marriage, money, food, sex, family, art and entertainment. Once we awaken, all bets are off, because there really is no right or wrong, good or bad, better or worse, winners or losers. Everything Matters, but not in the way it did before.

Integration prods us to honestly acknowledge our investment in outworn modes of behavior, in attitudes that are way beyond their "sell by" date. Bob Dylan's refrain still applies: the times, they are a changin'. Some of us are going along for the cosmic ride and enjoying the dips and turns, neither engaged nor resisting; others are choosing to stay ensconced in well-grooved tracks. Still others—that burgeoning collective of individuals who are awakening—are standing on a precipice, gaining courage to make the leap into the depths of the inward journey that, paradoxically, becomes a leap towards the stars of our unlimited potential. It is that contingent of seekers to whom those of us who have stood there too feel an allegiance, a moral imperative to lend encouragement. This is, for the most part, why I've chosen to divulge my most personal stories on these pages; if the retelling of them helps others to take that leap with more assurance, it's worth the possible wrath I might incur from those who don't agree that I should have revealed so much of myself.

Hawkins would add that when we transcend into higher states of consciousness, we have an obligation to others (especially loved ones) insofar as helping them "accept the required changes" that occur within those of us who are experiencing this transcendence. "This transition may . . . take considerable courage and patience as well as conviction, for it brings up residual doubts, attachments, guilt and the like," he says. I can relate! The perfection in this, however, is that by the time we reach a certain point in our personal alchemical process where we've burned away enough dross to reveal the gold within, all the gifts outlined in this book—intuition, contemplation, paying attention, knowing your inner self, encountering mentors and like-minded souls and (perhaps most crucial) the ability to witness—are now in our cosmic toolbox to draw upon.

As we integrate all aspects of our learning, we can take on, guilt-free, whatever kicking, moaning and screaming may go on around us in nonattached, dignified silence (at least for a greater percentage of the time) because we know that we cannot and should not make anyone do anything. In fact, I've discovered (and continue to learn) that the only way to help others accept the required changes is to just be the change you wish to see in the world, as Mohandas Gandhi said, and make choices based on that level of spiritual maturity.

"When an unawakened person tries to discredit the inner knowing of an awakened person, it is like a deaf and blind person attempting to convince a sighted-hearing person that there is no such thing as color or music," suggests author Patricia Cota-Robles (president of the nonprofit educational organization New Age Study of Humanity's Purpose, Inc.). "The difference in that situation is that the sighted-hearing person would understand perfectly why the deaf and blind person was having trouble grasping the concept of color and music. The sighted-hearing person would have compassion for the deaf and blind person and would respond to him or her with patience and understanding."

* * *

"So, what are you going for, enlightenment?" a wise man (wise guy?) asked me while we were chatting at a work-related cocktail party. Talk about Integration. There I stood, tipsy with a wine buzz, all dolled up in pink lipstick and high heels, waxing rhapsodic about the allure of communing with Spirit. And this simple, humble man, a Christian mystic—a self-professed carp out of water at this Hollywood gig whom I'd watched work the room like the Clintons at the Democratic National Convention—getting all over my shit about me wanting to find my Holy Grail.

"Do you even KNOW what you're going for?" he prodded. "Do you?" Woo wee. It was a fair question. I was in a mood to hear myself answer it.

"No, I'm not really going for enlightenment. Of what use is that to me now? That's the Big O, the cosmic climax. What stirs me most is the *pre-O*, living in the splendor of becoming, the full flush of adventure and emergence, where anything is possible, and where I can screw up and even get screwed, in the figurative sense, if need be . . . sort of like Anaïs Nin in *Henry and June*, don't you think?"

"How should I know? You're the writer."

Okay, I had gone a bit far, and he was having a hostile moment at my expense. I granted him that but couldn't resist extending the metaphor. "Yeah, that book is about her erotic awakening, how she wants to bite into life and be torn by it, how she swallows the laughter of her lover like bread and wine. Only replace sex with Spirit, lover with Beloved, promiscuity with piety. Life is my unexpurgated spiritual diary, my rendez-vous with full-frontal consciousness."

"Huh. You're speaking of love. Is it possible that you and God are having an affair?"

"How should I know? You're the mystic."

UNCONDITIONAL LOVE IS THE GOAL

Love and be loved! That's what I'm going for, not just in a human, physical sense but metaphysically—to bite into all that is seen or unseen, and not fear being torn by it. My awakening has taught me, in the empirical sense, that love is the grandest vibration of all. It is unending and unerring—and it is never wrong to love. Prismatic living has shown me that we are beings of light and love, and we are made to express emotion towards one another. It is only when we try to put ego-restrictions on these expressions that we become confused and overly cautious about sharing love. The truth about love is that it cannot be possessed, it can only be given. In love, we are always connected in heart and spirit. This cannot be severed by something as trivial as space and time. Love is eternal and cannot be "stopped."

We all crave love in our lives, sometimes out of need or lack—we want a physical body by our side, in our bed, with us on life's journey. Or we want love because it helps to complete some missing piece of ourselves. Sadly, we may believe that we are not total unless we are loved by someone else. Even more sadly, we may not feel worthy of this love that we so desire.

But once Christ consciousness enters a life, a heart, a body, down to the mitochondria of our being, we begin to realize that we are always loved, and we are always in love. There is no sense of incompleteness or need. All is as it should be. With this strength, we go forward with confidence into the world and do what we want or have to do, sharing the feeling we have within. When we are disconnected from Source, we instead go through life seeking that connection, and sometimes are misguided about where we think we can find it. (Could this be another possible explanation for why an artist or anyone with a known talent would feel tormented by his gift instead of fulfilled?)

Mary Magdelene, whom I consider to be the feminine side of Jesus, has been a great teacher to me about spiritual love and the truest meaning of how to love without condition. Intuitively, she told me this: "Spiritual love differs from physical love in this way: you are attracted to the divine within a person and witness it as a representation of God, in human form. The physical and the ego are, in a sense, circumvented. You see that person, but with reverent eyes. You enjoy the personality of that person, but don't need anything from him. You are happy to just be with him, even if you do nothing, as if sitting silently in a church, in complete rapture." As you can see, MM has set the bar pretty darn high—I'm not so sure I can ever live up to it. Nonetheless, I've set the intent that this is what I'm going for in all my relationships—with my family, friends, co-workers, pets, acquaintances and strangers. This is also the gold standard for my present relationship with the creative. As I write these pages about opening to Spirit, I realize that the majority of society (at least in the United States) is still not interested in exploring many of the intricacies of embracing God-consciousness as outlined here. And yet, redemption happens every day in countless ways. More and more people are awakening through some inner yearning or outer (quote-unquote) cause. Even those who could not have cared less about mysticism before some crisis came upon them or their lives fell apart, are now having intense spiritual experiences. Often, these individuals don't find God per se but they DO find love. And for those of you who say you want an evolution, you've got it. It's happening. It's an evolution of humanity becoming more humane.

"What's practical in this world is to try to reach a level called unconditional love—to be loving and kind and forgiving towards all, including yourself, with no exceptions," Dr. Hawkins shared with me. "The practical level for the average person is to try to reach a state in which you become loving at all times under all circumstances. It's a practical goal, very doable in this world. The world is extremely negative, and to even get to unconditional love is rare. So it's a realistic goal for the average person who doesn't want to withdraw from the world and go into specialized inner spiritual work—that's a whole different realm."

I do believe that unconditional love begins with the self. In order to love creation and Creator, we must first love ourselves and know that we are worthy of love. As an extension of that, we naturally believe in others and know that they deserve love, too. Even our yet-to-be-seen aspects, our unborn creations, are worthy of love without condition.

Forgiveness is the Fulcrum

How do we get there? Forgiveness, forgiveness, forgiveness. (I say it three times because it involves forgiveness of the self, others and the world.) Forgiveness isn't something that we say or do, as in "Oh, I forgive you for running over my cat." It seems more accurate to define it as a way of being or a way of thinking—and then what we say or do is an extension of that.

In *The Disappearance of the Universe*, Gary Renard talks about his nine-year journey of studying *A Course in Miracles* and how, in the process, two in-the-flesh ascended masters gave him direct instruction on advanced forgiveness, and detailed explanations about the existence of the universe. It was a period of powerful awakening for this private investor and former professional musician, a time of mind-blowing mystical experiences. But there was more. Renard writes:

"I had also learned that the REAL test of whether or not one was progressing on their chosen spiritual path had nothing to do with 'spiritual experiences.' Indeed, the real questions one should be asking were: Am I becoming more loving? More peaceful? More forgiving? Have I taken responsibility for my life? Do I understand the folly of judgment? THAT was how to tell if a path was working for someone. Still, my particular mystical experiences were giving me joy, especially because I had learned they were symbolic of my mind being forgiven—as a result of forgiving the world."

From this integrated perspective, Renard was able to reach peak states and not only extrapolate great meaning from his mystical experiences but use them pragmatically to improve his life in myriad ways. Years later, he took it many steps forward by publishing his story and speaking publicly about it so that others can benefit from his practical applications of forgiveness—the foundation for which is *A Course in Miracles*. Way to integrate, Gary!

A crucial piece of the forgiveness pie is forgiving ourselves. Listen as SFF Dan thinks on the page about just this, as well as his own integration towards the ultimate goal, love: "Upon self-reflection, much in my life hangs in the balance: my spiritual commitment, bringing my authentic self out to the world, my relationships and my business. For years, I have only talked about being this or doing that—with my wife and son, my business, making jewelry, playing the harmonica, chanting, working out, eating better. I regret none of that—it makes me who I am. But today I choose a new reality. I choose to be as alive, as present as I can bear. I choose to believe in little synchronicities—friends calling, feathers dropping from trees.

There's something to be said about being in the flow of life. For me, that means love. Reaching out to others and allowing them reach out to me. Surely, I have missed many openings, many doors and windows. Someday I will make a painting of them and call it Dan's Journey. Among the unopened doors and windows will be a scattering of life's gifts that I COULD see. I don't want to grieve anymore. I just want to paint my life with forgiveness and love, here and now—the glorious, passionate, absurdly funny goings on, the crap and the flat-out wow's."

As we allow forgiveness to exonerate us from past failings and clear our psychic pathways, we begin to teem with renewed creative energy. Without feelings of guilt, blame, bitterness and unwanted obligation, our reservoir begins to run deeper, richer. There is no limit to its content or quantity. And it is free. We don't actually need anything to have a creative experience, just as we don't need anything to have a spiritual experience—only the intention. When we live consciously we naturally create, because we are in the cosmic flow, the ultimate current of life. We are immersed in the emotion of being fully alive and allow that emotion to take us along its rightful course, like a river carries a branch. The branch does not concern itself with where it is going. It only knows that it is part of the energy that carries it. And while it may encounter obstacles along the way, it has a detached knowingness that it will ultimately arrive at the ocean's great expanse, if that is its destiny.

The future of our human existence, I believe, depends upon this integration of our conscious-creative selves. "The complexity of our time requires a greater and wiser use of our capacities, a rich playing of the instrument we have been given," Jean Houston said on this subject. "The world can thrive only if we grow."

So, let's grow!

At this juncture in our evolution, we are too emotionally intelligent, too aware, to grow apart and not together. When we bear in mind that we are one humanity, forgiveness takes on greater importance and urgency. "The pathology of our time is the illusion of separation," says Marilyn Schlitz, PhD. "The universal theme being played out right now is one of shifting from separation to integration—mainly, learning how to love and accept yourself and others, completely and unconditionally. We see others as part of the infinite being—no better, no less, just different from yourself. From this, you realize that consciousness isn't something that's 'out there'—it's inside each of us. Inner integration is a process that causes issues of separation to arise so that they can be resolved. Even societally, issues are coming up so rapidly that the world appears to be in turmoil. Hopefully, this is about issues becoming resolved once and for all."

Star Power: Creativity Leads Us to a Glorious Birth

With unconditional love as my compass, I know the direction my life journey is taking and welcome all who wish to come along. Let's pitch our pop tents together near the river, build a communal fire to keep us safe and warm through dark, wild nights, encourage each other into the dawn—and experience ourselves rising in spiritual awareness, like a phoenix from the ashes. And let's celebrate together when our journey endows us with elegantly appointed hotel suites, replete with sumptuous bed linens and fleecy robes in which to luxuriate as we sip DP and savor Godiva-covered berries. A fully conscious and creative life is all that: pitch-tents and suites, heart and spleen, ashen and sweet, rising and falling, swanky and fierce. So what if, at times, it's too cruel to bear? What happens to you happens to me, and vice versa. We'll endure together and ascend as one soul—the soul of Creation returning to Itself.

To once again quote the literary-spiritual legend Mirabai, as she speaks about her ecstatic union with the Divine:

O friends on this path,
My eyes are no longer my eyes.
A sweetness has entered through them,
Has pierced through to my heart.
How long did I stand in the house of this body
And stare at the road?
My Beloved is a steeped herb,
He has cured me for life.

I close this work, these writings, with a final story. The week before Christmas 2005, I was given a beautiful metaphor for how leading with love takes us straight to the Divine, and how uncovering our truest purpose on earth ultimately leads us home. My story is about the individual ways in which we express our creativity in the world through the inherent gifts we are given.

It began with a dream in which I'm cradled in the arms of the Beloved. I'm "with child." Upon waking, I feel well loved, blessed, complete. With my inner sight, the name Arcturus appears, which I know has something to do with the upcoming holiday season and birth of Jesus—but what?

I get the kids off to school, juice my morning greens, put them in the fridge to chill, and ease into meditation. The North Star appears in a mystical sky. I'm encouraged to follow it. I can't clear the thought of Arcturus from my mind so I ask to see this realm. I'm taken through the cosmos to a star system. It's celestial, very still yet amazingly alive, a place where a star is being born continuously. (Only later that day when I Google Arcturus do I make the connection: It's a bright star that presides over the northern hemisphere. It summons us to service and to prepare for great life journeys. In ancient cosmology, it was the Bold One, the Messenger, the Coming One.)

"What does this mean?" I ask for further clarification.

Answer: "Remain perpetually devoted to following your own North Star—your unique life purpose—and it will lead you ever closer to a glorious birth: the birth of Christ inside you."

Only recently, I discovered that the word "desire" stems from the Old French and Latin root de-sīder, "of the stars." To have desire, then, means to follow your inborn star. So I greet each dawn with a simple yet certain desire: put one foot in front of the other, making the very most of every step along the journey. Some days, I get creative and add a little soft shoe, a pirouette or leap. Some nights, I stumble and fall to my knees. Either way, I'm dancing due north in an upward spiral, euphoric with the knowledge that Everything Matters and Nothing Matters. Who needs enlightenment? Just to be alive is nirvana.

BEYOND 7

CONTEMPLATIONS AND SELF-CREATIONS:
EXERCISES TO HELP CLEAR YOUR CREATIVE
CHANNEL AND ACCESS HIGHER REALMS

*T*he following exercises are keyed to the themes of each chapter. They are, ultimately, about simplifying yourself so your essence can shine—paring down to what's essential in your life, tossing what's not, and growing into knowing the difference.

The Contemplations are inward practices that will serve to clear your creative channel. The Self-Creations are more tangible, outwardly focused actions that will provide access to realms of higher creativity. Some exercises are both internal and external. They are all deeply healing if approached with reverence and a true willingness to achieve spiritual clarity about yourself and others, and the world around you.

1. INTENTION

Contemplations

ASK AND YOU WILL RECEIVE
Begin by setting an everyday intention that speaks to the importance of taking small steps towards a desired outcome. Okay? Now set a logic-defying intention that invites the inexplicable into your life and announces to the universe that you are ready and willing to be delightfully startled by its brilliance and limitlessness.

HEAL THYSELF

Intention is vital to the process of healing the body or the spirit. The wise Rumi wrote, "We are pain and what cures pain, both. We are the sweet cold water and the jar that pours." Combine intention with a firm commitment to actions that support that intention. Don't stop any wellness routines or medical treatment you are receiving, just add to it a belief that "your faith has healed you," as Jesus said.

Self-Creations

CLEANLINESS IS NEXT TO GODLINESS

Clear space for the Divine to enter, bearing in mind that clutter can be seen or unseen. Physically clean your living space, then do a simple clearing ceremony. Light a smudging stick of sage or sweetgrass mixed with lavender, and say a prayer in every room. Intend to release the past and open the way for the new.

ALTAR-ED REALITY

After cleaning your home, choose a niche in it and construct an altar. Imbue it with sacredness by intentionally placing on or around it items, colors, scents, shapes, music and power objects that have significance to you. Ask the muses to come when you are in this holy space. "Your sacred space is where you can find yourself again and again," Joseph Campbell said.

HIGHER SELF INTENTION

Write a short, inspired (in-spirited) poem, mantra or catch phrase that reminds you of your greatest intention for yourself. It can be anything at all—no rules apply here. An example: "I turned myself into myself and I was Buddha." Here's one from SFF Dan: "He who dies with the most joy wins." Post this saying on your bathroom mirror, computer workstation, refrigerator...or anywhere that you'll see it daily.

2. DAILY PRACTICE

Contemplations

OM, AGAIN
In a word: meditate!

LET SPIRIT MOVE YOU
Choose a simple daily (or regular) routine that connects you to Spirit: cut flowers or herbs in your garden, cast runes or pull a card from an inspirational deck, take a morning walk or do gentle yoga stretches. Afterwards, allow the energy to carry you into a mood of contemplation. Go about your day. If this mood fades, return to doing something that reconnects you—even if it's just taking a few deep breaths or glancing at artwork that inspires you.

APPLY SPIRITUAL DRANO (SAFE WHEN USED AS DIRECTED)
Unclog your body's creative energy center by doing a meditation on the sacral chakra. Reflect on an incident or situation in which you were shunned or not allowed to express yourself during the ages of 6 to 12. Go there now, without hesitation, knowing that this experience may have helped define who you are but it doesn't necessarily apply to your future self. Write, paint, cry or scream out the story of then. While focusing light on your second chakra, breathe out this old story. Pause for as long as it takes to understand the greater purpose of this circumstance in your younger life. Bless it for its wisdom. Now you are free to begin writing the story of now.

Self-Creations

DREAM ON
Experiment with interpreting and even creating your own dreams. Place a notebook by your bed to be used as a dream journal. Upon

waking, write down the date and record whatever you remember from that night's dream. As you become skilled at interpreting your dreams' messages, you can invite a dream in order to solve a problem, gain perspective on a situation, or ask for creative inspiration. To do so, simply place a question that you'd like to ask in your mind, then release it. Give thanks for the insights you will be given as you sleep. Be aware of all dreams that you have in the coming days or weeks.

WRITE THE UNSEEN

As a form of divine inspiration, try intuitive journaling. Begin with a meditation or few moments of silence. Sit comfortably with a notebook or laptop. Center and clear your mind. Then state an intention, such as "I ask for the highest truth for myself in accordance with divine will." If you have a question, write it down then release it. When a word, phrase or thought comes to you, transcribe it verbatim. Don't analyze or edit it. After you've written down a thought, let it go; clear your mind again. Do this until you feel that the writing has ended. Give thanks for these insights. Read and interpret your message. With practice, you will learn to distinguish between what your logical mind is making up and what you are intuiting. Intuitive messages generally have a distinct language, tone and style, but they are always loving, supportive, honest and nonjudgmental.

3. PAYING ATTENTION

Contemplations

PAY ATTENTION TO WHAT COMES OUT OF YOUR MOUTH

Our voice is our song that we sing to the world. Pay attention to your song—meaning, how you say things, and the literal meaning of them, as well as the energy (the intention) that rides on the words. As I share in Chapter 2, I was encouraged by Spirit to replace the word "deadline" (ugh!) with "lifeline"—which better reflects how I feel about meeting my work goals. They are my livelihood, so their coming to fruition isn't a dead end, it's a "live beginning." Play with making up words to express what you're feeling. When I saw a group of dolphins in Hawaii, I got so excited that I blurted out to my son, "What an endolphin rush!" What words can you replace or invent that more adequately intend what you want to create in your daily life?

PAY ATTENTION TO WHAT GOES IN YOUR MOUTH

Nutrition is more than biological. As humans, bliss of any kind is first sensed through our physical body; spiritual elation is therefore obtained through a body that is optimally prepared for this experience. The best food to ingest is pure, raw (as much as possible), live food—unprocessed and close to the beginning of the food chain: vegetables, fruits, nuts, free range fish, poultry and (occasionally) lean meats. This diet helps to remove toxins and purify the body. As a result, it becomes a better conductor of kundalini (spiritual) energy—not to mention, you will look and feel healthier, more alive. Even taking one or two small steps towards this goal (like juicing a meal only a couple times a week) will reap rewards. To get started, read *Spiritual Nutrition* and *Conscious Eating,* by Gabriel Cousens, MD, a recognized yogi and medical researcher.

Self-Creations

LET YOUR LIFE SPEAK

The Quakers have a saying: "Let your life speak"—referring to the language of your soul. Taking this one step further, consider writing your soul's desires on paper then speaking them aloud. Affirmations aren't just intellectual confection. They sway the power of intuition in your favor. Think of some thing or some situation you'd now like to manifest in your life, and speak of it—and to it—with affection.

Appreciate that it has already happened. Give glory to the Divine for this showing up in your life—in a form that is greater than the one you've already imagined for yourself.

MAKE THE MOST OF THE MOMENT YOU'RE IN

Paying attention is all about being present. The more we're in the moment, the greater our sense of flow, joy and gratitude. For instance, one winter evening when my kids were very young, the electricity went off in our home. Not able to do anything in the dark, the kids sat by the fire while I lit candles all around. Carlin had a battery operated cassette player and because it was mid-December, he had a tape of Christmas music in it. So, Carlin created a game—which he called Kissing Carols—to pass the time. Basically, he would kiss my hand or arm to the rhythm of a holiday melody and have me guess what song it was, then I would do the same with him. Gianne gleefully joined in. For the next 30 minutes, we made the most of the power outage by pecking and giggling our way through *Jingle Bell Rock, Silent Night* and *The Nutcracker Suite.*

4. TURNING WITHIN

Contemplations

ABANDON PERFECTIONISM

As we turn within, we may have a tendency to look back at certain situations with regret or remorse. We all make mistakes. Guess what? That's a good thing. In fact, nothing is as successful as a string of mistakes. Remember, Nothing Matters—everything is already perfect. Our alleged errors help us refine ourselves. Creativity is about change and experimentation; trial without error is unlikely, and constraints hamper creative flow. Do a special meditation in which you forgive yourself for your perceived mistakes (which are really gifts of insight in disguise). Going forward, allow yourself to have greater tolerance of mistakes—yours and others.

HOW DELICIOUS IS YOUR SLIVER OF THE DIVINE?

Every one of us is an aspect of the Creator. As such, we all have a piece of that divine essence. Think of it this way: God is a gigantic cake—angel food, perhaps—and you are a perfect sliver of it. Your slice, albeit tiny, contains every ingredient of that wonderfully complex Original Secret Recipe. Your task is to turn within and replicate what's already there. So, what are your basic ingredients? Of them, which ones are your most delicious attributes?

Self-Creations

CHOOSE YOUR MAIN COURSE

Benedictine monk and Christian writer Macrina Wiederkehr penned this: "O God, help me to believe the truth about myself, no matter how beautiful it is." As you contemplate the basic ingredients that you listed above, add some descriptors to it in the form of symbols or analogies. What is the beautiful truth about yourself? You may think you're shellfish (ha, ha) when, really, you're a sweet tart. Don't assign value to your traits or compare them to anyone else's qualities. Just sit with them until they gel in your consciousness.

HOLD YOUR CREATIONS UNTIL THE RUNWAY IS CLEAR

As I mention in Chapter 4, be careful with whom you share your unpolished creative gems that have been mined from a very deep place or high source. Create a tarmac in your consciousness (or on your hard drive) where your ideas can lie in wait for real-time takeoff. Allow this holding pattern to further incubate your creative outpourings. If others scoff about not being privy to your ideas, tell them you're awaiting clearance from the Tower.

5. WORKING WITH A MENTOR

Contemplations

INTEND A MENTOR

If appropriate for you, set an intention for the right teacher to enter your life at precisely the right time. Give gratitude for the appearance of the highest and best individual or group of like-minded others (see below), then release the intention into the hands of the Divine. It will happen—probably when you least expect it.

MANIFEST A (CREATIVITY) GUIDE

At any time, you can ask for a guide or archetype to assist in your creative process and strengthen your own sense of identity. Go to your sacred space, enter meditation and simply ask for higher inspiration. Remember these words from novelist Stephen King: "Ideas seem to come quite literally from nowhere, sailing at you right out of the empty sky: two previously unrelated ideas come together and make something new under the sun. Your job isn't to find these ideas but to recognize them when they show up." Ask your creative guide to help you recognize them when they show up.

Self-Creations

KINGDOM COME AGAIN

Revisit your childhood religion with fresh eyes, whether in practice or by reading materials that resonate with its wisdom and beauty. Feel very free to create your own personal forms of prayer and ritual around it. Doing so takes nothing away from this faith—in fact, it can serve to deepen your appreciation of it.

CREATE A GATHERING CIRCLE

Connecting with others is an essential part of any personal growth practice. Group energy can be a powerful force in elevating its members to a higher level. Churches and synagogues are one option (see above), as are recognized support groups such as AA. Another option is to form a small circle of compatible folks who collectively intend to inspire and challenge one another. Begin by answering the question: In what way do I want to grow right now? Establish some simple ground rules (for example, no giving advice...just attentive listening!). Be creative by opting to go on outings, intuiting what should be talked about (as opposed to always having a set agenda), or ending your circle with something fun—like chocolate all around....mmmmm.

6. WITNESSING

Contemplations

FLY WITHOUT AN AIRPLANE

We've all had moments of effervescent joy—the kind that make you want to hug strangers, dance a little jig or run through a field of daisies. Sure, external events can prompt such random behavior but our awakened state allows us to tap into this sensation at will. India's ancient art of health and well being—Ayurveda—refers to this joie de vivre as your *ojas*. We can cultivate ojas by slowing down, making conscious choices and non-personally observing our own reactions. Starting today, take a few moments to up your ojas-factor in this manner. Even if you're handling a difficult situation, truly and fully be in that experience instead of wishing it away.

LIVE THROUGH SOMEONE ELSE'S EYES

Take this one step further by non-personally observing others' actions and reactions. For a few minutes every day—or when the opportunity arises—put yourself in another person's shoes. Suspend all judgment about that individual and simply view things from their perspective. See how it feels . . . and feel what you see. It might help to think of yourself as an actor taking on the part of a character.

DON'T TRY TOO HARD . . . BETTER YET, DON'T TRY AT ALL

When cavorting with the concept of witnessing, remember: don't over-think this or try too hard to make it happen. Go nice and easy; eventually it will become second nature. Spirit gave me a clever analogy one day when I was struggling with this. With my inner vision, I saw a picture window with lush greenery outside. Behind the windowpane was a high powered magnifying telescope, like the kind used by astronomers in a space lab. I knew this represented my behavior at that time of gazing intensely at a situation and analyzing the heck out of it. I was guided to step away from the telescope: "It's very simple" I heard. "All you have to do is look through the window with your eyes!"

Self-Creations

DEFINE A PRISMATIC ACTION IN YOUR LIFE AND JUST DO IT

What takes your life from sepia-tone to prismatic? Define the activity that most brings you alive and get busy doing it on a regular basis. For me, that thing is dance. I was born loving ballet and will until I die. And there's nothing like the sheer adrenaline rush of performing—the ojas soar! I recently met a woman at a dinner party who performs for Ringling Brothers. As soon as I saw her, I knew she was a dancer, so we hit it off. I made a comment about getting too old to train and stay in shape, that I'll just take class for a few more years then stop. She blurted out with much drama, "NO! You must dance until your last breath!" What is it that you love to do so much that you'd choose to do it until your last breath?

WITNESS UNIVERSAL FLOW THROUGH TRAVEL

Travel not only teaches us about other places and people, it oftentimes leads us inward to a richer understanding of who we are. When we change our environment and leave our comfort zone, we learn varied rules, boundaries, tolerances and ways of being. Anything and everything can happen: from a lost set of eyeglasses to crime and even war (depending on where you're going). Because our antennas are up when traveling, it increases our capacity to witness people, places and situations. Sometime in the next few months take a trip to a place you've never been, even if it's only to a part of your own community you aren't familiar with—and explore witnessing.

CHANGE IT UP

This action will aid in your ability to witness: Do something different on a regular basis—switch to your non-dominant hand, take a different route home, introduce yourself to a new neighbor, listen to an alternative genre of music, change your hair style, or close your eyes and walk around the room using your other senses. Observe yourself doing these things while you are doing them.

7. INTEGRATION

Contemplations

LIVE IN THE PRE-O

Don't wait for the Big O, the crescendo, the ephemeral brass ring of future success, wealth, personal achievement or self-improvement. Opt right now to live in the pre-O, the splendor of becoming, where anything is possible in this moment. Savor the fullness of your emerging potential, instead of the lack of what hasn't yet come to fruition in your life. Integration isn't about waiting for the climactic highs. It's about the heart being perpetually aroused. The way to achieve this is by allowing the ordinary to open you over and over again, as if you're a rose that can't stop blooming. Take this idea into your daily meditations.

SO . . . BE IT

Integration occurs when we decide to be the change that we want to see in the world, our relationships, our work, our own home. How to do this? Ignite your passions, burn down any resistances to them, be a flame of dynamic light, warmth and quiet, humble strength wherever you go—and stay ablaze regardless of what happens to you. Integration is not about avoiding our feelings and emotions, but being conscious of how we react to them no matter what the outer circumstances. So feel whatever issues arise in as non-personal a way as possible, and help those around you to do the same. Be the change.

JUXTAPOSE TWO THINGS YOU LOVE

When we integrate, we afford ourselves the ability to juxtapose disparate things to form uniquely new creations. Years ago, I had the idea to open a sandwich shop in my town and name it The Deli Llama—serving up sandwiches and spiritual wisdom. (I might still do it someday.) Contemplate the things in your life that are essential, and how you might be able to align and integrate them.

Self-Creations

LOVE AND BE LOVED

"My God, these folks don't know how to love, that's why they love so easily," wrote novelist D. H. Lawrence. Higher consciousness love isn't casual. It's profoundly sweet, mysterious and has the power to change everything, at once, forever. Remember this, and allow yourself to be loved—even if it's something small like accepting a compliment. By the same token, give love repeatedly with no thought of anything in return (expectations are premeditated resentments). Give it not just to your family and friends, but to the cashier at the grocery store and the person who cuts you off in traffic. Send love and more love to the politician you abhor and the criminal you fear. As an aware person, you have only two fundamental obligations: show up and be loving.

END (AND BEGIN) WITH FORGIVENESS

To successfully integrate, we first need to clear the lower emotions of guilt, shame and remorse. Is there someone you need to forgive? Mend the fence. Does someone deserve your forgiveness? Build a bridge. As A Course in Miracles says, "Today it's time to practice forgiveness. Every tomorrow will profit from it."

FOLLOW YOUR OWN NORTH STAR

Gaze at the night sky. Choose your own North Star. Follow it until you find the Christ inside you. Awaken to your own life. Give all glory and praise to God.

ACKNOWLEDGMENTS

$\mathcal{J}$ bow in gratitude to the dream team at St. Lynn's Press: publisher Paul Kelly, for his generous spirit, confidence in the work and faith in me; and Catherine Dees, a true editor's editor, for her gracious heart, keen insight on the topic and divine perfectionism with words. With recognition to literary agent Michael Murphy, whose early encouragement of these writings stirred me to complete the draft.

To New Thought pioneers and prose writers whose work has influenced mine: Dr. David Hawkins, David Whyte, Julia Cameron, Jean Houston, PhD, Joan Borysenko, MD, Arjuna Ardagh, Ma Deva Padma and John O'Donohue. With respect for the eternal teachings of Paramahansa Yogananda, Joseph Campbell, Carl Jung and Baird Spalding; and admiration for the ecstatic poetry of Rumi, Gibran, Rilke, Hafiz, Mirabai and Neruda—whose words never cease to stagger and unfold me.

To my soul group incarnate: Lee Ann Heltzel, Jennifer Evanko, Nancy Kelmeckis and Kathleen Pasley—for unwavering friendship, wisdom, honesty, and loving me through my shortcomings; Annette Alemán, for being the sister I've always wanted, near or far; Sven Hosford, Dan Cavanaugh and David Smolensky—for lending a masculine touch, spiritual intelligence and warm caring to my journey; everyone in the Intuitive Dialogue group (a.k.a. Traveling Light Show) for bravely sharing their stories and listening to mine; Sallie Christensen, for setting me on this phantasmic ride; and especially, Edemir Rossi, for showing me the higher meaning of devotion and vocation.

To my soul group *in spiritus*, whose scintillating wisdom inspired and enhanced these writings—in particular, Philomena, Rose, Scribe and Sage; and the blessed personal insights of Isis, Magdelene and Ashtar.

To Don, for his loving plenitude and enduring my metaphysic-artistic sensibilities; Gianne and Carlin, for making my heart brim with joy every day; *la mia famiglia*, Joe and Jerome, for the comfort of brotherly love, as well as the ever-amazing Dee, the other sister I've always wanted; and ultimately, to the purest light in my life: my mother, Sarah, for demonstrating daily the essence of unconditional love.

ABOUT THE AUTHOR

Gina Mazza Hillier is a freelance journalist, editor, writing consultant, dance enthusiast and advocate of living with creative abandon. She is a partner and founder of Epiphany Works, an "inspired event planning" company that creates public entertainment to celebrate world cultures, spiritual traditions and the beauty of community. Co-author of two nonfiction books, Gina lives with her family in a town called Harmony.

For more about the author and her work:
www.EverythingmattersNothingmatters.com
www.ginawriter.com
www.epiphanyworks.org